POLICIES F AFRICAN DEVELOPMENT

From the 1980s to the 1990s

POLICIES FOR AFRICAN DEVELOPMENT

From the 1980s to the 1990s

Editor
I. G. Patel

Papers presented at a symposium held in
Gaborone, Botswana, February 25–27, 1991

INTERNATIONAL MONETARY FUND
Washington • 1992

© 1992 International Monetary Fund

Cover and interior design by IMF Graphics Section

Joint Bank-Fund Library Cataloging-in-Publication Data

Policies for African development : from the 1980s to the 1990s / editor, I. G. Patel.—Washington : International Monetary Fund, 1992.
        p. ; cm.

"Papers presented at a symposium held in Gaborone, Botswana, February 25–27, 1991."
Includes bibliographical references.
ISBN 1-55775-232X

1. Africa—Economic policy—Congresses. 2. Africa—Economic conditions—1960– —Congresses. 3 Finance—Africa—Congresses. I. Patel, I. G. (Indraprasad Gordhanbhai), 1924– II. International Monetary Fund.
HC800.P55   1992

Price: US$24.00

Address orders to:
International Monetary Fund, Publication Services
700 19th Street, N.W., Washington, D.C. 20431, U.S.A.
Telephone: (202) 623-7430
Telefax: (202) 623-7491
Cable: Interfund

Foreword

Africa, despite great economic adversity during the past twenty years, has managed recently to record positive real growth, steadily transform and improve its economic structures and systems, and improve the living standards of the rural population. This has been achieved through the perseverence of nearly thirty African countries in following growth-oriented adjustment programs, with the support of the International Monetary Fund (IMF).

A seminar held in Gaborone, Botswana, from February 25–27, 1991, sponsored by the Association of African Central Banks and the IMF, provided an opportunity for frank evaluation and discussion of the progress made by Africa during the 1980s and of the prospects and needs for continued development in the 1990s. The propositions that regional cooperation in Africa has formidable potential in enhancing economic efficiency and that the industrial countries have a special responsibility in helping Africa drew broad agreement. In view of the importance of the issues discussed, it has been decided to publish the proceedings of the seminar so as to make them available to a wider audience.

There is no doubt that for Africa the road ahead is hard, but it is my deep conviction that many African countries during the 1990s will be able to successfully launch homegrown programs, deserving strong international support and leading to increased regional cooperation. The responsibility for development and economic adjustment is a shared one. The IMF is ready to do its part in helping Africa face the challenges that lie ahead.

M. CAMDESSUS
Managing Director
International Monetary Fund

Acknowledgment

I should like to say what a great pleasure and privilege it has been to participate in this symposium and what a rich and rewarding experience it was. I am grateful to the Association of African Central Banks and to the IMF for providing me with this unique experience. The staff of the Central Bank of Botswana and Governor Hermans spared no effort in making our stay comfortable and our discussions fruitful; and special thanks are due to Mrs. Hermans for keeping our spouses safely and happily away from the conference hall.

I am grateful also to all the participants for the rich fare they served. I have done scant justice to the actual discussion at the symposium in this introduction. Unlike the invited authors whose papers are reproduced here, those who spoke on the spur of the moment, and thus rose splendidly to the occasion so to speak, have to be content with what I can recollect and record in a short introduction in which I have not been able to resist the temptation of inserting my own overtones.

Perhaps it is not too much to hope that it is interactions such as those that have taken place at the symposium—free from rancor, clearheaded, hard-hitting, and yet not allergic to delineation of agreement as well as disagreement—that give grounds for hope that the transition from the 1980s to the 1990s in Africa may well be a journey from stagnation and decline to revitalization and renewed vigor.

I am greatly indebted to the IMF staff, Ahmed Abushadi, who ably coordinated the seminar, and Juanita Roushdy, who edited and prepared the volume for publication, and to Varghese Thomas and his associates of the Indian Petrochemicals Corporation Limited, Baroda, for voluntary assistance so readily given at every stage.

I. G. PATEL
Editor and Moderator

Contents

	Page
Foreword	v
Acknowledgment	vii
Introduction	
I. G. PATEL	1
Opening Remarks	
ABDUL R. TURAY	15
M. CAMDESSUS	19

I Structural Adjustment in Africa: Future Approaches and Lessons Learned from the Past

A View from Africa	
A.K. MULLEI	29
A View from the IMF	
JACK BOORMAN	48
Tanzania's Experience	
G. RUTIHINDA	69

II Africa's Adjustment and the External Debt Problem: Issues and Options

A View from the African Development Bank	
A. SANGOWAWA	83
A View from the Paris Club	
DENIS SAMUEL-LAJEUNESSE	92
An Unofficial View	
G. K. HELLEINER	97

	Page
Discussants	
Africa's Adjustment and the External Debt Problem PERCY S. MISTRY	115
Issues and Options JACK BOORMAN and AJAI CHOPRA	126
Official Debt Reduction: Toronto Terms, Trinidad Terms, and Netherlands Initiative FRANCESCO ABBATE and ANH-NGA TRAN-NGUYEN	140

III Financing Growth and Development in Africa: Outlook and Issues

Estimating the Cost of Financing African Development in the 1990s MARIA CRISTINA GERMANY, CHARLES P. HUMPHREYS, and STEPHEN O'BRIEN	153
A View from the UN Commission for Africa OWODUNNI TERIBA	171
Discussants	
Resource Gaps and Financing for Growth in Africa BENNO J. NDULU	188
Just How Important Is Finance for African Development TONY KILLICK	198
Structural Adjustment Program: Lesotho's Experience in a Nutshell A. M. MARUPING	210

IV Trade, Investment, and Growth: Prospects for Africa

A View from UNCTAD K. S. DADZIE	221

	Page
A View from Africa	
BEKELE TAMIRAT	237
A View from Africa	
KERFALLE YANSANE	244

Panel Discussion

Adjustment, Resources, and Growth: How to Manage in the 1990s	
ROBERT J. BERG	255
G. K. HELLEINER	265
MATTHEW MARTIN	270
G. E. GONDWE	281
List of Participants	291

Introduction

I.G. Patel

The joint symposium of the Association of African Central Banks and the International Monetary Fund (IMF), held in Gaborone, Botswana, February 25–27, 1991, was a sequel to a similar gathering held in Nairobi, Kenya, May 13–15, 1985. The contrast in the mood on the two occasions was remarkable. The 1985 symposium had a hint of confrontation, or, put another way, illustrated a need for much greater understanding, between the IMF and Africa. The 1991 symposium had a marked positive and constructive tone, and the views expressed had a remarkable degree of correspondence. Emphasis was on the dynamics of a suitable policy framework for the 1990s rather than on dialectics, which had been the emphasis of the 1980s. There was a strong undercurrent that the primary emphasis should be on African development, which had sadly received such a serious setback in the 1980s.

The African central bankers in Gaborone were noticeably free from any tendency to minimize the magnitude of their task or to explain away the mistakes of the past. While emphasizing the importance of the external environment and of the policies of the rich, they were unsparing in highlighting the far-reaching responsibilities that Africans alone can shoulder. The representatives of the IMF, the World Bank, the Paris Club, and the Western intelligentsia present were also remarkably free from dogma. Quite clearly, neither the earlier debates nor the experience of recent years had gone unheeded. As Governor Yansane of Guinea so aptly put it, one important consequence of the experience of structural adjustment is that it has brought about some adjustment of minds as well.

One should perhaps be somewhat wary about the signs of an emerging consensus at the conference. Consensus can be a kind of tranquilizer that dulls our perception about vital differences and nuances. These can get lost in catchphrases that easily roll off our tongues. One has also regretfully to admit that while more powerful now than before, central bankers do not always reflect correctly the public mood nor the perceptions and compulsions of political leaders. Some might even suggest that those present at the conference—the Managing Director of the IMF not excluded—could well be a little ahead of their respective constituencies! The evidence so far as to the right recipe for countries that differ in circumstance as much as they resemble each other in terms of policy responses generally is such as to warn against any simplistic view about a policy framework for the development of Africa as a whole. All these caveats notwithstanding—and they were made during the discussion—it has to be reckoned as a hopeful sign that there is now considerable common ground on which our analysis and aspirations rest.

The tone for the entire conference was set admirably by the two "keynote" speeches given by Governor Turay, Chairman of the Association of African Central Banks, and Mr. Camdessus, Managing Director of the IMF. Governor Turay, while emphasizing the limited successes so far in structural adjustment and the almost total absence of growth and of progress toward diversification, which alone can make African economies fully responsive to policy stimuli, recognized that far-reaching changes were inevitable. His emphasis on technical assistance from the IMF and elsewhere to enable Africans to draw their own blueprint for adjustment and growth was echoed during the conference in different contexts.

Mr. Camdessus was emphatic that what was needed was growth-oriented structural adjustment and that antipoverty policies and programs were not just additives or correctives but should be an integral part of structural adjustment. He could well have added that this would be easier if antipoverty concerns were already an integral part of longer-term development plans or programs. Mr. Camdessus was equally clear that African development was a shared responsibility and that international institutions had to prod the richer countries to do their part just as they had to insist on appropriate policies by the developing world. Above all, one has to recognize that there is room for improvement and for learning from experience so that an appropriate policy framework for any country—let alone a continent—is not a closed book, even if there are some basic economic laws that none can evade. Difficult as the task is and, indeed, because it is so difficult, there is no escape from perseverance for all concerned in the partnership. While emphasizing this, Mr. Camdessus was hopeful of a more positive response all round.

The first session of the symposium was devoted to an assessment of structural adjustment. The term "structural adjustment" no longer refers only to a stable macroeconomic framework with excess demand and inflation under control and major distortions in key prices, such as the exchange rate or interest rates or prices of wage-goods and labor, removed. There is now general agreement that it should embrace an appropriate set of microeconomic policies as well. They should include less reliance on government control and public ownership and more on individual initiative and signals from the markets, incentives by way of moderate tax rates, a less discriminatory and more transparent set of rules and regulations to the extent required, greater integration into the world economy, and, above all, the creation and maintenance of a competitive environment conducive to greater efficiency and resilience.

But the Gaborone conference was also clear that, structural adjustment even so widely defined, greatly abridges the policy agenda. Economic growth or development requires going beyond this to positive steps to stimulate savings and investment, to develop human resources, as well as control population growth, and to prevent the degradation and destruction of natural resources—to mention just the important things. Participation of the people and concern for the poor are not luxuries but essential ingredients for the success and sustainability of any sensible set of policies. Structural adjustment, development, social justice, and environmental protection have all to proceed side by side; and in the real world, countries have also to reckon with uncertainty and shocks whether external (oil prices) or internal (crop failures). Adjustment to unforeseeable shocks and factors is as much a part of the policy agenda as are sustainable growth, or social justice, or financial stability and a competitive environment.

It is this diversity and depth of the policy agenda that makes for complexity and difficult judgments. While all important objectives have to be pursued and means wielded, it is not possible to do everything at the same time. Priorities have to be set, and policies and programs have to be phased appropriately—a point made most forcefully by Mr. Boorman of the IMF. There are some sequences that one can confidently recommend. For example, it would be suicidal to liberalize imports extensively unless a substantial degree of macroeconomic adjustment had already taken place, excess demand had been greatly reduced, and realistic exchange rates and interest rates were in place.

But everything is not so clear or obvious. There is a temptation to think—perhaps more so among donors and international financial institutions—that as long as structural adjustment in the wider sense is not completed, investment for development must be postponed or greatly reduced. But, as Mr. Helleiner rightly points out, without some evidence of continued growth, it may well be impossible to muster enough political support for structural adjustment. In any event, the agenda for structural adjustment, at least in the microeconomic sense, is so vast and far-reaching that there cannot be agreement on all elements of it. Nor can it be implemented except over a number of years. A stop-and-go policy on growth can be self-defeating. And yet, in practice, developmental ambitions may have to be curtailed, even when there are no major distortions to begin with, for example, in response to a severe shock. How to minimize the adverse consequences of unavoidable and indeed generally beneficial adjustment is not an easy question, particularly when growth as well as social justice are borne in mind. We may all agree that public expenditure needs to be reduced. But how to do this without harming development or the consumption of the poor is not that easy to prescribe.

Not only is it that our knowledge of economic facts and relationships is imperfect or that our experience so far gives no clear answers to such detailed questions of priorities and phasing in a particular environment, but also by their very nature most economic policies are double-edged; even good policies have bad side effects. At any given time, the art of making economic policy is the art of choosing the second or even the third best—of trading off and recognizing realities even as we seek to change them. For example, if tax incentives are necessary for private enterprise and risk taking, cannot subsidies also be so justified at least in some contexts? One may agree with Mr. Boorman that, even so, subsidies must be minimized and made transparent and even add that they must be pinpointed as far as possible. But there is no room for either/or here.

Major prices, like exchange rates, interest rates, wages, and prices of key wage-goods, have not only to be realistic but also stable so as to provide a stable framework for private decisions. Stability in these areas cannot be guaranteed by government fiat. It requires sound fiscal and monetary policies. But few governments in actual practice refrain from stabilizing action in such vital areas and rely exclusively on the free play of markets. Or to take a more relevant case for most of Africa, as the Governor of the Bank of Swaziland, Mr. Oliver, pointed out, customs revenue is such an important part of government receipts that one cannot sacrifice it unduly in a hurry to open the economy to external competition and thus jeopardize financial stability.

The much greater agreement on fundamentals should not obscure the fact that we do not know enough and cannot, in any case, be dogmatic about the details of any program that has to take many specific things and trade-offs into account. When one is concerned with the nitty-gritty of actual programs, there must be room for argument, debate, discussion, further research, and revisions and reformulations and a certain degree of humility and give-and-take on the part of all concerned.

It is good that the debate has shifted from first principles to concrete programs and that there is no great inclination nowadays to look for alternative strategies or approaches—although the terminology of the past may still linger on in some quarters, as is evidenced by some of the papers published here. No, we do not have a major alternative to follow, be it socialist or statist, autarchic, or even ascetic. Austerity, discriminatory protection, state guidance in investment, and an active role in many spheres, as well as concern for social justice, remain valid. Words like "socialism" and "a mixed economy" or "autarchy," in the sense of "self reliance," and "retreat from consumerism" will not disappear altogether from the dictionary of development. But the concerns underlying these words can only supplement the policy agenda; they do not provide a substitute for the logic and discipline inherent in structural adjustments.

The main point is that policies fo African development must be homegrown, and there should be room for argument and open-mindedness when individual country programs are under consideration. The debate must be conducted not on first principles but on a case-by-case basis. But for that, the developing countries, and Africa in particular, have to be better equipped. There is need for improvement of statistics and analytical skills and for better awareness of experience elsewhere and of changes in technology and the external environment in general. Negotiating skills are also scarce and strained unbearably by the demands of a multiplicity of donors and institutions to which Mr. Martin's paper draws pointed attention. There needs to be better coordination among donors and a readiness to give the benefit of doubt to those who have to implement the program—something very difficult for donors and even international institutions to accept. The developing countries have come a long way in giving the benefit of doubt to the essential features of structural adjustment. It is only reasonable that on details of priorities, or phasing, or speed and trade-offs, or appropriate mix at a particular stage, the benefit of doubt be given to those who are nearer the ground.

It is in this context that Africa's need for technical assistance deserves the greatest emphasis. Programs for structural adjustment and development must not be only seen as homegrown; they must actually be so. This requires that many more Africans be trained—in the highest academic standards in economics; this can only be done by greater access to the finest universities in the world. It is regrettable that, except perhaps in the

United States and France, in large parts of the Western world the welcome extended to students from the Third World is waning. This has to be remedied—if need be by private foundations and international institutions. Without that, creative and constructive dialogue on equal footing between Africa and the IMF or the World Bank or the donor community will remain an ever-receding dream.

All this has relevance also to the vexing question of conditionalities. The instinctive reaction against any kind of conditionality is much less in evidence now—although one should never expect it to disappear altogether. But areas for genuine worry remain. I have already referred to the complexity of any agenda for reform and revitalization and for the consequent need for the benefit of doubt being given not to the stronger party in negotiations but to the party that ultimately takes the blame and is, therefore, truly accountable. The rich are rich enough to afford this additional risk, which can have a high payoff.

More important perhaps, when there is so much uncertainty and so many variables, is whether there is any justification for the kind of sudden-death conditionality involved in the credit ceilings prescribed by the IMF. Even a modest breach of these ceilings leads automatically to a withdrawal of promised assistance. It does not help to argue that IMF conditionality is related to instruments rather than to objectives. Whether that is valid or not is not the point; the point is whether it is better to continue with assistance while resuming negotiations whenever a condition is not observed or to hold the gun and then argue. Bad cases of noncompliance can occur, despite clear warnings; in such cases, stoppage of further aid would be justified. But a breach of a credit ceiling does not somehow seem to command that much pre-eminence in the overall context of a wide-ranging reform of policies. It seems like a vestige from the past and deserves another look.

On the other hand, the temptation to multiply the area of conditionality or policy undertakings with precise time frames (even if there are no specific sudden-death criteria)—to which the World Bank seems to be prone—is equally at odds with what can be realistically expected. For example, the World Bank's structural adjustment program for Zaïre included 102 measures to be introduced in 24 months; this evoked more than a little laughter from the conferees. Yes, there is some merit in preparing a detailed and comprehensive shopping list, but if some items are not actually bought, we cannot allow that to become a source of family discord.

At the heart of any argument about performance is the reasonableness of the time frame during which certain measures are to be taken or certain results achieved. Apart from questions of judgment and the intervention of the unexpected, the issue of a reasonable time frame is further complicated by the fact that African development is recognized as a partnership where the partners have unequal strength and very different responsibilities. If the need for internal policy changes and if the need for external support or finance are recognized, what is an appropriate or optimum mix of the two? It is true that programs can fail because of lack of political will or strength at home, but they can also—and do—fail because they are underfunded. It will not do to assert—as international institutions are sometimes tempted to do—that the availability of external resources has to be taken as given and the programs adjusted to that. A country does not have an unlimited ability to adjust on a wide front within a short time, and underfunded programs can be worse than none, as they squander away scarce resources of political will and generate cynicism and despondency all round.

To put it in reverse, forcing undue speed on poor countries guarantees that programs will fail or will impose unacceptable hardship on the vulnerable sections of society and may even retard growth. It is now more generally accepted that international institutions should not be guided too much by what might appear to be financially feasible. They have to strive to stretch these limits when sensible programs are available; and there is some evidence that this is beginning to happen, at least in the African context. Whether this will continue when more and more countries are ready to implement realistic programs remains to be seen. In the meantime, programs may even have to be front-loaded in terms of external support if, as Mr. Mullei points out, there are to be tangible early results to steady the political and public will for more difficult steps.

True, lapses, willful or otherwise, could occur on the part of the developing countries. But policy infirmities are not the prerogative of the poor only, and strident didacticism seldom behooves the rich, who have less excuse in terms of the suffering of their people for their own aberrations. If the message, as Mr. Camdessus pointed out, is perseverance, we have to persevere with the successful and the not-so-successful, with the political heavyweights, as well as the lightweights. Donors, as well as recipients, have to be urged to stay the course and not cut and run at the first sight of failure.

Needless to say, resources will always be limited, and difficult questions about the distribution of available funds among all recipients will remain to be solved. Should support be concentrated on those who are making the sharpest of breaks with the past? Is there not moral hazard in this? Should concentration be on those who are already reasonably successful rather than on those who are just coming along? There was a feeling that the most successful examples of structural adjustment were precisely those that received much larger support in relation to their size. However attractive rewarding success and punishing reluctance may be, one has to be careful—if staying the course is the message (and it should be). There are many examples of the good having turned bad and of the bad eventually returning to the fold. Bridges, therefore, have to be maintained everywhere and the sinners and the weak of will should not be abandoned altogether. At the other end, there was a feeling among African central bankers themselves that those who pay their debts should not be penalized because others do not or cannot and that even middle-income African countries have a claim on external support, as they too have large areas of poverty and underdevelopment. These are difficult questions that cannot be resolved fully.

Even more difficult are the truly hopeless cases for the foreseeable future—whether as a result of internal discord and strife, folly, tyranny, or some quirk of rapidly deteriorating natural resources and high rates of population growth. It would be idle to pretend that there are no such cases. To paraphrase Isaac Bashevis Singer, it is nowhere written that progress must be possible everywhere at all times. But even these unfortunate cases cannot be abandoned altogether even if aid to them can only be temporizing and for survival more than for growth.

Conferees recognized that what is expected from the richer countries is not just finance or even assistance, including technical assistance, or a less protectionist trade policy, but consideration by them of the effect of their domestic policies on the developing world and particularly on Africa, where external influences had a tendency to reverberate more vigorously. Stop-and-go policies in developed countries or recessionary trends can cripple African trade volumes, as well as terms of trade. Lack of macroeconomic adjustment in major industrial countries tends to divert too much of the world's savings to some of the rich countries and to increase interest rates to levels that make a great deal of investment unremunerative in the poorer countries. Financial institutions like the IMF have a surveillance role in the industrial countries as well, and the IMF could do more to urge, for example, higher rates of saving everywhere. The tendency sometimes to solve the problems of those who save too little by asking others to consume more can be a disaster not just for the developing world.

One of the most heartwarming aspects of this symposium has been the emphasis on regional cooperation transcending mere sound policies in individual countries. Mr. Camdessus highlighted the importance of such cooperation while emphasizing that it should be outward looking and that it can be more successful when there is greater harmonization of domestic policies as well. These sentiments were echoed widely; and despite the poor record of such cooperation in the past, it was felt that recent experience was more promising. The experience of the Southern African Development Coordination Conference (SADCC), of which all countries in Southern Africa with the major exception of South Africa were members, was often quoted approvingly; and the hope was expressed that once South Africa returned to more civilized norms, the scope for mutual cooperation would increase greatly in a region that had the highest potential for growth in Africa if not in the developing world as a whole.

In sum, the discussion on structural adjustment became truly a discussion on the whole range of policies relevant, both internal and external, to Africa.

The subject of the second session, Africa's adjustment and the external debt problem, proved in some ways to be the most rewarding, as it dealt with a number of specific issues and options. That debt relief cannot be a substitute for more traditional aid was recognized and that it should indeed be an integral part of the total aid package. Africa's debt problem may appear small in relation to that of Latin America, for example, but it should not receive less attention for that reason. It is much more difficult for Africa to service debt because of the rigidities inherent in highly undiversified economic structures; and dollar for dollar, the suffering involved in debt repayment in Africa is much greater. Africa's debt problems, thus, deserve greater attention; and they are indeed receiving it in recent years, although much more remains to be done.

Debt relief, as a mechanism for transferring real resources, clearly enjoys several distinct advantages. It can translate almost immediately into higher imports without any question about absorptive capacity; and one thing that is beyond question is that African development has been held back by lack of import capacity—a consideration that will remain valid for the 1990s as well. What is more, debt relief permits imports that are most in need as it is akin to availability of free foreign exchange through exports, which aid more often is not. If, as Mr. Ndulu points out, there is considerable scope for increasing the productivity of capital in Africa by greater use of capacity already created, debt relief can certainly be most beneficial, as it would permit the import of raw materials and components, as well as spares and miscellaneous capital goods.

Progress toward debt relief in Africa has been significant in respect of official bilateral debt, and as Mr. Lajeunesse of the Paris Club points out, radical steps forward are actively under consideration. One can only hope that agreement will soon be reached on Prime Minister Major's proposal even if one cannot go as far as Mr. Pronck of the Netherlands.

The Paris Club insists on a prior agreement with the IMF before debt relief is extended, which is understandable, but excessive linkages may at times be counterproductive. There must be sufficient flexibility to act in time. The willingness to consider the debt problems of the middle-income countries is welcome. Should the formula for debt relief have too many options for donors, resulting perhaps in the lowest common denominator to prevail, or should the Paris Club insist on greater uniformity? These are matters of judgment that might vary from time to time. But the reluctance to deal with the entire stock of debt at one go is less understandable, as members of the Paris Club have enough hold over all debtors anyway— including those who may be freed for a number of years from the annual pilgrimage to Paris. Given the transaction cost of negotiation for the African countries, more radical solutions may have other side benefits in that they will release managerial resources better utilized for implementation of policies than for negotiation of debt relief.

Progress in securing relief for commercial debt has been particularly tardy in the case of Africa and more attention needs to be paid to this despite the fact that the share of private commercial debt in total is rather small for Africa. This is also true of commercial or official debt owed to countries in Eastern Europe and elsewhere, which are not members of the Paris Club.

As for official financial institutions, where there is a perverse negative flow of resources at present in most cases, there has to be a departure from the traditional policy of no rescheduling even when this is done indirectly. The reservation of $100 million from the World Bank's profits for reducing the debt burden of the neediest African countries is welcome; and the Bank could and should do more in future. As for the IMF, it has made a beginning with the "rights" approach to tackle the problem of countries most seriously in arrears. But this is hardly an adequate answer. The African Development Bank, it was noted, has taken no initiative in this field.

Mr. Mistry draws pointed attention to the rather insignificant results achieved so far and asks why some of the radical measures suggested for securing greater and more concessional resources for debt relief should not be pursued. Perhaps Mr. Boorman is right when he suggests that gold sales or a special issue of drawing rights are not practical politics at present. But this should not be true at least of a concerted move to lower IMF charges, which were raised substantially in the recent past. The IMF is an instrument of international cooperation, and there is no intrinsic reason why creditor positions in the IMF should earn market rates of return. This was not so until the early 1980s when something akin to fundamentalism of the "right" had a brief sway. There are already signs of at least partial retreat in the light of experience from the mood of the early 1980s. There is also the market-related consideration that a reserve asset virtually fully guaranteed against depreciation and default should be content with a lower rate of return. A sizable reduction in IMF charges should be high on the agenda of policy reform in the IMF itself, and it is to be hoped that the Managing Director will throw the full weight of his authority behind this proposal. Beyond this, perhaps the atmosphere in the era after the Gulf war may be conducive to a more statesman-like attitude to the needs of developing countries; and this could be harnessed to secure greater and more concessional resources under existing arrangements like those of the International Development Association (IDA) and bilateral aid without opening any new channels.

There were somewhat conflicting worries expressed about too much linkage among donors so that debtors are faced with a virtual cartel with no room for maneuver and the wastefulness of having to negotiate in so many forums. One participant was so oppressed by the latter that he suggested that the IMF retreat entirely into technical assistance leaving the financial field to the World Bank (and bilateral donors) and perhaps nothing for the United Nations Development Program (UNDP). It is perhaps an index of the rapidly declining unpopularity of the IMF, at least in Africa, that this proposal went unsupported.

Discussion at the third and fourth sessions, which dealt with financing growth and development and trade, investment and growth prospects, inevitably got intertwined and indeed somewhat squeezed for want of time. The subjects are closely related, and a good deal of ground was covered earlier. Fortunately, the papers published here, particularly the one by the Secretary-General of the United Nations Conference on Trade and Development (UNCTAD), Mr. Dadzie, and the other by Governor Yansane are comprehensive enough to compensate for the brevity of discussion on issues relating to trade and investment.

If African development must be accelerated after the disastrous but educative decade of the 1980s, what can one reasonably say about the prospects for the 1990s? A useful point of departure in answering this question is provided by the World Bank paper presented in Session III, which presents at least one possible scenario. The rate of growth in Africa could accelerate to 4 percent a year in the early 1990s increasing further to

5 percent by the year 2000 if the rate of investment could be increased from 15 percent to 25 percent of gross domestic product (GDP), the incremental capital/output ratio reduced from 10 to 5 and the present rate of growth in official development assistance (ODA) in real terms of 4 percent a year, as well as the present framework of debt relief, continues. Even so, per capita incomes in Africa in the year 2000 would not quite return to the not-so-enviable level of 1980.

Can anything less be acceptable? But, is even this feasible? Some of the assumptions, for example, those regarding savings and the incremental capital/output ratio appear, prima facie, heroic. But already there are signs that things will be much better than assumed in some respects, for example, debt relief. Assumptions on aid are also not unrealistic and may well be conservative—there were suggestions that the World Bank tends to assume conservatively what is feasible on resource transfers and treats domestic effort as the residual for achieving the desired results. Undoubtedly, this reflects caution rather than callousness. But whatever it may be, there were African voices that supported the feasibility of a substantial improvement in the productivity of capital. Mr. Ndulu, as already noted, drew attention to unutilized capacity, and there were telling illustrations of how far productivity in Africa lags behind that in Asia in comparable fields. Also, authorities now are set more firmly against wasteful or grandiose investment.

As Mr. Killick rightly points out, finance is by no means the only or even the major constraint on growth. Shortage of skilled labor is perhaps a greater bottleneck, as several African governors noted. Clearly, this is not to discourage external support or internal effort to generate more savings and establish more effective financial intermediaries. But the effectiveness of financial intermediaries is perhaps greater in terms of the improvement in the quality of investment they can bring about rather than in promoting savings or reducing the transaction cost of bringing savers and investors together.

There are, contrary to the conspiracy of silence generally observed in this regard, political dimensions to growth as well, and these go far beyond the maintenance of law and order and the like. We know now that governments are not embodiments of objectivity and wisdom any more than they are trustees of the national interest. But they are there and are not likely to wither away despite the prophecies of the left and the proclivities of the extreme right. What can be done to minimize the harm they can do and to maximize the good they are capable of doing? There are no soothing or simple answers.

It is a sobering thought that the much-heralded four Asian tigers (Hong Kong, Korea, Taiwan Province of China, and Singapore) do have teeth that bite deeply into democratic norms and individual freedom with varying degrees of frequency and ferocity. Even so, one can perhaps say in favor of democracies that the transparency and possibility of change they imply is a safeguard against things going too far in the wrong direction. Even flawed democracies are less arbitrary and have a semblance of equality before the law. These and other aspects of freedom and individual dignity are essential parts of the kind of quality of life that alone can justify the emphasis on growth.

Whatever political system is desirable, it cannot be imposed from outside or guaranteed from inside. But international financial institutions and bilateral donors are concerned about at least some aspects of good governance, including a measure of transparency, evenhandedness, accountability, decisiveness, and good housekeeping. This was confirmed by Mr. Langley, who is at present an Executive Director of the World Bank. Somehow, even if a week is too long a period in politics and pleasing the voters is an integral part of the democratic tradition, a way has to be found whether through statesmanship or statecraft to minimize shortsightedness and to limit pork-barrel populism.

Africa's trade prospects are rendered particularly difficult by its narrow productive base and the concentration on a few markets. It will be a long time before this situation changes. The structural weaknesses are further enhanced by the technological threat to commodity exports. And yet, these exports are far too important to be neglected. Africa will have to strive hard to retain whatever advantages or preferences it has, for example, under the Lomé Convention. Nor can it abandon the search for greater stability in its commodity terms of trade. Conventional commodity agreements, such as those that require production sharing, may be feasible only in a few cases. But there are other possibilities of individual action or cooperation between producers and consumers, as Mr. Dadzie points out.

Above all, Africa cannot be indifferent to international negotiations on trade, such as the current round of the General Agreement on Tariffs and Trade (GATT) in which Africa's voice is muted. Liberalization of trade in agriculture, for example, may well affect adversely food importers, which is what most African countries are. But there was no African voice in GATT forums to draw attention to this and to demand at least transitional relief. In short, while Africa's trade options may be limited now and its stake in a more open world-trading system not so clear, it still has such an excessive dependence on imports over a wide range that it has to fight even harder for its corner than the newly industrializing countries who can, in a pinch, be more self-sufficient.

The last session in which four panelists and myself provided their own summations or emphasis was a wrap-up session and I have drawn greatly in this introduction on what was said then. A new and important note was, however, struck in this session by Mr. Berg, who emphasized the extreme urgency of the problems and the moral imperative of tackling issues that go far beyond mere technical virtuosity. His reference to population and environment was one of the few references to these most vital matters; and if I have any regret, it is that more was not said on these matters by our African friends. But as they say in my country, you need one small blemish to enhance the beauty of the whole.

Opening Remarks

Abdul R. Turay

That Africa is in the throes of an economic crisis of major dimensions hardly needs emphasizing. Country variations notwithstanding, there are numerous manifestations of this situation: poor agricultural and industrial performance, deteriorating institutions and infrastructure, declining levels of per capita income, dismal levels of social welfare indicators, weak export performance, and high and unsustainable levels of external indebtedness.

A number of explanations have been posited for the causes of this crisis. The economies that evolved from the ravages of the colonial period were structured to cater to the needs of the colonial powers; these economies were sources of raw materials and markets for their finished products, rather than integrated entities, with mutually supporting production structures. Also, inappropriate models of development were adopted, which neglected the agricultural sector but emphasized suboptimal import-substituting industrialization strategies. Another problem not to be downplayed was the ubiquitous intervention of the state in economic activities that are best suited for the private sector. Closer to our responsibilities was the use of inappropriate macroeconomic policies resulting in unsustainable fiscal deficits, expansionary monetary policies, and external disequilibrium. But at the top of these factors was the impact of a hostile external economic environment characterized by adverse terms of trade, inadequate access to markets, declining flows of financial resources, and the perpetuation of a generally peripheral status in international economic arrangements. It is against this background that the subject of this symposium, "Structural Adjustment, External Debt, and Growth in Africa," should be appreciated.

The goal that our national leaders have never lost sight of is the achievement of long-run sustainable growth. However, past attempts at accelerated development financed through substantial external borrowing to supplement meager domestic savings have, in the face of the structural inadequacies just referred to, yielded only minor successes and caused other problems. Prominent among the new problems is the debt crisis, which has hit African countries hard and has resulted in making international capital markets inaccessible to us.

The evident solution of going right to the source of the problem by reforming the structures of our economies is now upon us. But, structural adjustment programs are impossible to implement and sustain without financial support from foreign sources. It is consequently necessary that some framework be established within which past indebtedness and future funding requirements could be successfully addressed so that the goals of structural adjustment and growth do not become impossible to achieve. The interlinkages between structural adjustment, external debt, and growth are thus inescapable. These are important issues not just at the present conjuncture but also for the very future of our continent.

Structural Adjustment and Growth

Structural adjustment programs are now a common feature of the African scene. Numerous African governments, in their determination to correct the growing external and internal economic disequilibria that have become quasi-permanent in our countries, have adopted packages of reform measures, mostly in close consultation with the International Monetary Fund (IMF) and the World Bank and with their financial support. These measures embrace both facets of macroeconomic stabilization and structural reforms, and they aim at inducing our economic structures to be more responsive to free market signals. The implementation of these policies is closely watched by the international financial community and is invariably interpreted as an indication of willingness to change the direction of economic management in order to engineer sustainable growth and development.

Questions have been raised regarding the internal economic consistency of the measures built into the typical reform package, including its purely macroeconomic stabilization aspect. Their effectiveness in achieving the desired ends, especially in the context of African economies, is in doubt, and this doubt is strengthened by empirical studies. For example, doubts have been expressed regarding the compatibility of exchange rate devaluation and reduction of inflation and, indeed, the positive response of export sectors to such exchange rate changes. In this context, it has been stressed that rigidities and bottlenecks in our economic structures defy adjustment by the traditional preferred policy instruments of the Bretton Woods institutions.

In addition to these economic concerns are the practical issues, such as the cost of adjustment in human and political terms. This concern is now analyzed under the rubric of the social costs of adjustment. There is the admission that labor retrenchment and higher prices of goods and services resulting from the removal of subsidies, especially in the areas of health care and education, are regressive in their effects on the populace. Subsidiary or integrated programs have been devised in response. Special attention is consequently being paid to the needs of those considered least able to absorb these shocks. But it is not certain that these subsidiary programs are adequate in their scope and intent, or reach the target groups. Societal reactions to the austerity brought in the wake of structural adjustment programs continue sporadically to cause governments to abort programs because of fear of political and social unrest.

Regarding the achievement of desired goals, empirical research reveals major shortcomings in terms of the effects on the balance of payments, the rate of economic growth and its composition, the reduction of inflation, or the more imponderable social adjustments. Indeed, it is questioned whether African governments have concluded structural adjustment programs because of their conviction that the programs would yield desired results or merely because they appreciate the importance of being perceived to be cooperating with the Bretton Woods institutions, in order to have access to funds from donor countries and other international capital markets.

That the external debt problem of Africa is as severe as Latin America's, from the point of view of the debtors, if not more severe, is now widely recognized. However, it is still not receiving the attention it deserves, because Africa's debt problem is now primarily noncommercial bank debt and is, therefore, considered less of a threat to the international banking and financial system than is Latin America's. This is deplorable because the human costs to Africa are far higher, far more dramatic.

The statistics show a very sharp increase of over 600 percent in the aggregate debt of the region over the 1970s and 1980s, with an equally staggering burden in the region's debt-service requirements. This predicament is aggravated by the recent catastrophic evolution of the terms of trade of the region, compounded by the rise in world interest rates during the 1980s. Net capital movements for a couple of years were negative, translating into outflows rather than inflows.

Africa's debt problem had its origins in external borrowing to finance development. The a posteriori pronouncement for the course of the failure is that the projects financed with borrowed funds had not been selected wisely; little consideration had been given to their economic return. The important element from our point of view is that in most cases funds were expended on infrastructural projects that indeed facilitated the process of economic and social development. They did not, however, yield returns directly usable for the servicing of the debts incurred for their realization. The resulting inability to service these debts promoted even more foreign borrowing, to settle past obligations. This strategy did not lead to the enhancement of capacity or the creation of production facilities. A further complication arose from the pressure on available tax revenue to meet not only debt-servicing requirements but also the servicing of other governmental responsibilities. Deficit financing became inevitable, with its associated monetary expansion.

The conclusions call for a search for new approaches to the African debt problem. Most pressing is the problem of countries in arrears to the IMF. The new IMF approach of "rights accumulation" programs does not guarantee that these countries will be able to manage a credible adjustment program without front-loaded external support being in place. The African countries are experiencing intense anxiety in the face of a relapse into the negative capital flows of a couple of years back, the diversion of scarce funds to newly liberalized East European countries, the marginalization of their external debt worries, and prolonged loss of ground in development. New ways need to be found to address these concerns.

African countries in turn are committed to continue implementing adjustment programs to achieve a greater degree of self-sufficiency. In particular, growth-oriented programs should focus on action to increase domestic savings and attract the return of flight capital. The encouragement of private savings should be pursued through the offer of attractive rates of interest and the promotion of appropriate financial institutions. Public savings should also be boosted where possible by exploiting untapped tax avenues and containing public expenditure within limits consistent with the efficient provision of service. With regard to the latter aspect, expenditure patterns should be scrutinized carefully and realistically, with a view to eliminating wasteful and avoidable outlays. The quality of development projects should also be scrutinized to ensure maximum social returns. Attention should also be given to the policy of contracting loans. Given the present debt overhang, contracting loans of comparatively short maturity at market interest rates should be avoided as far as possible. Concentration should be on loans obtained on concessional terms for the realization of worthwhile projects.

The foregoing survey is unavoidably incomprehensive. It no doubt leaves out some vital issues and oversimplifies others in its broad sweep. The intention, however, was first to attempt to show the interrelationship between debt and economic growth in Africa, and second to provoke you to a more detailed and specific discussion of the relevant issues that I have not covered. The subject for our discourse is not only topical but of such importance to the future of Africa that it deserves the most intensive and comprehensive discussion possible.

The ongoing search for solutions to our problems will require African central bank governors to probe with increased urgency the implementation of regional economic and monetary cooperation, beyond matters that we shall discuss in this symposium. In addition, I should like to call the attention of the Managing Director, Mr. Michel Camdessus, to the urgency we central bank governors attach to the development of technical capacities in our institutions if we are to efficiently proceed with the implementation of the program of reform in our respective countries.

M. Camdessus

Allow me to tell you it is my pleasure to have, thanks to the generous hospitality of the Government of Botswana and its Central Bank, this unique occasion to meet with my former colleagues, the central bank governors of Africa and so many of my present Governors. My pleasure is very special as I have just visited three African countries, Mozambique, Zimbabwe, and Zambia, with which the IMF shares very important cooperation, and we are here in a country all of you consider a remarkable example of wise and efficient macroeconomic management. What a good time and what a good place for sharing experiences and thoughts!

Yet Africa is experiencing difficult times: times of natural disasters and setbacks, times, also, of man-made problems including wars and civil disorders. After some twenty years of disappointing performance in much of Africa, resulting in lower real per capita incomes, it is easy to understand why many feel tempted to despair about the prospects. Moreover, the global economic environment is worsening, with the Middle East war and the slowdown in some industrial countries, while the suspension of the Uruguay Round raises questions about the prospects for world trade. These setbacks compound the existing external difficulties, including the shortage of external financing and slow progress toward resolving the debt problem.

But in contrast to all this, we also see the encouraging achievements of those countries that have prudently managed their resources and steadfastly pursued their reform programs. Consider the encouraging recent record of the nearly thirty African countries that have been persevering with growth-oriented adjustment programs. The programs are producing results—positive real growth, the steady transformation and improvement of their economic structures and systems, and, in particular, an improvement in the living standards of the rural population.

This very difficult global situation, and the experience of the three countries I have just visited, reminds me forcefully that African countries and the international community together cannot escape a joint responsibility. More solid economic progress is achievable, but only if we reinforce what I call the unwritten law of international cooperation: that countries should implement appropriate policies to the best of their ability, and that these policies should be supported by creditors and donors.

What does this mean at present?

In terms of *domestic policies,* it means steady macroeconomic discipline and far-reaching structural reforms to achieve sustainable growth in a medium-term context. This is the approach that the lessons of experience suggest. I have welcomed such pragmatism in the economic strategies of many African governments. We see strong evidence of this in the countries whose economic strategies the IMF is supporting with financial and technical assistance. This realistic approach holds the promise of sustained positive growth per capita, an objective nobody could consider overambitious.

It is true that structural reforms do not produce their full results quickly. One cannot expect to correct in a few years what has sometimes been decades of structural misadjustment. The results so far have been modest in some cases, at least partly because of the legacy of mistaken investment priorities and development strategies that were for too long inward looking and based excessively on state interventionism. It is taking time to rectify these policies and to move toward a more productive economic system—in which private entrepreneurship is encouraged, given sufficient scope, and allowed to flourish. It is also taking time to adjust the role of the public sector to its proper function in a modern market-based economy.

It is not surprising that those African countries (such as Botswana and Mauritius) that were quick to deal with their economic problems and showed firm economic management have achieved an enviable economic performance. Equally important, a significant number of African countries

(The Gambia, Ghana, Kenya, Malawi, Morocco, Nigeria, Senegal, Togo, and Tunisia —but of course that is not a complete list!) have been implementing far-reaching structural reforms for several years. These reforms are yielding encouraging results, and their long-term benefits will be reaped increasingly in the period ahead. Certain countries—including Mozambique, Tanzania, and Uganda—that are still experiencing severe economic difficulties are already seeing significant results from their commitment to effective adjustment programs, including a revival of economic growth or slower domestic inflation, or both. I was particularly delighted to be in Harare, Zimbabwe, at the moment when our common friend Senior Minister Chidzero was launching, with our full support, a comprehensive "Framework for Economic Reform" covering the 1991–95 period. The sheer diversity of these programs—even if they reflect common basic principles—demonstrates clearly the importance we attach to support really homegrown programs, thereby increasing the chances of being better understood and supported by public opinion.

Truly, in many countries, we see encouraging signs. Clearly, there is a definite need for further structural improvements. In each country there are sectors where the progress has been inadequate. One of these is of particular concern to the central bankers gathered for this symposium; I refer to the urgent need to reform and strengthen the commercial banking sectors in several countries. This is particularly important where we see insolvent banks, an overhang of nonperforming loans, a banking structure that does not promote competition, and the persistence of negative real interest rates. These weaknesses in banking systems hamper the development of competitive and productive economies and render more difficult the conduct of sound policies. And in most countries, I believe, there is scope for more vigorous measures to promote private sector activity, decentralize decision making, and reduce the stifling impact of excessive state intervention and unnecessary bureaucracy. All this simply underlines the need for persistence in forcing through the structural and systemic changes that are a necessary condition, though never sufficient in themselves, for the creation of a more productive and viable economy.

So far I have stressed the responsibility of the Africans themselves. They know that the primary task rests with them, with their governments, and with their people to forge their own destiny. Help from outside is indispensable. But it can only supplement these countries' own efforts. The experience of the Fund in recent years has been that governments are more likely to find success if their programs are both well designed technically and broadly supported by the public. This implies, in particular, that these programs ensure that the vulnerable members of society are cushioned from the most severe transitional consequences of necessary adjustment. This is not only compatible with, but effectively supportive of, the process of adjustment for growth.

Increasingly, we are seeing that effective political leadership involves a complex process to marshal a consensus behind a coherent medium-term strategy. Hence the increased emphasis in Africa on improving the "qualitative" design of economic programs. This is reflected in a greater concern to ensure that revenue systems are efficient and fair, and public expenditure is channeled in accordance with economic and social priorities. In many countries, we hear loud and really justified criticism of expensive, if not extravagant, projects or excessive military spending. In times of such scarce saving and such pressing basic needs, this has got to be corrected. I do hope that the relaxation of regional tensions, particularly in Southern Africa, will be seen by the governments of this area as a favorable occasion to demonstrate their commitment to reduce such expenditures to a minimum. Acting simultaneously and, why not, in a coordinated fashion, could allow them to be bolder than acting on their own. Let us hope that this could enable all countries of Southern Africa to use the resulting "peace dividend" to meet pressing needs, and to pay greater attention to the development of human capital.

These are only a few aspects of the growing demand in Africa for "good governance," meaning more responsive and accountable governments, and for more pluralistic systems of political representation. These trends are improving the chances for economic and systemic reforms to be better understood, better accepted, and so more successful. That is why they are particularly welcomed by Africa's friends.

In discharging these demanding responsibilities, governments can be most effectively supported by bold regional cooperation as underscored in the Lagos Plan of action. If anything, my recent stay in Southern Africa has further brought to my attention the formidable potential for additional economic efficiency your countries could release in forging closer regional ties. There is no need to tell you that we, in the IMF, look forward to strengthening our relationships with key regional organizations in Africa and particularly with the Southern African Development Coordination Conference (SADCC).

In retrospect, the experience of Africa with regional cooperation offers some useful lessons. First, it may be helpful to start with modest but feasible programs of cooperation, by focusing on selected areas where the prospects for mutual benefit are largest. Cooperation along this line, as exemplified by SADCC, can concentrate on specific areas, such as transportation, energy, industry, and banking. Second, efforts at economic integration stand a better chance of succeeding if they are also outward looking. Economic integration at the regional level and in the world economy are not incompatible. It is important that a reduction of trade barriers within any region be accompanied by measures to reduce domestic distortions, liberalize markets, and improve competitiveness. Regional cooperation is most effective if it is accompanied by careful harmonization by the cooperating countries of their policies in key areas; in particular, to increase the scope for trade with the outside world. The ultimate aim must be to ensure that African exports are competitive in the industrial countries. And here also, how could I refrain from mentioning that seeing key countries in the area now implementing economic policies inspired by the same principles, I do believe that prospects for fruitful regional cooperation are made even more promising and could at the appropriate time culminate in various forms of monetary arrangements.

More effective policies in African countries will not succeed—however—and this is my second main proposition—unless their reform programs are adequately supported by the rest of the world. I repeat, *the responsibility for development and for economic adjustment is a shared one.* The industrial countries, in particular, have a special duty to Africa. In the more difficult global economic environment of today, I would like to focus on three main areas: the level of activity in the industrial countries, finance, and trade.

First, the long expansionary phase in the industrial countries has recently faltered, with slowdowns in some major countries. It will be important for Africa that the industrial countries, which are the major market for its exports, resume growth at sustainable rates. The Fund expects that the present slowdown will be relatively shallow and short. Because any artificial boost to their activity would be self-defeating, the IMF is recommending a cautious fiscal and monetary policy stance for the industrial countries. We think that policies should be geared mainly to ensuring that the next expansionary phase will be a healthy one. Therefore, we are stressing the desirability of continued fiscal consolidation, as the most effective means of bringing about a rise in national savings rates. This will be very important, in view of the global shortage of savings, as will the need to provide for substantial levels of investment in the period ahead, not only in the industrial countries themselves, but also in Eastern Europe, Latin America, Africa, and elsewhere. It is only through an improvement in savings performance that a consolidation of the present downward trend in global real interest rates will be possible—which would be very helpful to the developing countries.

Second, finance. The prospects for some of the traditional sources of external finance are not encouraging. It would be unwise to expect a buoyant provision of bilateral or multilateral development assistance in the period immediately ahead. The most recent projections of the Development Assistance Committee (DAC) point to only a modest nominal rise. The commercial banks are showing a reluctance to extend new finance to developing countries on the scale of a few years back. Of course, we should beware of overgeneralizing. The banks *are* lending, on a careful and selective basis, to the most creditworthy countries. But much of Africa will clearly need to rely heavily in the period ahead on domestic sources of finance (including the return of flight capital) and on nonbank types of private foreign capital.

In my view, the industrial countries can improve their provision of finance to Africa in three ways. First, even if their provision of official development assistance (ODA) is not expected to grow substantially in the years immediately ahead, they can do much to ensure that these scarce resources are channeled in ways that contribute to development in direct and productive ways. I am encouraged by the growing evidence that donors are working to enhance the usefulness of their assistance, while streamlining their procedures for approval and disbursement. Second, they could increase the proportion of grants in total ODA. And a third avenue is in the area of debt relief; much progress has already been achieved, in the cooperative framework of the Paris Club, particularly under the active and talented chairmanship of J.C. Trichet and D. Samuel-Lajeunesse. There have been several useful initiatives on debt—including that proposed by Mr. Major when he was still Chancellor of the Exchequer—and I understand that the industrial countries are working hard to provide these initiatives with constructive responses. In our view, in many cases they can be of critical importance.

Trade is the third area where the industrial countries need to act soon, and forcefully, to improve the global economic environment. A meaningful reduction of trade barriers, in the context of the Uruguay Round, is essential. It will reinvigorate the expansion of the industrial countries themselves, and create the prospects of stronger trade for all countries. The importance of this open door policy for Africa, and in particular for those African countries that are implementing outward-looking reform programs, is self-evident. *The present opportunity should not be missed.*

Last, let me add a brief word on the IMF's own contribution. The Fund also shares the responsibility for Africa's future. As many of you know, this is a subject that is close to my heart! Nobody needs to be reassured here that the Fund will help Africa face the challenges that lie ahead. We now have concessional facilities, the structural adjustment facility (SAF) and the enhanced structural adjustment facility (ESAF)—quite essential in the case of Zambia and Mozambique—which are tailor-made mechanisms for helping any low-income African country that seeks to achieve long-term and sustained growth through structural reforms. We are ready, as we have shown with the creation of the rights approach, from which, I hope, Zambia will promptly benefit, and with our response to the recent oil shock, to adapt as needed our instruments to the emerging problems. The Fund, as I noted, is currently supporting the programs of nearly thirty African countries. The Fund stands ready to help all others, and is impatient to do so, both with technical assistance and with financial support as soon as they are ready to embark on sound programs. If the quota increase is promptly ratified—and for that a positive vote on the Third Amendment of the Articles of Agreement is essential—we will have the financial resources: what we need are more countries to come forward with well-designed programs.

I should like to end by mentioning something that has come up in each of the African countries that I have visited in the last week. Everywhere, I have been asked if the large amounts of assistance that the IMF is extending to others, including Eastern Europe, will oblige it to shortchange Africa. My answer is a definite "no." No Fund resources will be shifted. The Fund will support good economic programs in all member countries and with the same heartfelt commitment continue to help to catalyze support from other sources. That is our basic mandate.

After visiting Mozambique, Zimbabwe, and Zambia, and being today in Botswana, I believe more than ever that mediocre performances in this continent are not inevitable. It is my deep conviction that many countries in Africa can find in the 1990s their own window of opportunity for successfully launching homegrown programs, which could deserve strong international support and find added efficiency in active regional cooperation. We will be proud to support them.

I
Structural Adjustment in Africa
Future Approaches and
Lessons Learned from the Past

A View from Africa

A.K. Mullei

Economic distortions affecting the balance of payments in the late 1970s, particularly the sharp shift in the terms of trade, spurred an increasing number of African countries to undertake both stabilization and structural adjustment programs. Some countries (e.g., Algeria, Botswana, Ethiopia, Lesotho, Libyan Arab Jamahiriya, and Nigeria) designed their own approaches (i.e., homegrown programs), which did not differ significantly from the widespread programs undertaken with the assistance of the International Monetary Fund (IMF) and the World Bank. As a result of the new programs, important and long-lasting changes have been applied. In many of the countries, austere budgetary and monetary policies have been effected with a view to containing balance of payments and inflationary pressures and to promoting economic confidence. A much stronger role for the private sector has been encouraged, and significant efforts have been made to make it adapt to market signals. Policies that recognize private initiatives in production and investment have been pursued, even in some socially oriented countries. The adoption of, and perseverance with, stabilization programs and structural adjustment reforms in the 1980s reflected an expectation on the part of African governments that the IMF and the World Bank would play a catalytic role in facilitating the flow of large financial resources from the two multilateral institutions and other external sources. It was also expected that the adoption of structural adjustment reforms would help African countries eliminate their balance of payments deficits, manage their external debts, and resume growth of their economies.

Notwithstanding the policies and measures applied throughout the decade of the 1980s, Africa's economic crisis has presented an extraordinary challenge to the development community. As the crisis continues to deepen, the concern of academics and policymakers has heightened and, naturally, some searching questions have been raised. The concern has also led to the search for alternative models for formulating structural adjustment programs. Some of the suggestions have focused on policy instruments and approaches.[1] Others have emphasized the need for a human-centered approach to protect particularly the vulnerable groups in society. The IMF and the World Bank staffs have also modified their views on the formulation of structural adjustment programs over the years, paying more attention to structural factors.

As we begin the new decade of the 1990s, it is proper to evaluate the trends of the crisis and the measures applied. It is also useful to assess the successes and failures in order to draw lessons and chart a course for future approaches. While my paper is intended to make only a modest contribution in this direction, it is admitted that no single paper can hope to do full justice to the diversity of Africa's experiences with structural adjustment strategies and the differing views on how to tackle the problems associated with them. The paper does not pretend to present full answers: its goal is to sift carefully through available information and to set forth an assessment of the lessons learned and the measures and approaches needed to improve Africa's development prospects in the 1990s.

The paper is organized as follows. The first section relates the need for a larger volume of imports to promote growth and investment in Africa and the necessity, therefore, for stabilization and structural adjustment programs to provide a larger volume of financing on terms that are more appropriate for the African situation. The second section discusses the problem of linking additionality of external assistance to stricter conditionality and unrealistic repayment schedules for outstanding external debts and argues that the current conditionality prescriptions in the absence of substantial debt relief and more adequate external financing can only lead to excessive idle capacity, rising unemployment, forgone output, and deterioration in living standards for African countries.

The third section suggests that for stabilization and structural adjustment programs to be successful and viable in the 1990s, larger flows of external financing are needed. Also needed is a longer time horizon for carrying out important aspects of structural reforms, particularly those aimed at improving the response capacities of African economic systems, such as the strengthening of the performance of the public sector and its

---

[1] Such as the popularized *African Alternative to Structural Adjustment Programs: A Framework for Transformation and Recovery,* by the Economic Commission for Africa (ECA) (Addis Ababa, 1989).

savings-generating capacity, providing the private sector with a more efficient regulatory environment, removing obstacles to supply bottlenecks, and introducing an efficient policy framework for overall management of the African economy.

The paper concludes by underscoring the point that African countries have lost a terrible amount of ground and time for growth over the period of stabilization and structural adjustment programs.

African Experience with Stabilization and Structural Adjustment Programs

In a spirited attempt to provide an in-depth evaluation of the impact of structural adjustment programs, the World Bank undertook a study in 1988 of the experience of Africa with stabilization and structural adjustment programs. The study states that "[t]he adjustment lending (AL) countries were on average hurt more by changes in the terms of trade, real interest rates, and external indebtedness than countries that did not receive adjustment loans (NAL countries)."[2] The study indicates that the hoped-for switching and growth-augmenting effects of adjustment lending are not apparent in adjustment lending countries in Africa and emphasizes that the forgone gross domestic product (GDP) of countries that have received adjustment loans was more than 1 percentage point greater than that of those that did not receive loans.

The study further presents some macroeconomic indicators of performance that show that for countries in sub-Saharan Africa that received adjustment loans (1) the investment/GDP ratio fell from 20.6 percent *before* adjustment lending to 17.1 percent *after*, a decline of 3.5 percent; (2) the annual growth rate of GDP fell by 0.9 percent after adjustment lending; (3) the budget deficit worsened, falling from 6.5 percent to 7.5 percent; and (4) debt service and private consumption per capita either deteriorated significantly or remained unchanged after adjustment lending. The study asserts that the falling investment shares in GDP suggest that the required reduction in expenditures fell disproportionately and more heavily on investment than on consumption, thereby jeopardizing future growth.

---

[2]World Bank, *Adjustment Lending: An Evaluation of Ten Years of Experience*, Policy and Research Series, No. 1 (Washington: The World Bank, 1988), page 20.

Even more dismal are the results presented for social indicators. The study shows that, between 1980 and 1985, for 33 countries in sub-Saharan Africa that received adjustment loans, the social indicators showed no progress. Although "[l]ife expectancy at birth improved from 46 to 48 years, . . . the infant mortality rate remained at 126 per thousand, and the daily caloric intake declined from 2,060 to 1,911. In the same period, for a subgroup of 11 low-income sub-Saharan countries, per capita education outlays fell from US$10.80 to US$6.30 and per capita health expenditures from US$3.60 to US$2.80."[3]

The adverse impact of stabilization and structural adjustment programs on social conditions of the poor during the 1980s had been confirmed earlier by United Nations Children's Fund (UNICEF) in a widely publicized study.[4] UNICEF's latest appraisal in *State of the World's Children* also estimates that at least half a million young children have died in developing countries (particularly in Africa and Latin America) as a result of economic setbacks precipitated by structural adjustment policies that focus solely on macroeconomic indicators.[5] The UNICEF study also emphasizes that the effects of disinvestment in human capital in the 1980s will extend to the next generation, and its result will be reflected in the undereducation of many adults in the next century. In August 1990, the World Bank confirmed this assessment when it reported that real per capita spending in the social sectors decreased in many developing countries, especially those adjusting intensely, and that undernutrition increased in low-income African countries.[6]

To complement the above studies, this paper analyses the experiences of 17 African countries that have experimented with traditional stabilization and structural adjustment programs. The analysis uses the traditional before-and-after analytical framework to capture the impact of stabilization and structural adjustment programs on selected key variables, including real rates of growth in GDP, domestic savings, investment, inflation, exports and imports, debt-service ratios, and net transfers. These macroeconomic aggregates are selected because they can measure the impact of the economic measures currently used for reforms. They are also widely

---

[3] Ibid., page 29, Box 2.2.

[4] C.A. Cornia, Richard Jolly, and Francis Stewart, eds., *Adjustment with a Human Face: Protecting the Vulnerable and Promoting Growth* (New York: Oxford University Press, 1987).

[5] UNICEF, *State of the World's Children* (New York: United Nations, 1989).

[6] See Nanak Kakwani, Elene Makonnen, and Jacques van der Gaag, "Structural Adjustment and Living Conditions in Developing Countries," Working Paper No. 467 (Washington: The World Bank, Population and Human Resources Department, 1990).

accepted targets and are consistent with the purposes of structural adjustment, which is to permit countries to restore long-term growth.

While the methodology adopted in this paper compares post-adjustment situations with preadjustment situations, it is recognized that different approaches are possible, such as a comparison of the actual performances with targets or of simulations with actuals. It is also recognized that while results may vary, depending on the methodology chosen, using prior-and-post comparison is attractive because it reflects the conditions that countries actually undergo. Besides, it is difficult to obtain complete information on the targets for all countries. It should be noted that the results of this analysis measure short-term impact effects rather than long-term effects. The short-term effects are critical in determining the sustainability of a structural adjustment program.

The 17 countries chosen for the empirical analysis include Côte d'Ivoire (1981), Kenya (1981), Tanzania (1981), Zambia (1981), Malawi (1982), Zimbabwe (1982), Ghana (1983), Morocco (1983), Zaïre (1983), Niger (1984), Senegal (1984), Sudan (1984), Madagascar (1985), Tunisia (1985), Burundi (1986), Nigeria (1986), and Uganda (1987).[7] The selected countries were determined strictly on the basis of data available. In each case, the analysis is based on data relating to at least three years before the announcement date of the structural adjustment reforms. The announcement date is chosen for two reasons. First, it is the date on which implementation of a program starts. Second, it is the announcement date that changes economic behavior of the country by modifying or conditioning its expectations. The ending date for "after" analysis for all cases is 1988. All the figures are given in real terms.

The data for the analysis were assembled as follows: for Sudan, Niger, and Senegal, 3 years before and 5 years after the structural adjustment loan; for Zaïre, Ghana, Morocco, and Zimbabwe, 3 years before and 6 years after; for Malawi, Tanzania, and Kenya, 3 years before and 7 years after; for Madagascar and Tunisia, 3 years before and 4 years after; for Uganda, 3 years before and 2 years after; for Nigeria and Burundi, 3 years before and 3 years after; and for Zambia and Côte d'Ivoire, 3 years before and 8 years after. Table 1 presents a summary of country performance with respect to the eight macroeconomic indicators.

The general picture that emerges from Table 1 is that eight countries, namely, Burundi, Ghana, Kenya, Madagascar, Malawi, Morocco, Nigeria, and Zimbabwe, showed improvement from structural adjustment policies;

---

[7] The date in parentheses is the year that the structural adjustment began.

Table 1. Summary of Country Performance with Respect to Key Macroeconomic Indicators

Country	1 INFLA	2 GDPG	3 GDIY	4 GDSY	5 EXPG	6 IMPG	7 DEBSY	8 NERT	Percent Success
			(In percent)				(In millions of U.S. dollars)		
Nigeria	22.8 (17.0)	1.0 (3.0)	8.6 (10.8)	9.0 (13.5)	2.6 (–11.8)	–18.0 (2.1)	32.0 (24.0)	–1050 (–491.0)	87.5
Niger	10.7 (–0.8)	4.2 (–1.5)	23.6 (9.0)	8.0 (3.0)	–6.2 (–3.5)	1.7 (–5.8)	41.0 (39.0)	77 (–41.0)	37.5
Ghana	63.0 (44.8)	0.1 (2.3)	4.7 (7.4)	3.0 (6.0)	–13.8 (7.8)	–4.6 (8.5)	13.6 (38.0)	51 (118.0)	87.5
Côte d'Ivoire	14.8 (5.4)	7.6 (–0.1)	28.7 (16.9)	25.3 (21.2)	6.9 (–1.9)	5.9 (–9.4)	20.0 (44.0)	609 (211.6)	12.5
Senegal	11.6 (5.0)	5.1 (2.6)	16.1 (14.8)	9.7 (6.4)	7.9 (–0.1)	5.0 (–4.5)	11.6 (25.0)	215 (96.4)	12.5
Morocco	10.8 (6.7)	3.0 (3.0)	28.0 (21.0)	7.4 (18.0)	–7.9 (12.4)	7.4 (17.9)	37.6 (34.0)	634 (35.0)	50.0
Tunisia	10.3 (6.8)	3.3 (2.8)	31.0 (30.0)	21.0 (19.0)	2.9 (1.5)	–3.9 (5.5)	19.3 (26.1)	196 (–114.5)	37.5
Sudan	27.0 (38.0)	4.4 (0.3)	17.7 (10.3)	3.6 (4.5)	16.9 (–1.3)	10.9 (–3.9)	25.1 (25.9)	574 (139.0)	12.5
Kenya	11.2 (9.8)	4.4 (3.9)	27.0 (23.0)	18.2 (21.0)	–7.7 (3.7)	–10.0 (2.1)	23.4 (39.0)	165 (–25.0)	62.5
Uganda	114.4 (210.8)	–3.7 (2.5)	12.4 (9.2)	11.0 (3.0)	4.3 (–18.3)	–3.1 (27.7)	40.6 (43.5)	56 (179.0)	37.5

A VIEW FROM AFRICA

Burundi	8.8 (4.5)	4.9 (1.3)	23.0 (18.0)	3.7 (5.7)	4.8 (5.8)	3.8 (6.9)	19.2 (38.3)	71 (79.0)	75.0
Tanzania	23.2 (31.3)	0.3 (1.7)	16.8 (17.0)	11.7 (5.3)	18.8 (−4.2)	−10.2 (0.2)	16.2 (32.3)	242 (171.0)	25.0
Malawi	10.8 (18.0)	−0.8 (3.2)	31.0 (16.7)	11.0 (12.5)	8.9 (−2.4)	−8.7 (3.1)	(26.5) (24.9)	67 (66.0)	50.0
Madagascar	20.2 (14.2)	−0.4 (0.9)	13.4 (14.7)	6.4 (11.2)	0.3 (1.9)	0.4 (2.8)	23.0 (52.0)	133 (93.0)	75.0
Zimbabwe	15.8 (14.2)	7.6 (1.7)	19.0 (19.5)	14.8 (21.0)	3.9 (7.0)	14.0 (−5.5)	6.6 (32.6)	199 (−35.2)	50.0
Zambia	10.0 (13.7)	0.2 (0.2)	20.4 (15.8)	21.0 (14.0)	−6.7 (0.0)	−4.7 (−1.3)	22.6 (28.0)	151 (100.9)	25.0
Zaïre	37.7 (59.7)	0.8 (2.6)	24.7 (16.7)	6.0 (14.8)	13.3 (18.5)	23.1 (14.6)	19.2 (20.1)	93 (13.0)	37.5
Percent Success	64.7	41.2	35.3	58.8	52.9	64.7	25.5	23.5	

Sources: International Monetary Fund, *International Financial Statistics Yearbook* (1989); The World Bank, *World Tables* (1989/90) and *World Debt Tables* (various issues).

Note: INFLA = the rate of inflation; GDPG = the rate of growth of the economy; GDIY = the investment rate; GDSY = the savings rate; EXPG = rate of growth of export; IMPG = rate of growth of import; DEBSY = debt-service ratio; NERT = net resource transfer. The numbers in parentheses represent performance after structural adjustment.

the remaining nine showed deterioration in their performances. Out of the eight macroeconomic indicators, success was achieved in four, namely, rate of inflation, of growth of export, of growth of import, and of savings; the performances of the other four macroeconomic indicators—growth rate, investment rate, debt-service ratio, and net resource transfer—were not encouraging. The summary evidence suggests that the expectations that were assumed to follow from the application of stabilization and structural adjustment have not materialized in most cases. This reflects rigidities in the structures of African economies and also asymmetries in the behavioral responses of governments, donors, producers, and suppliers of loan funds, which call for caution in the nondiscriminate expectations.[8]

Based on the outcome of the foregoing analysis, it is possible to surmise that the mixed performances of African countries, as indicated from the empirical evidence of the sample countries discussed above, result from the structuralist contentions that (1) austerity measures may adversely affect the supply of imports for export-oriented countries; (2) the long gestation period required for certain agricultural exports may not provide results in the short term; (3) when the supply of exports from adjusting countries is increased during stable global demand, the terms of trade might deteriorate; (4) where the larger part of domestic production is either agricultural export commodities or mining products, the cutback in domestic demand brought about by monetary contraction may not produce a greater share of output available for exports, since only a very small share of exportable commodities is consumed locally; (5) the contraction of money supply (credit restraint), and compression of government expenditures in the presence of curb markets for finance and monopolistic or oligopolistic price-setting behavior, may lead to an increase in price inflation in the short run; (6) with supply and demand both determining prices, a policy package that tries to restrict demand but ends up reducing supply, may well be inflationary; (7) in countries with severe institutional rigidities and less open markets, the potential for supply-side policies

---

[8]It is readily conceded that there are qualitative variables that are not captured in the figures, but their omission reinforces rather than undermines the case made in the paper that the evidence for success of adjustment programs is at best mixed. The imponderables—the social and human costs of adjustments mainly, but also possibly other factors—that do not show up in the figures are negative effects. The positive effects, such as improvement in growth performance, easing of inflation, among others, are well captured.

is likely to depend on the amount of time allowed for adjustment reforms.[9]

In recognition of the above limitations, investigations have been made and the search continues for alternative approaches to the analysis of interrelationships in economies that are semi-industrialized, have marked dualism, are beset with the existence of parallel informal markets, in particular a curb market for loan funds, and are significantly dependent on imported intermediate inputs as a factor of production.[10]

The Search for an Alternative Policy Approach

The case for searching for an alternative approach in the design of stabilization and structural adjustment for African countries can be best explained in the first instance by delineating the plausible effects of the expenditure-changing policies that are applied rigorously, to reduce aggregate demand and eliminate external deficits, and the expenditure-switching policies used to change relative prices of domestic and foreign goods. This traditional approach to stabilization and structural adjustment has been costly for African countries for two reasons. First, while income-dampening policies can be relatively inexpensive for countries with high-income and open economies, for those with low incomes and limited degrees of openness and supply response, the cost of income dampening can be very high. This point has often been neglected in formulating adjustment programs for African countries, where foreign trade sectors are very small indeed. A further point that has also been overlooked is the size of the imbalance in the external

---

[9]The argument of the paper is not that the removal of structural rigidities should be the focus of policy in *all* countries, irrespective of their specific situations. Clearly, the problem is country-specific. In many countries, the substitution of production, say from cash-crop export production into manufacturing or other value-added activities, is limited because of rigidities. External shocks are no doubt important, but where structural rigidities exist, substitution in production is harder. In countries where substitution possibilities are more significant, traditional measures may be very effective. In other countries, different approaches are more appropriate.

[10]By *alternative*, parallel is meant, not opposite, with focus on different aspects. Thus, demand-reduction through monetary contraction may adversely affect investment rather than consumption. Alternative sequencing of policies and financing could leave investment intact or even stimulate it, while consumption demand is met by supply-expanding policies. Other variations and permutations are possible and therefore more can be done to further attune adjustment programs to Africa's specific needs and peculiarities. Foremost among them is the financing and performance criteria monitoring sequence on which the paper lays due stress.

account that has to be eliminated by income dampening. When the imbalance is very large (as has often been the case in African countries), the income forgone, as a result of austerity measures, will be large and unbearable.

A second argument for searching for an alternative approach to structural adjustment is that in African countries, where there are severe institutional rigidities, the magnitude of an import or export response to a policy change will depend heavily upon the amount of time that is allowed for adjustment. The longer the time horizon, the greater will be the response to price or exchange rate changes. This last observation has important implications for stabilization and adjustment policies, because it implies that the attempt to force the entire adjustment within a short period necessitates larger deflation of the economy than would be called for if a longer period were allowed. The larger deflationary effects usually run the risk of overshooting and thus engendering further instabilities accompanied by additional costs, not only in the form of increased risk and uncertainty but also in the form of misapplication of resources in terms of forgone employment and output.

A more serious argument for alternative stabilization and structural adjustment relates to the absence, so far, of credible adjustment programs that are truly growth oriented, that take adequate account of the needs for health, education, and other essential social services, and that, at the same time, take into account the fact that major changes in the structure of production do take a long time to yield results and require specific investments.

The necessity for designing adjustment programs that contain growth has recently been reflected by the search for alternative approaches to the design of adjustment policy packages. One important line along which this development is taking place is the growth-oriented adjustment program research project that the research staff of both the IMF and the World Bank are currently engaged in; they are trying to develop a stabilization and structural adjustment design that includes aspects both of the IMF focus on external financing dynamics and balance of payments correction and the World Bank's growth and investment concerns. Although it is still being formulated, the approach holds the promise of wider applicability for the African countries in the 1990s.[11]

---

[11] See for instance, Mohsin Khan and Peter J. Montiel, "Growth-Oriented Adjustment Programs: A Conceptual Framework," IMF Working Paper, No. 88/64 (unpublished, Washington: International Monetary Fund, 1988) and Ernesto Hernandez-Cata, "Issues in the Design of Growth Exercises," IMF Working Paper, No. 88/65 (unpublished, Washington: International Monetary Fund, 1988).

It is worth emphasizing that the growth-oriented approach put together by the IMF and the World Bank augments the traditional model. It first builds in a growth dimension with an incremental capital/output ratio relationship as a focus and then enhances that with supply-side inspired support policies. Although the reformulation can be seen as a step in the right direction, it does not go far enough. It still depicts smooth market-type reaction functions. Such relationships are not typical of African countries.

Another approach, which the African Centre for Monetary Studies has termed the "neo-structuralist synthesis,"[12] goes further toward introducing the structural rigidities of developing—and African—countries into the argumentation. It derives policy packages that are distinct in their characteristics from the traditional ones and that evidently address African specificities. The neo-structuralist synthesis approach consists of three main arguments. First, it contends that inflation and balance of payments difficulties are not the results mainly of domestic excess demand but also of specific supply bottlenecks and external shocks. Often, excess capacity exists in the economy, but the missing element is the extra supply of foreign exchange for intermediate inputs in critical sectors. Second, it argues that the composite goods sector model exemplified in the monetary approach to balance of payments does not reflect the sectoral composition of production in African countries, which relies heavily on imported components. At least three goods sectors should be discerned: importables, exportables, and nontraded goods, all of which have significant amounts of imported components, so that their price elasticities of supply may depend on the exchange rate, export subsidies, and other policy variables. The third argument is that the mix between financing and adjustment is as important as incentives and financial liberalization. To smooth out structural rigidities, front-loaded financing is necessary so that when policies take effect with a lag, supply can expand in a timely fashion.

According to this approach, correction for disequilibrium in the balance of payments should be built more on the growth of exports and less on the reduction of imports. It emphasizes that a policy aimed at boosting the contribution of export growth to balance of payments management should consist of "differential devaluation" that would raise the local currency

---

[12] While a concrete model for this approach has not been proposed, the main outline recurs in the writings of authors such as Tony Killick, R.H. Green, A. Floxley, and Edmar Bacha.

revenue from the export of industrial products or semi-finished goods by setting the incentives received by each sector at a level comparable to the total production costs. The neo-structuralist synthesis also focuses on the sectoral approach. Besides the greater emphasis laid on structural adjustment with longer-term programs and financing, the approach advocates mostly supply-oriented policies that use as main instruments price reform, the raising of institutional efficiency, the upgrading of investment policy to refocus priority on agricultural and food self-sufficiency, and the improvement of foreign-debt management to ensure a sustained inflow of funds over an estimated long-term debt cycle.

Two important developments have resulted from the neo-structuralist synthesis approach. First, the specificities of borrowing countries' economies are more strongly emphasized, with a prominent role given to the possibilities of rigidities (elasticity-pessimism), the existence of curb markets, and possible perverse effects of devaluation, financial reform, including interest rate liberalization, and inversion of priority on investment. Second, under the thrust of protests from advocates of this new approach, the double imposition of generally sound World Bank policies and often severe demand-management policies on borrowing countries is giving way to a more coordinated approach in which greater recognition is given to nuances underlined by this new orientation. The problem with the approach, in which disequilibrium is the central theme, is that only various disjointed aspects of the dual economy are rigorously modeled, and the task of bringing these rigorous parts into a coherent whole has yet to be addressed. Furthermore, disequilibrium analysis and the dynamics of adjustment through the short run to the longer term make difficult a robust mathematical modeling of the neo-structuralist synthesis approach. Yet, the policy conclusions that derive from the imperfectly formulated model seem more intellectually satisfactory in the tracking of African economies' adjustment problems.

Another approach, developed by the United Nations Conference on Trade and Development (UNCTAD), puts African countries' problems more markedly in the international exchange framework. The UNCTAD approach proposes "unequal exchange" (that is, self-perpetuating unfavorable terms of trade) as the cause of the persistent monetary disequilibrium problems of African countries. In its analysis, UNCTAD derives a policy package for adjustment that carries a strong component of foreign aid, restructuring of the international terms of trade, and discretionary intervention in commodity markets to correct the unfavorable terms of trade effect. Economic integration in Africa and cooperation both subregionally and regionally are other important elements of the policy measures recommended.[13]

The UNCTAD approach is grounded in the belief that the prevailing market structures in African countries cannot be changed in the course of one, two, or even three medium-term structural adjustments, and since imperfect market structures send the wrong signals of what patterns of production, consumption, investment and saving are required, a policy of price and direct credit control is well inspired. Furthermore, if the repayment of externally contracted loans and the maintenance of the balance of payments equilibrium without resort to measures that impair the free movement of trade and payments goals are to be strived for, the maintenance of a relatively equitable distribution of income is an even greater priority; otherwise not only will it happen that no program of financial discipline will be sustainable, but also that larger economic disruption may ensue. Third, and most important, market imperfections and structural deficiencies require the continued intervention of the public sector in production, in investment, and in control. It is, however, readily conceded that inefficiencies exist in the public and parastatal sector, but that these shortcomings must be addressed by more pronounced training, capacity building, and institutional innovation, research and technology transfer, and development.

A fourth approach, developed by the Economic Commission for Africa (ECA),[14] rightly identifies the structural rigidities in Africa and other specificities, but lacks both a time frame for implementation and a rigorous model and restricts itself to a "framework." The general framework may be its strength, however. It is argued that each country should develop policies that address its own problems and that models cannot be transported from one economy to the other. At the same time, however, the ECA approach itself succumbs to the temptation to treat African countries as homogeneous in some of its recommendations. More important, there seems to be in the ECA framework a wish to refrain from integration into the world economy, which flies in the face of the evidence that more pronounced integration into the world production structures could vastly increase welfare in developing countries. The strength of the ECA's framework is, however, to be found in some of its recommenda-

---

[13] UNCTAD, *Revitalizing Development, Growth and International Trade: Assessment and Policy Options* (New York: United Nations, 1987).

[14] ECA, *African Alternative to Structural Adjustment Programmes: A Framework for Transformation and Recovery* (Addis Ababa, 1989).

tions, which suggest that the long-term development issues should be taken into account when formulating stabilization and structural adjustment programs. Issues, such as the need to establish international and domestic enabling environments, including governance and accountability, institutional capacities, and human dimensions, are, to say the least, very important.

Possible New Orientations

Against the background of limited success with conventional stabilization and structural adjustment programs and drawing on several of the ideas suggested in the various alternative approaches, it is possible to outline broadly a consistent set of considerations that need to accompany new stabilization and adjustment programs in African countries.

First, it should be recognized that the challenge for stabilization and adjustment programs in the 1990s is to help African countries restore growth, while promoting the use of efficient policies. It should also be recognized that for these countries higher rates of growth in imports and investment are key elements in resolving their balance of payments and growth problems. It should be accepted that since the onset of traditional adjustment programs, adjustments in trade balance have produced a reduction in import volumes rather than an increase in exports. Lagging exports coupled with the virtual drying up of foreign capital have meant that the burden of adjustment has fallen on imports and growth. The strategy to improve Africa's balance of payments performance and growth in the 1990s should, therefore, be built more on encouraging greater growth of imports; excess capacity often exists in the economy but the missing element is the supply of foreign exchange for intermediate inputs. Reducing imports can only aggravate this excess capacity problem. The implication is that the international community has a duty to improve the terms of trade of African countries and to encourage the flow of resources to them. The UNCTAD approach discussed earlier is not without great merits in emphasizing this aspect.

Second, it should be appreciated that weak investment, which has reflected the domestic counterpart of the adjustment in the external current account, has harmed both the public and private sectors of the African countries. Private investment has been affected because import compression has tended to reduce anticipated rates of return. Moreover, private investment has also been "crowded out" by the increased pressure of public sector demand on domestic savings to finance external debt-service payments. Public investment has also fallen, primarily because of the political sensitivity to reductions in some social sector spending and also because of the massive increase in payments on government debt induced by the depreciation of the domestic exchange rates and the increase in the domestic interest rates.

A third consideration to bear in mind is that the prolonged period of import compression and retrenchment of investment is no longer sustainable; the rate of expansion of import volume will have to increase, or the rate of economic growth will continue to decline and have serious repercussions for Africa's short- and medium-term stability. Stabilization and structural adjustment programs to be formulated in the 1990s should rely on non-import-compressing policy measures, which require significant expansion in net flow of resources from the international community and a marked reduction of the external debt of the African countries. While the international community has taken initiatives to deal with the burden of official bilateral debt, there is need for new approaches to provide real relief for multilateral debt and commercial debts, which also burden African economies. Moreover, despite the recent initiatives on debt, the flow of resources in real terms continues to remain below the requirement levels for African countries. It is important that the World Bank, the IMF, and the international community accept that the economic problems of African countries are exceptionally and uniquely difficult and require special treatment.

The new orientations of stabilization and structural adjustment programs as suggested above should draw on the past experiences of the IMF, the World Bank, and the international community in financing growth and development in African countries. Prior to the 1980s, it was generally recognized that Africa's economy was basically weak and dependent on a narrow range of commodity exports whose prices fluctuated erratically. It was also generally accepted that Africa's physical infrastructure was grossly inadequate and required substantial external financing to develop its potential. In the period up to 1978, the multilateral aid institutions and the donor countries had provided Africa with development assistance on a substantial scale enabling the countries to achieve a level of public investment in infrastructure that would, otherwise, have been impossible to undertake. The World Bank played an especially crucial role in promoting economic growth (which was occurring in the great majority of the African countries) and concentrating on lending for individual projects in agriculture, industry, health, education, and infrastructure in rural and urban areas.

In that earlier period, the IMF's approach was also to some extent praiseworthy, although there was criticism of the short-term frame of the programs it supported and the economic policy instruments emphasized. Consistent with its Articles of Agreement, which refer to maintenance of high levels of employment, income, and economic development as "the primary objectives of economic policy," the IMF recognized that the balance of payments deficits of African countries were basically externally induced and better handled through larger interventions by international agencies and the surplus countries. The IMF's attitude then was essentially geared toward assisting African countries, especially the low-income ones, to overcome their balance of payments difficulties, while maintaining a reasonable rate of economic growth. Up to the late 1970s, the IMF established special facilities (the Trust Fund, the Subsidy Account) for low-income countries and maintained a low-conditionality, compensatory financing facility to finance shortfalls in overall export earnings. In addition, SDRs were regularly allocated, and part of the gold of the IMF was sold to support low-income members. The European Community (EC) moved along a similar track establishing its commodity-specific STABEX window, which enabled African countries to finance shortfalls in commodity export earnings.

Fourth, the necessity to introduce new orientations in stabilization and structural adjustment programs for African countries is also supported by a finding of the World Bank in its 1987 Annual Report, which applauds the depth of the reforms in many African countries and the persistence of policymakers in implementing these reforms. The Bank even calls this a "major achievement." While the Report admits that adjustment has taken longer than was envisaged originally, it says:

> In the absence of needed resources on appropriate terms, these countries, [many of which are highly indebted,] will find it difficult to maintain, let alone expand, education and health services, nutritional programs, and improved water facilities . . . shelter for the poor [p. 15]. The overall picture on capital flows remains disappointing: Strong financial support for adjusting countries from the Bank and the Fund has not been accompanied by any significant new financing from commercial banks. Multiyear rescheduling agreements have not evolved as anticipated into a financial underpinning for medium-term adjustment programs [p. 17].

This is a devastating judgment with regard to possibilities for conventional structural adjustment. The Bank admits that, because of this, resistance to further reforms is hardening and adds that the ability of a country to persist with adjustment will depend on its ability to achieve tangible results in terms of economic growth.

Fifth, it should be recognized that the compelling argument for a new orientation in stabilization and structural adjustment derives from the fact that the need to resolve the debt crisis and achieve long-term sustainable growth and development was one of the reasons why African countries, one after the other, undertook structural adjustment programs. During the 1980s, however, a solution to the debt problem and growth have proved more elusive. Compared with other regions, Africa's rate of economic growth, averaging 1.9 percent in the 1980s, is the lowest and its burden of external debt the most severe. Although repeated reschedulings have been given to many African countries on a continuous basis for a long time, their debts have intensified and arrears have accumulated. Thus, viewed against the background of the experiences of African countries with a variety of remedial measures since 1987, the debt crisis has become not only unmanageable but also intractable.

In outlining the nature of possible alternative adjustment programs in the 1990s, one should, therefore, be guided by the shortcomings of the conventional approach outlined earlier in this paper, in particular the need to account for supply rigidities and to place emphasis on development targets rather than extreme reliance on quantitative targets. The new structural adjustment programs will need to concentrate more on monitoring the fulfillment of well-conceived, clearly defined development programs in the 1990s, with import constraint being seen as the single most important factor limiting both domestic and export growth in African economies. Accordingly, programs should provide for adequate external assistance as far as possible, before major policy changes. The argument for this is that unless consumer and intermediate goods are available, increased prices and other incentives will achieve little by way of stimulating exports or production in general and will tend, simply, to be inflationary. Yet, there are time lags of several months between the receipt of foreign exchange assistance and the local availability of intermediate products. It will be much easier for an economy to absorb the strains of policy adjustments if programs are front-loaded in terms of finance.

The new stabilization and structural adjustment programs must also incorporate explicitly specified percentage rates of growth. Such a real economy approach to adjustment implies greater emphasis on financing, in contrast to too heavy reliance on the control of aggregate demand. Adjustment with growth would permit equilibrium to be restored at a higher overall level of economic activity and it would minimize the conflicts between the policy objectives of stabilization, growth, and social welfare.

Finally, in the new approaches to stabilization and structural adjustment, sustained efforts need to be devoted to exploring avenues for increased resource mobilization and plugging the several leaks that do exist. Specifically, a generous handling of the debt problem, including substantial cancellation of debts, will be necessary if Africa is to sustain its ability to continue perseverance with stabilization and structural adjustment policies. In the absence of substantial debt relief and more adequate financing, it is difficult to see how countries in Africa can overcome adjustment fatigue, already rampant, and, at the same time, underpin the political support necessary for structural adjustment programs to succeed. Finally, the scope for market forces to correct distortions and to generate the incentives to mobilize domestic resources should neither be considered as unlimited, as orthodox enthusiasts would depict it, nor as negligible, as pure neo-structuralists argue it is. Public or para-public enterprises should be recognized as often being inefficient, wasteful, and aggravating distortions. A more important dose of market-based incentives in the context of new programs would send the correct signals to producers, consumers, investors, and savers alike and would help mobilize domestic financial, entrepreneurial, and labor resources.

The new orientations and approaches suggested above for the 1990s call for the adoption of alternative perceptions, attitudes, and more dialogue if African countries are to have better prospects for the future. Of course, the commodity issue is also important and must be addressed within this new orientation. The fact is that the fortunes of African countries, since they are basically primary commodity producers, depend critically on the fluctuations in the export prices. There is the need, therefore, for improvement in the international environment to ensure that African countries receive remunerative prices for their commodity exports.

Conclusion

This paper has presented an evaluation of the experiences of African countries with stabilization and structural adjustment reform measures using the traditional before-and-after analytical framework. The evidence from the sample countries used in the study indicates that the expectations that are assumed to follow from the application of traditional stabilization and structural adjustment programs have not materialized in more than 50 percent of the cases examined. While 8 countries, out of a sample survey of the 17 countries studied, recorded some significant improvement from prestructural adjustment performances, the remaining 9 in the sample survey have shown appreciable deterioration in poststructural adjustment performances. Furthermore, out of the eight macroeconomic indicators chosen for the analysis significant success was achieved only in four, namely the reduction in the rate of inflation, the increase in the rate of domestic savings, and improvement in the rate of growth of exports and imports. The other four macroeconomic indicators, namely, the growth rate, investment rate, debt-service ratio, and net resource transfers recorded a deterioration of performance in the poststructural adjustment period.

A new approach, adequately espoused in the paper, suggests the urgent need to design credible adjustment programs in the 1990s that are truly growth-oriented, and also to take adequate account of the needs for health, education, and other social services, while being conscious of the fact that major changes in the structures and production fabric of the African economy will take time to yield results and require substantial investment. The new "adjustment-with-growth" strategy, which is being advocated for the 1990s, should draw on the past experience of the international community in financing development in Africa. Up to the mid-1970s the multilateral institutions and the donor community had accepted that the African economy was basically very weak and its infrastructure grossly inadequate, requiring substantial resources to develop. Recognition and adoption of this earlier approach would mark an important and positive turning point in relations between the IMF, the World Bank, and African countries.

A View from the IMF

Jack Boorman

The Context for Adjustment

The performance of the African economies in the last two decades, and of sub-Saharan Africa in particular, has been disappointing.[1] For Africa as a whole, real per capita gross domestic product (GDP) showed no improvement; the growth of about 1 percent a year during the 1970s was offset by a similar rate of decline during the next decade (Table 1). For sub-Saharan Africa, real per capita GDP remained stagnant during the 1970s and fell by nearly 1 percent a year during the 1980s; during the same time, other developing countries recorded moderate growth.

Unfavorable external factors have clearly played a significant role in this outcome. By far the most important was the decline in Africa's terms of trade. A 60 percent improvement in the terms of trade during the 1970s (largely attributable to developments in oil prices) was followed by a drop of about 50 percent during the 1980s—consistent with a continuing decline for many non-oil exporting countries. Terms of trade developments were particularly adverse for sub-Saharan Africa, where a 9 percent drop in the 1970s was followed by a further 33 percent slide during the 1980s, or over three times the decline experienced by other developing countries. Africa also suffered from the international recessions during the mid-1970s and again in the early 1980s, and the sharp rise in real interest rates associated with the turn by industrial countries to anti-inflationary policies in the early 1980s.

---

[1] In this paper, sub-Saharan Africa is defined as all African countries, except Algeria, Morocco, Nigeria, South Africa, and Tunisia. Unless otherwise indicated, all data are drawn from the IMF's *World Economic Outlook*, and from IMF staff papers on programs supported by the structural adjustment and the enhanced structural adjustment facilities (SAF and ESAF) of the IMF.

Table 1. Selected Economic Indicators: African Countries and Other Developing Countries, 1971–90

	African Countries		Other Developing Countries[1]	
	All	Sub-Saharan countries	All	Low-income countries
	(Average annual change in percent)			
Per capital income				
1971–80	0.9	—	3.2	2.0
1981–90	–0.9	–0.8	1.1	–2.0
Terms of trade				
1971–80	5.1	–0.9	8.9	1.8
1981–90	–4.4	–3.9	–1.2	–0.9
Export volume				
1971–80	2.1	1.1	4.1	1.6
1981–90	–1.5	1.9	4.3	6.9
Inflation				
1971–80	14.1	18.5	21.4	9.7
1981–90	16.6	21.8	58.4	32.6
	(Average share in national income in percent)			
Domestic investment				
1976–81	27.6	. . .	27.3	16.0
1982–88	20.2	. . .	24.1	15.8
National saving				
1976–81	24.1	. . .	27.3	11.7
1982–88	17.7	. . .	23.2	12.7
	(Percentage)			
External debt, 1990				
Relative to exports	233.3	359.3	125.7	454.2
Relative to GDP	53.3	75.7	28.8	61.4

Sources: Bijan Aghevli, and others *The Role of National Saving in the World Economy: Recent Trends and Prospects*, Occasional Paper No. 67 (Washington: International Monetary Fund, March 1990); and International Monetary Fund, *World Economic Outlook: A Survey by the Staff of the International Monetary Fund*, World Economic and Financial Surveys (Washington, various issues).

[1] Excluding Africa.

For the 1980s, several indicators signal major difficulties in the structural transformation of Africa.[2]

Investment activity. Our data suggest that Africa's domestic investment rate fell sharply to about 20 percent of GDP, well below that for other developing countries (see Table 1). More important, the rate of return on

---

[2] Aspects of Africa's external indebtedness in relation to recent economic performance are addressed in the discussion paper by Boorman and Chopra.

investment has been dismal, declining to 2.5 percent in the period 1980–87 (World Bank (1989)), reflecting inefficient use of resources and unproductive investment priorities.[3]

Savings performance. Africa's domestic savings rate also fell sharply, to an average of only 18 percent, again well below the average level registered for other developing countries. This steep decline is not solely related to adverse external circumstances; it may also indicate inappropriate domestic policies.

Exports. Its export volume fell at an average rate of $1^{1}/_{2}$ percent a year, compared with an annual increase of 4 percent for other developing countries. More important, looking behind the aggregates, various studies indicate that for primary products, traditionally a major source of export earnings for Africa, the region's share of total world exports fell significantly—in some cases drastically—between the early 1970s and mid-1980s (Akiyama and Larson (1989)).

Unfavorable external circumstances undoubtedly complicated the tasks of economic management for policymakers in Africa. Abrupt policy shifts, sometimes reflecting swings in the ideological pendulum, created further uncertainty and instability in the environment for economic decision making in many countries.

Thus, the starting point for structural adjustment in Africa was considerably weaker than in other regions, the challenges facing governments more daunting, and the economies more vulnerable to further external shocks. Furthermore, adjustment has been made more difficult by weaknesses in basic institutions, infrastructure, and social services. In many instances, ineffective public administration over time eroded the institutional framework. For example, unsound banking practices, excessive financing of state budgets and of parastatal enterprises, and lack of competition have kept banking systems fragile. Inadequate legal frameworks for protecting private sector activity hampered the development of a dynamic private sector and, sometimes by plan, but sometimes by default, economic development came to rest unduly on the public sector.

Within the public sector, a number of constraints limited the administrative capacities. Because of financial difficulties, wages were often kept too low and not differentiated sufficiently to attract qualified personnel, essential for the design and implementation of policy reforms. In many instances, the public sector became overextended and inefficient, intervening in areas in which it lacked the necessary technical and managerial

---

[3]See World Bank (1989).

expertise. Furthermore, expenditure policies did not always give priority to the maintenance and improvement of physical infrastructure, nor of human capital. Mechanisms for budgetary control and monitoring were often found wanting.

These structural rigidities would, under the best of circumstances, take many years to correct; for Africa, the precarious external environment adds another dimension to the problem.

Despite this discouraging background, signs of progress have emerged. For an increasing number of countries, economic performance is improving. Moreover, consensus on the requirements for effective economic policies is growing in Africa. It is now widely recognized that sustainable economic growth and a strong external position can only result from comprehensive macroeconomic and structural policies. Recent experience in Africa shows that well-designed and implemented structural adjustment policies can lead to a recovery in growth, and views are converging on those specific policies that are likely to succeed.

The scope of the tasks ahead is broad. A collective effort on the part of the donor community, the World Bank, and the IMF is needed to support Africa. Central to this process is a favorable global economic environment. Key factors include an open world trading system, the level of real interest rates, and the adequacy of external financing on appropriate terms. At this time, when Africa is making difficult policy choices, much is at stake in the outcome of the Uruguay Round, in the macroeconomic policies of the industrial countries, and in further progress in resolving debt problems.

At this stage and for the foreseeable future, adequate external financing will be crucial for investment to help maintain and build infrastructure and to meet other pressing social needs, given that domestic saving takes time to respond to policy reforms. For those countries with the heaviest debt burdens, financing will have to be provided by the official sector on concessional terms. Given Africa's structural difficulties and macroeconomic imbalances, the World Bank and the IMF are naturally expected to provide policy advice, help mobilize official assistance, and provide financing as appropriate.

The results of structural adjustment are not likely to be immediate. As structural adjustment takes hold, the effects of policies should begin to emerge and the financing need be thereby reduced. It is to be hoped that Africa's reliance on official assistance for exceptional balance of payments financing would decline over time. In some cases, this is already evident. In the interim, of course, there is a clear need for an appropriate policy setting in Africa to ensure productive use of scarce domestic and donor resources and to foster a better return on investment (see below). Over the longer term, aid could be expected to shift gradually from exceptional balance of payments financing assistance to more traditional forms of assistance to directly develop infrastructure and human resources.

Recent Approaches to Structural Adjustment

In the second half of the 1980s, 35 African countries adopted structural adjustment programs supported by the IMF, primarily in the context of arrangements under the structural adjustment (SAF) and enhanced structural adjustment (ESAF) facilities, but also through stand-by and extended arrangements. The experience of programs under the facilities has been relatively encouraging as regards the resumption of growth, including export diversification in some cases.

For a large number of countries undertaking comprehensive structural adjustment,[4] growth in the last few years has improved, compared with earlier periods; in many cases, real growth rates have averaged 4–5 percent annually, representing a considerable gain in per capita terms (Table 2). Where progress was substantial, policy implementation was strong in both macroeconomic and structural areas. This suggests a close link between the comprehensiveness of policies and improvement in economic performance. This recent experience is broadly in line with the World Bank's findings, for all regions of the world, that countries adopting structural adjustment have on average grown faster than other countries.[5]

It should be stressed that any assessment of the contribution of structural adjustment programs—for example, as in a comparison of economic performance during the pre- and post-adjustment program periods—is a complex undertaking.[6] Such assessments need to include a comparison of the actual results against possible, alternative outcomes in the absence of such an adjustment. The assessment also needs to sort out the role of exogenous factors and the strength of policy implementation—factors that cannot always be quantified in summary indicators. For structural adjust-

---

[4]For example, Burundi, The Gambia, Lesotho, Madagascar, Malawi, Mozambique, Niger, Senegal, Tanzania, Togo, and Uganda.

[5]The World Bank (1990). It was concluded that after taking account of the effects of initial conditions, external shocks, and the amount of external financing, those countries that entered full-fledged adjustment programs in 1985–88 had a larger increase in the average rate of GDP growth than other countries.

[6]For a recent survey of research on the effects of Fund-supported adjustment programs, see Khan (1990).

ment, an added complication is that structural changes cannot be readily quantified, nor can the effects be easily measured. More important, structural effects may not yet have been reflected in shorter-term economic outcomes. To the extent that there has been a basic redirection of policies toward market-oriented reforms in an increasing number of instances in Africa and that there has been qualitative improvement in economic management, the contribution of structural adjustment programs may have been greater than that captured by the typical quantitative indicators of economic performance.

Elements of Structural Adjustment

Growth-oriented structural adjustment has typically involved the following core elements: an enhanced role for market forces, a stable macroeconomic environment, an adequate scope of structural reforms, and gradual integration with the world economy.[7] For Africa, with a legacy of structural rigidities, there is also an urgent need to build infrastructure and strengthen regulatory and institutional systems. In addition, successful reform efforts cannot ignore the linkages between economic and social objectives.

An Enhanced Role for Market Forces

A priority in recent reform efforts has been to adjust prices to levels that reflect resource scarcity. This often entails easing or removing administrative controls on most prices and adjusting the administered prices that remain. Appropriate price signals and incentives can help strengthen the private sector, on which rests much of the economic future of Africa. By largely removing day-to-day management of prices from the authorities' policy agenda, greater attention can be given to other, more pressing, issues such as financial and structural reform. With a transparent mechanism in place for pricing, the issue also becomes less politicized.

Correct price signals are needed urgently in the area of agricultural output. Until the mid-1980s many African countries relied on state enterprises to market their main agricultural products, using administratively determined producer prices. By and large, these enterprises were unable to maintain producer prices in real terms, thereby discouraging agricultural production in favor of urban employment and leading to smuggling at the

---

[7] For an overview of the main conceptual issues underlying structural adjustment, see the paper by Streeten (1987).

Table 2. Growth Performance in African Countries with IMF Arrangements, 1986–90

Country	Average GDP Growth Rate During Three Years Preceding First Program	Average GDP Growth Rate During Program Period and Subsequently[1]	Overall Experience	
			Improved growth performance[2]	Gain in per capita income[3]
	(In percent)			
Arrangements under the SAF or ESAF				
Benin	−1.0	...[4]		
Burundi[5]	2.9	3.5	x	x
Central African Republic	5.1	1.0		
Chad	7.0	5.1		x
Equatorial Guinea	...	...		
Gambia, The[5]	−3.4	5.4	x	x
Ghana[5]	6.4	5.5		x
Guinea	5.6[6]	5.7[6]	x	x
Guinea-Bissau	4.8[6]	5.8	x	x
Kenya[5]	5.1	5.0		x
Lesotho	2.7	8.3	x	x
Madagascar[5]	1.6	2.4	x	
Malawi[5]	2.3	4.2	x	
Mali[5]	7.3	4.5		x
Mauritania[5]	3.0	3.6	x	x
Mozambique	−2.1	4.4	x	x
Niger[5]	−2.0	1.7	x	
Sao Tome and Principe	...	2.3[6,4]		
Senegal[5]	0.8	3.1	x	x
Sierra Leone[5]	2.5	1.4[4]		

	(1)	(2)	(3)	(4)
Somalia[5]	5.0	3.0[4]		x
Tanzania[5]	2.8	4.2[6]	x	x
Togo[5]	2.6	4.4[6]	x	x
Uganda	-0.3	5.3	x	
Zaïre[5]	2.6	2.6	x	
Stand-by and extended arrangements[7]				
Algeria	1.7	..[4]		
Cameroon	-2.5	-4.9[4]		
Congo	3.9	-1.3		
Côte d'Ivoire	-2.1	0.6		
Egypt	6.7	-0.7[6]	x	
Gabon	3.9	-2.9		
Morocco	4.4	4.9	x	x
Nigeria	-1.3	3.2	x	x
Tunisia	3.4	2.7		
Zambia	-0.1	3.3[4]	x	x

[1] Average GDP growth over three or more years, starting with the program year and including program and nonprogram years.
[2] Country whose average growth rate was higher during the program period and subsequently than during the three years preceding the first program.
[3] Country where growth during the program period exceeded estimated population growth.
[4] Program in place for fewer than two years.
[5] Country had stand-by or extended arrangement in addition to SAF or ESAF arrangement.
[6] Average over fewer than three years.
[7] Except for countries that had SAF or ESAF arrangements. See footnote 5.

expense of legal export activity. Against this background, reforms of agricultural marketing systems and setting producer prices at competitive levels have, therefore, been key elements of structural adjustment. We have found that the supply response to adjustments in producer prices can be swift, not least through redirecting flows of output through the official instead of parallel channels. For instance, in Ghana, maintaining realistic producer prices at internationally competitive levels over time has reversed the declining trend of cocoa production, as well as provided timely signals for export diversification.

Adjustment and flexibility is most urgently needed in those prices that have a direct bearing on the macroeconomic environment, such as the exchange rate and interest rates. Through the mid-1980s, there was reluctance in most of Africa to adjust official exchange rates, despite growing overvaluation that impeded the development of exports and led to parallel exchange rate markets. In a recent study of commodity exports, the major African producers of such crops as coffee, cocoa, and cotton on average allowed much greater increases in their real exchange rates from 1970 through the mid-1980s (Table 3) than did competing producers in other regions (Akiyama and Larson (1989)).

During the second half of the 1980s, however, exchange rate policy shifted substantially; more countries were willing to adjust their exchange rates to more competitive levels and to move toward market-determined systems. Empirical evidence for Africa suggests a clear correlation, particularly over the medium term, between exchange rate movement and growth in export volume. For example, strong export growth was experienced in The Gambia, Ghana, and Lesotho following substantial real effective depreciation. In contrast, export performance in Tanzania and Uganda was weak when the real effective rate either remained unchanged or appreciated. The experience also suggests that exchange rate policy needs to be supported by early removal of related structural rigidities. In some instances, a substantial depreciation of the exchange rate in real effective terms was not sufficient to promote exports because other essential policy elements were missing. For example, in Madagascar, notwithstanding a substantial real effective depreciation in the mid-1980s, export volume picked up only after liberalization of imports in 1987 and the abolition of state monopolies and liberalization of domestic and external trade in 1988.

Recent experience in Africa and beyond would lead to the conclusion that where economic progress has been satisfactory (including export diversification), a common factor has been depreciation of the real exchange

Table 3. Real Exchange Rates in Selected Countries, 1970–87[1]

Country	1970	1975	1980	1985	1986	1987
Sub-Saharan Africa	100	179	376	319	298	306
Burundi	100	170	314	357	384	381
Côte d'Ivoire	100	185	405	250	346	420
Cameroon	100	213	358	278	372	470
Congo	100	189	300	240	319	376
Ethiopia	100	144	299	430	388	379
Gabon	100	212	395	295	407	465
Ghana	100	193	1,095	503	382	310
Gambia, The	100	190	324	269	236	286
Burkina Faso	100	178	300	206	260	292
Kenya	100	88	160	135	142	147
Liberia	100	167	258	304	315	331
Madagascar	100	201	318	252	283	206
Mauritius	100	164	280	215	250	263
Niger	100	186	374	253	317	341
Nigeria	100	220	549	793	425	205
Rwanda	100	208	357	448	512	586
Sudan	100	207	337	292	334	336
Senegal	100	243	342	282	389	429
Sierra Leone	100	139	231	370	212	279
Somalia	100	165	451	459	342	300
Swaziland	100	155	277	195	212	268
Seychelles	100	224	398	435	504	570
Togo	100	204	343	223	301	347
Tanzania	100	182	322	564	399	264
Zaïre	100	233	559	193	236	239
Zambia	100	157	259	165	101	118
Zimbabwe	100	161	229	184	204	230
Brazil	100	147	179	145	162	186
Colombia	100	136	265	241	210	207
Indonesia	100	213	283	254	233	199
Malaysia	100	183	251	276	267	276

Source: Takamasa Akiyama and Donald F. Larson, *Recent Trends and Prospects for Agricultural Commodity Exports in Sub-Saharan Africa,* Working Paper WPS 348 (Washington: The World Bank, December 1989).
[1] A rise in the index indicates an appreciation of the real effective exchange rate.

rate and liberalization of trade policies, both supported by financial restraint. Thus, priority needs to be given at an early stage of structural adjustment to moving rapidly toward a realistic exchange rate, and to achieving adjustments in other key prices. Liberalization of trade, at least in terms of allowing market-based allocation of scarce foreign exchange and of abolishing import quotas, has been shown to be particularly significant for efficient allocation of imports; it often permits higher capacity utilization of the existing capital stock and much needed modernization (and hence some transfer of new technologies) and promotes export diversification. Greater attention to trade liberalization in the early phases of the structural adjustment process could thus improve the overall outcome.

In this context, it could be noted that the debate on exchange rate policy continues in Africa, with some postulating a return to multiple exchange rate systems based on administrative choice rather than on market-based solutions. IMF experience has shown these systems to be highly inefficient; they introduce distortionary elements in exchange rate management and drain scarce administrative resources.

Much of the criticism of exchange rate adjustments has focused on their potential inflationary impact. Nominal devaluations, if not supported by firm fiscal and monetary policies, can indeed lead to inflation. The experience in Africa suggests that where monetary expansion was kept under effective control after an exchange rate adjustment, inflation decelerated after the initial price impact had subsided. For example, in Madagascar, the real effective exchange rate was depreciated by as much as 50 percent during 1986 and 1987, but the rate of inflation still remained around 13 percent until the end of 1987. Inflation only picked up subsequently when monetary expansion accelerated. Thus, firm financial policies are the key to avoiding frequent adjustments of the nominal exchange rate, and to securing a sustainable improvement in competitiveness.

There has also been some advocacy of differential interest rates and selective credit control policies. In practical terms, a major weakness of credit controls is that the final allocation of credit may not be altered as desired while administrative resources are wasted in the evaluation process. More generally, such policies constitute implicit taxes or subsidies. Artificially low deposit interest rates are an implicit tax on depositors, discouraging savings. When banks lend at below market rates, because they rely on the central bank to refinance loans to favored sectors, they promote inefficient industries and weaken monetary management. Interest subsidies provided by the central bank also reduce transfers to the budget and thus affect the fiscal position. The accumulation of contingent liabilities resulting from such loan operations places the burden of risk on the government, which may be forced to intervene to guarantee the stability of the banking system. Also, direct controls on interest rates and credit may retard the development of the financial sector, including the introduction of new savings instruments to better mobilize domestic resources.

Financial sector reforms aimed at the mobilization and more effective allocation of domestic savings need to be supported by better supervision

Role of Macroeconomic Stability

Experience under structural adjustment has shown that for sustainable growth, macroeconomic stability must be achieved in a lasting way. The World Bank has also concluded, from its recent experience with adjustment programs, that a stable macroeconomic framework contributes to the success of structural adjustment in every major area of the economy and that programs that focus mainly on microeconomic and sectoral policies are more likely to fail when a stable macroframework is not in place.[8]

Key policy elements of successful macroeconomic management have included financial restraint and the correction of cost and price distortions, including those of the exchange rate and interest rate (as noted above).[9] Such policies along with a sound financial system, have helped to raise domestic financial savings, discourage outward capital outflows, and over time attract private transfers from abroad (e.g., Bolivia, The Gambia, Ghana, and Senegal). In contrast, overexpansionary fiscal policy, high inflation, and distorted prices have led to declines in savings rates and have failed to attract private transfers from abroad in several cases (e.g., Burundi, Niger, and Zaïre).

In Africa, experience has shown the importance of a two-pronged approach to economic management, with stabilization and structural policies playing a mutually supportive role. Demand-management policies need to be buttressed by strong structural measures, focusing in particular on basic fiscal and public sector reforms necessary for lasting macroeconomic stability. Conversely, a stable macroeconomic environment is essential for carrying out structural adjustment, as well as effective sectoral policies. High rates of inflation and financial instability have frequently

---

[8] World Bank (1990).

[9] A narrow interpretation of the policy content of Fund programs has at times given way to the misconception that such programs are designed with the sole objective of reducing aggregate demand, through the use of contractionary monetary and fiscal policies. Supply side policies intended to increase domestic output at any given level of domestic demand are, however, an integral part of Fund programs. These include policies aimed at improving the efficiency of resource use, such as through the reduction of distortions caused by price controls, trade restrictions, and rigid tax systems. Other policies, designed to enhance incentives for domestic savings and investment and to increase the inflow of foreign savings, seem to raise in the longer term the rate of growth of capacity output.

disrupted or complicated the implementation of structural and institutional reforms. The momentum of structural policies is weakened when economic managers must divert limited technical and administrative resources to deal with crisis management. Banking sector reform is often not feasible in the absence of a minimum degree of financial stability. Trade liberalization can be costly in terms of foreign exchange when it is not accompanied by a realistic exchange rate and sufficiently tight domestic policies to moderate the pressure on imports. Price adjustment—often a first step in public enterprise reform—and civil service reform is even more politically sensitive in the face of accelerating inflation.

A fundamental strengthening of the financial position of the public sector is itself a key structural element. This is necessary to rebuild social and physical infrastructure. For fiscal adjustment to be compatible with strong economic growth, the revenue base must be broadened and wasteful expenditure curtailed. To maintain public sector services at an appropriate level and efficiency, such services must be economically priced. Overall, financial discipline by both the central government and the public enterprise sector is a critical underpinning of structural adjustment.

Adequate Scope of Structural Reform

Consistency and Sustained Implementation

For successful structural adjustment, careful attention needs to be given to the sequencing of reforms, the speed of their implementation, and the ability of institutions and economic agents to respond to a changing environment. From the experience so far, two main lessons seem apparent.

First, reforms must be carefully conceived and sequenced because of the underlying linkages. For instance, for countries with severe debt problems, large fiscal deficits, and high inflation, a certain degree of macroeconomic stability needs to be achieved before undertaking trade policy reforms. Where there are serious distortions and institutional and infrastructural deficiencies, trade reforms may need to be complemented by other policies aimed at improving domestic competition and easing market rigidities. This would imply a parallel easing of unduly restrictive labor laws, price controls, and marketing regulations.

Second, structural reform measures must be better prioritized. This need is particularly urgent in the African context, given weaknesses in the administrative framework and the careful technical preparation required in each structural area for successful implementation. Limitations of technical and administrative capacity have given rise to difficulties and delays in implementing structural measures in the past. This experience should not be taken to imply that the pace for structural reforms should be gradual. Rather, emphasis should be placed on careful prioritization, concentrating initially on reforms aimed primarily at securing a smooth working of macroeconomic policies. These include, for example, tax reform and the reform of the public sector. Because some reforms in these areas take time to develop, technically and politically, early attention should be given to them.[10] The financial environment in a number of countries has been very weak, with a virtual breakdown of the basic functioning of the banking system in some extreme cases. Technical assistance to strengthen the banking system should be stepped up to promote private financial savings and financial intermediation.

More generally, technical and financial assistance from international organizations and bilateral donors (e.g., in such areas as public expenditure review, public investment and public enterprise, and civil service reforms) should also be strongly encouraged since these reforms are critical to improving savings performance and the efficiency of investment. In all areas, close attention should be given to ensuring a timely provision of assistance. At the same time, donor assistance is likely to be more effective when it is well coordinated and supports a coherent set of policy reforms. There is need to avoid conflicting advice, reduce demands on the already strained administrative capacities of recipient countries, and further streamline procurement and disbursement procedures. In coordinating this international effort, the policy framework paper process, with the recipient countries in a central role, can be useful. The policy framework paper could set out the policy objectives, the required measures, and the financing requirements in a medium-term framework. Strengthening technical assistance among donors will have an important bearing on enhancing the structural content of programs.[11]

---

[10]The IMF has sought to strengthen technical assistance in the areas of tax reform, improvements in tax and customs administration, and expenditure control mechanisms. Additional technical assistance is required in such areas as budgetary formulation, monitoring and control, and the development of macroeconomic information systems for policymakers.

[11]The IMF has been paying increasing attention, including in the context of policy framework papers, to ways in which the technical assistance provided by it and by donors could help strengthen policy implementation in its member countries under Fund-supported adjustment programs. Attempts have begun in recent policy framework papers to identify more systematically the needs for such assistance and its proper sequencing, and there would seem to be scope for further improvements in coverage in this area.

Because the structure of each economy and its social and political context is different, the optimal approach to reform will vary from one country to the next. There are no simple formulas; careful study and preparation are required, supported by a willingness to make adjustments as the reform process proceeds. The Fund's experience thus far with structural adjustment programs supported by the SAF and ESAF has shown that satisfactory performance has depended on the strength and coherence of agreed policies and sustained implementation over time, and close working relations with the Bank and donors in sectoral areas.

The Regulatory Framework and Institutional Reform

The effectiveness of structural adjustment policies will depend on the support given by institutional improvements. Freeing agricultural output prices, for instance, will encourage a supply response, but its magnitude is likely to be larger under an adequate infrastructure for transport and sound credit institutions. Recent reform of agricultural marketing boards in Africa is a good example of the way in which institutional reforms play a key complementary role to such policy adjustments as price decontrol (e.g., Malawi and Zambia).

Experience suggests that a recovery in private activity has generally taken longer than expected and followed—with a lag—credible assurances of fundamental reforms in economic management. This experience applies to Africa as well. Recognizing the problem of weak administration and institutions, several countries have embarked on comprehensive programs of administrative reforms (e.g., the Central African Republic, The Gambia, Ghana, Madagascar, Mauritania, and Senegal). The seemingly slow private sector response so far may have reflected, in part, the long gestation period involved in such reforms, and the need for strengthening the legal and regulatory framework. The response of the informal sector, however, may have been considerably stronger but difficult to measure.

In addition to a leaner, better disciplined, better trained public service with adequate incentives for highly qualified employees, special attention has been given to strengthening the economic management capabilities of governments. This includes redefining the role of the public sector from that of control and direction, to provision of physical and institutional infrastructure to support the private sector. This approach has aimed at setting a simple regulatory framework based on transparent rules and eliminating excessive intervention to give confidence to private sector investment. For public enterprises, financial discipline has also called for giving them clear mandates, managerial autonomy, and monitorable performance indicators.

Early attention needs to be given to promoting foreign direct investment and a return of flight capital. Until recently, the macroeconomic environment and investment policies of most African countries have not been sufficiently enticing to investment from abroad. A more stable financial environment would promote foreign direct investment, which could also be further encouraged through a variety of policies, such as the removal of administrative allocation of foreign exchange and streamlining other regulatory requirements, a competitive banking system, reasonable marginal tax rates on company profits, and adequate expenditures for maintenance and investment in socially productive infrastructure.[12]

A stable and transparent judicial system is also a key element of institution reform. Absence of a well-defined legal framework for foreign investors, for instance, is thought to have been a major obstacle to investment flows into Africa. A legal framework that clearly defines contract and property rights can reduce uncertainty and promote a more stable and competitive business environment. Adequate legal underpinnings and a framework for public accountability are key elements of institution-building reforms. In all these processes the role of the government is critical.

Linkages Between Economic and Social Objectives

Structural adjustment can significantly effect the distribution of incomes and thus social equity and welfare. There is growing recognition that adjustment efforts must take into account the effects of certain measures, especially on the most vulnerable or disadvantaged groups of society.[13] Closer attention is therefore being paid to the social aspects of adjustment, for example, the effects of civil service retrenchment, and protecting basic health and education expenditures from budgetary cuts. The international community should support efforts by governments to ease the short-term adverse impacts of certain adjustment policies on these groups, through appropriate adjustments to the policy package, or through targeted assistance without sacrificing the overall objectives of economic reforms. The aim should be to bring the necessary adjustment with the least amount of hardship to the most vulnerable groups. Donor

---

[12] In this connection, see International Monetary Fund (1985).

[13] For a discussion of the issues, see the paper by Heller and others (1988).

assistance is important, both financially and in terms of technical advice. Proper consideration of the impact of economic policy measures on the poor can produce stronger public support for an adjustment program, making it more socially sustainable.

Integration with the World Economy

A more outward orientation of policies has been an essential element of successful structural reform. Greater openness imposes on domestic producers the discipline of international competition and enhances prospects for growth through efficiency and exports. Thus, structural adjustment programs have sought to open the economy to foreign trade, through policies aimed at reducing or eliminating discrimination against tradables and promoting private enterprises that are competitive by international as well as local standards.

In Africa, as elsewhere, past strategies of import substitution often misdirected investment and led over time to balance of payments difficulties. Import restrictions, in effect, are a tax on exports and inhibit export-led growth. We are learning from the experience of many East and Southeast Asian countries that have had strong growth led by dynamic export sectors. Efforts are now under way in Africa to reform trade policies. A more open orientation along with a stable macro policy environment has already led to strong export growth and diversification and attracted much needed foreign capital and technical expertise in a number of cases (e.g., The Gambia, Mauritius, and, more recently, Madagascar).

Concerns have been expressed to the effect that rapid import liberalization may undermine the development of nascent industries and lead to a deterioration of revenue performance and to shifts in expenditure patterns, with the consumption of imported luxury goods increasing. In our experience, the problem of revenue loss typically stems from inefficient tax and customs administration, rather than from the removal of import restrictions and tariff adjustments. When revenue loss might be expected, alternative revenue-raising measures and a broadening of the tax base should be considered, giving due regard to equity and efficiency aspects. Reforming the tax system is complex and difficult, and increasing levels of technical assistance may be required for these purposes.

Questions have also arisen concerning possibilities for African economic integration. Regional projects with large externalities should have the potential of being cost efficient; however, regional trade integration requires the elimination of domestic distortions as well as the harmonization of policies in a number of key areas, particularly trade policies with the rest of the world. Such regional policies should also ensure that African exports are competitive in industrial countries, which are potentially by far the largest markets for Africa. In the context of their adjustment program, individual countries can facilitate efficient regional integration by eliminating distortions in domestic economies, reducing trade barriers, liberalizing markets, and securing competitiveness. The Fund is placing increasing importance on these issues in its country work and is undertaking more in-depth analysis of trade issues in developing countries, including those in Africa.

The industrial countries can contribute to successful integration of Africa with the world economy, through further opening of their markets. As noted earlier, an open global trading system and adequate levels of financial assistance will play a key role in the future growth performance of Africa.

Conclusions

Economic performance in Africa during the past decade has been disappointing: for sub-Saharan Africa, real per capita GDP fell by nearly 1 percent a year on average. External circumstances have played an important role, with the unfavorable terms of trade being the leading factor. But there is now a broad consensus that part of Africa's decline rests with domestic economic policies that have had the effect of discouraging production, exports, and investment and have not dealt effectively with exogenous shocks. To promote sustainable growth, policy reforms are often now needed in the areas of exchange rates, credit policies, government budgets, and a range of structural reforms to ease deep-seated rigidities.

Recent experience offers some grounds for optimism. A number of countries have embarked upon comprehensive programs of structural reform, reflecting a significant change in the economic thinking and priorities among the leadership in Africa. Early results have been encouraging, with a recovery of growth having been experienced in a significant number of cases. More important, a consensus is developing in Africa—as in other parts of the world—regarding the nature of effective economic policies. It is now widely recognized that sustained growth and external viability can only result from consistent and steady implementation of comprehensive policies in both the macroeconomic and structural areas. Furthermore, there is a growing convergence of views concerning the specific types of policies that are likely to be successful, even though their application must vary according to the circumstances of each country.

This paper has examined in some detail the main elements of this emerging consensus on the main policy requirements of sustainable structural reform. The core elements that have been emphasized include the need to give greater scope at the earliest stage to market forces, and to adjust key prices to reflect resource scarcity; the need to create and maintain a stable macroeconomic framework; the need for structural policies with appropriate scope and sequencing; the need to better integrate the domestic economy with the world economy through more open trade and exchange systems; and the overriding need to rebuild institutions and social infrastructure.

Recent experience also suggests that the structural adjustment process in Africa could take more time than initially expected. Removal of deep-seated rigidities through structural reforms can add flexibility and adaptability to the region's economies and help reduce their vulnerability to future shocks. The process is still evolving, however, and lessons are still being learned. Most important, we have come to the conclusion that design and implementation of structural measures are technically complex and time consuming and that many difficult issues on the appropriate sequencing of certain measures remain. Until structural reforms take hold, macroeconomic stability is also fragile, prone to setbacks. Thus, the entire adjustment process is challenging; it requires sustained commitment from governments, the private sector, and the donor community.

The experience of Africa in recent years provides evidence that comprehensive structural adjustment policies of the types described above, when well designed and implemented, can indeed contribute to a recovery of growth. The effectiveness of adjustment depends as well on adequate external assistance in policy and financing, and a favorable global environment. The IMF, in collaboration with the World Bank and the donor community, stands ready to support the reform process in Africa in the 1990s by helping countries design and implement appropriate macroeconomic and structural policies, helping to catalyze additional assistance, and providing direct financial support through its various facilities.

Over the next few years and under current policies and prospects, a large number of countries in Africa could be expected to remain engaged in full-fledged structural adjustment. On present trends, a number of countries would have graduated from reliance on exceptional balance of payments support while several others will have just initiated their reform effort. In many cases, comprehensive structural and institutional reforms will need to be deepened and broadened in a medium-term process with the collective support of the international community—both in terms of technical advice and financial assistance.

The IMF can play an important part in this process. In assisting Africa, our effort will continue to be focused on the macroeconomic and related structural policy areas, in close collaboration with the World Bank. As described in this paper, reducing macroeconomic imbalances is a key precondition for initiating structural adjustment, and continued macroeconomic stability and structural policies are mutually supportive. We will continue to ensure that IMF resources—a large part of which will be in concessional terms through the structural adjustment and enhanced structural adjustment facilities over the next few years—are available to member countries pursuing strong policy reforms and having a balance of payments need. Our aim would be to help them achieve a financial situation in which the structural adjustment process can be sustained primarily with development assistance, and a domestic policy framework that is sufficiently flexible to cope with external shocks. At the same time, we also recognize that even with a strong headway having been made in economic restructuring, some African economies will remain vulnerable to adverse external developments and the macroeconomic framework fragile over the next few years, given the size of the initial problems that need to be addressed.

To help countries buffeted by external shocks, we will ensure timely IMF support—in policy advice and financial resources as appropriate to return countries to a stable financial path. More generally, we will continue to operate the various facilities in a flexible manner and continue to examine how best to adapt or extend some of the existing facilities to support reform programs, including those in Africa. We have also committed ourselves to examine more closely the social aspects of adjustment, with a view toward better addressing them in adjustment programs. We are working with donors as well as with the World Bank to coordinate external assistance more effectively in support of structural adjustment.

Bibliography

Aghevli, Bijan B., James M. Boughton, Peter J. Montiel, Delano Villanueva, and Geoffrey Woglom, *The Role of National Saving in the World Economy: Recent Trends and Prospects*, Occasional Paper, No. 67 (Washington: International Monetary Fund, March 1990).

Akiyama, Takamasa, and Donald F. Larson, *Recent Trends and Prospects for Agricultural Commodity Exports in Sub-Saharan Africa*, Working Paper WPS 348

(Washington: The World Bank, International Economics Department, December 1989).

Fischer, Stanley, and Vinod Thomas, *Policies for Economic Development*, Working Paper WPS 459 (Washington: The World Bank, June 1990).

Heller, Peter S., A. Lans Bovenberg, Thanos Catsambas, Ke-Young Chu, and Parthasarathi Shome, *The Implications of Fund-Supported Adjustment Programs for Poverty: Experiences in Selected Countries*, Occasional Paper, No. 58 (Washington: International Monetary Fund, May 1988).

International Monetary Fund, *Foreign Private Investment in Developing Countries: A Study by the Research Department of the International Monetary Fund*, Occasional Paper, No. 33 (Washington, January 1985).

———, "Investment, Financing, and Growth in Developing Countries," Supplementary Note 5 in *World Economic Outlook: A Survey by the Staff of the International Monetary Fund*, World Economic and Financial Surveys (Washington, April 1988).

———, *World Economic Outlook: A Survey by the Staff of the International Monetary Fund*, World Economic and Financial Surveys (Washington, October 1989).

———, *World Economic Outlook: A Survey by the Staff of the International Monetary Fund*, World Economic and Financial Surveys (Washington, October 1990).

Khan, Mohsin S., "The Macroeconomic Effects of Fund-Supported Adjustment Programs," *Staff Papers*, International Monetary Fund (Washington), Vol. 37 (June 1990), pp. 195–231.

Mussa, Michael, "Macroeconomic Policy and Trade Liberalization: Some Guidelines," *The World Bank Research Observer* (Washington), Vol. 2 (January 1987), pp. 61–77.

Streeten, Paul, "Structural Adjustment: A Survey of the Issues and Options," *World Development*, Vol. 15 (December 1987), pp. 1469–82.

United Nations, Economic Commission for Africa (UNECA), *An African Alternative to Structural Adjustment Programs: A Framework for Transformation and Recovery* (Addis Ababa, 1989).

Weissman, Stephen B., "Structural Adjustment in Africa: Insights from the Experiences of Ghana and Senegal," *World Development*, Vol. 18 (December 1990), pp. 1621–34.

White, Louise G., "Implementing Economic Policy Reforms: Policies and Opportunities for Donors," *World Development*, Vol. 18 (January 1990), pp. 49–60.

World Bank, *Sub-Saharan Africa: From Crisis to Sustainable Growth, A Long-Term Perspective Study* (Washington, 1989).

———, *Report on Adjustment Lending II: Policies for the Recovery of Growth* (Washington, 1990).

Tanzania's Experience

G. Rutihinda

By all standards, Tanzania's economy was in a deep macroeconomic crisis by the mid-1980s. The downturn in the economic performance, which started in the mid-1970s, manifested itself in imbalances in the external account, huge unsustainable budget deficits (financed by monetary accommodation), an accelerating rate of inflation, declining growth performance (and the consequent decreases in per capita incomes and consumption), falling savings, and the general deterioration of the social and physical infrastructure. The proximate causes were both of internal and external origin. Inappropriate pricing policies resulted in a downturn in the production of exportables and promoted misallocation of resources. These effects were compounded by the hostile external environment: adverse movements in the country's terms of trade, reduced inflow of foreign assistance, periodic droughts, the war with Idi Amin, and the break up of the East African community. The existence of the economic crisis was well-known and acknowledged by the authorities, and they attempted to correct the imbalances and restore economic growth within the overall social economic goals of the society as enshrined in the Arusha Declaration of 1967.

The main purpose of these remarks is to briefly review the performance of the recently completed Economic Recovery Program and in doing so to point out the pertinent lessons derived from its implementation. My comments will be divided into five main headings. First, I will outline the basic social economic policies of Tanzania as enshrined in the Arusha Declaration. The outline is important for one to appreciate and understand the nature and extent of policy interventions practiced in Tanzania. Second, a brief macroeconomic review of the period of the crisis, 1975–85, will be presented, followed by a brief outline of the home-based stabilization measures. The fourth part of my remarks will be devoted to the recently completed Economic Recovery Program of 1984/85 to 1988/89, and last, I will draw some lessons from our experience in implementing the program.

Basic Tenets of Tanzania's Social and Economic Policies

Prior to 1967, the basic macroeconomic goals and policies pursued in Tanzania were identical to most other developing countries. Growth in per capita incomes and self-sufficiency in high-level manpower were the main economic goals. The role of the government was limited mainly to providing social overhead capital and to promoting a conducive investment climate in which the private sector can operate. But in 1967, a major policy shift transformed large aspects of the economy and institutions. This policy change is commonly known as the Arusha Declaration.

The main goals of the declaration are building an agricultural system based on collective villages, socialism, and self-reliance, and egalitarian distribution of incomes and opportunities. To accomplish these objectives, numerous institutional changes were introduced, for example, the nationalization of banks, insurance companies, export-import trade, and the main manufacturing enterprises. This resulted in the creation of numerous parastatals, which by the early 1980s accounted for 60 percent of total fixed investment and between 30 percent and 40 percent of the value added in the manufacturing sector.

An important feature that emerged from the Arusha Declaration was a system of direct controls on the macroeconomy. These included investment allocation, foreign-exchange licensing, credit, and price controls. The direct controls and allocation, supplemented with a few doses of market-oriented policies, were thus the main policy instruments used in the overall management of the economy for the period up to the mid-1980s.

Macroeconomic Review, 1975–85

The economic crisis that beset Tanzania is deep-rooted and started way back in the mid-1970s. For this presentation only the salient features of the economic performance for the period 1980–85, as compared with 1976–80, will be reviewed.

With respect to the overall economic performance, as measured by the growth of the gross domestic product (GDP), there was considerable deceleration of the growth performance during 1980–85. Overall, GDP increased, on average, merely by 1 percent a year, compared with a registered growth of 2.5 percent during 1976–80. With population growth estimated at 2.8 percent a year, there was considerable increase in the decline of per capita income. Output in the manufacturing sector tumbled by about 5 percent during 1980–85, despite the relative high investment in the sector during the 1970s. As a result, capacity utilization dropped to between 20 percent and 30 percent in the sector. Though agricultural performance rose by 3 percent during 1980–85 (against an increase of 1 percent experienced during 1975–80), export volumes did not increase, largely on account of relative price structures, which favored nontradable goods production.

Despite the economic crisis, the proportion of output invested did not significantly decline as it did in other countries. In actual fact, the ratio of investment rose by 16 percent during 1980–85, compared with 1975–80, to 26.6 percent of GDP. This additional capacity did not result in increased production, which suggests that investment was misallocated and its productivity was low. On the other hand, the proportion of personal consumption to output remained more or less static, but there was considerable upturn of government absorption. On the external front, the value of total exports decreased from $500 million in 1980 to $286 million by 1985. As a result, coupled with reduced external inflows, imports tumbled from $1,200 million in 1980 to $1,000 million by 1985. The external balance worsened and the country's dependence on foreign savings to finance domestic investment increased.

This increased external debt and debt-servicing difficulties. The overall external debt rose from $2.6 billion (about 330 percent greater than exports of goods and services) in 1980 to $3.9 billion (or about 880 percent greater than exports of goods and services) by 1985. As a result, the debt-service ratio—on a commitment basis—increased from 7.5 percent in 1980 to about 80 percent during 1985. Consequently, external payments arrears rose from $65 million in 1980 to $1,000 million by 1985.

As indicated above, the fiscal situation also deteriorated during the period. Growth rates in public expenditures by far exceeded revenue growth and resulted in large budget deficits. On average, about 40–50 percent of the deficit was financed by external grants and the remaining balance by domestic sources, particularly by the banking system. The bank financing of the deficit increased the growth of money supply and partly contributed to the general inflationary pressures experienced by the economy. The rate of inflation, which averaged 18.5 percent during 1975–80, rose to 30 percent during 1980–85.

"Home-Based" Stabilization Measures During 1975–85

Confronted with these adverse macroeconomic trends, the Government embarked on a series of adjustment measures that would restore economic growth and, at the same time, conform to the broad social economic goals of the Arusha Declaration. In particular, care was taken to ensure that the most vulnerable groups would be insulated and that adjustment would not compromise the overall development objectives nor increase income inequalities.

Before the crisis of the 1980s, two other shocks struck the economy: a drought in 1969/70, and in 1973/74 a drought and the adverse repercussions of the oil price hike. Though the economic performance during 1975–78 was favorable—thanks to the commodity beverage boom—the foundation for the crisis of the 1980s was laid nevertheless during these favorable times. The increased foreign exchange earnings encouraged the Government to liberalize the foreign trade regime; the result was an unprecedented increase in capital goods imports at a time when evidence of capacity underutilization was beginning to emerge. This was not all. The increased government revenues further increased public spending, mainly in development. When the commodity boom collapsed, foreign borrowing and deficit financing were relied upon to continue the spending pattern. All this exacerbated both internal and external imbalances. Thus when additional shocks struck the economy during 1978/79, its ability to recover was severely constrained by the existing imbalances.[1]

In order to deal with the macroeconomic crisis, the Government launched two stabilization programs: the National Economic Survival Program (NESP) of 1980/81 and the Structural Adjustment Program (SAP) of 1982/83. In line with the Tanzanian official view of the crisis, NESP was designed to resolve the economic crisis within the context of policies and instruments that were in use then, in particular, the greater use of administrative controls. Its main objectives were:

(1) an aggressive export drive in order to increase substantially foreign exchange earnings;

---

[1] These other shocks included the collapse of the East African Community, which necessitated the diversion of both human and financial resources from other priority areas to the transport and communication sectors—formerly a joint responsibility of the Community; the economic strains of the war with Idi Amin; and the oil price increase in 1979 and the associated recession in advanced countries, which resulted in further deterioration of Tanzania's terms of trade and import capacity.

(2) a judicious use of available foreign exchange so as to enhance future earning capacity, as well as to save on imports;

(3) the elimination of food shortages through inexpensive small-scale village irrigation projects and the cultivation of drought resistant food crops;

(4) the strict control of public spending by both government and parastatals;

(5) an emphasis on consolidation rather than expansion of new activities; and

(6) the expansion of the scope and capacity for self-reliance in all sectors of the economy and raising the productivity of the workers and farmers through appropriate incentives.

The objectives of the NESP clearly reflected a structural program that, to be successful, lacked basic elements of stabilization policies, including demand management. Yet, such a program needed an injection of foreign exchange if the productive capacity in the import-dependent industrial sector was to remain at a reasonable level of utilization. Refusal by the donor community and the Bretton Woods institutions (the International Monetary Fund (IMF) and the World Bank) to support the program rendered it ineffective and exacerbated the crisis.

The SAP, prepared in conjunction with an independent advisory group, for the period 1982/83–1984/85 did not differ significantly from the NESP in its diagnosis of the problems of the Tanzanian economy. Nevertheless, the SAP included stabilization policies—specifically stricter fiscal and monetary policies. Notwithstanding, SAP was not supported by the Bretton Woods institutions, because the active use of exchange rate policy was not considered a basic instrument.

The SAP was relatively successful, however, particularly during its last year of implementation when foreign trade was liberalized. Own-funded imports considerably reduced the shortage of consumer goods, and the foreign exchange retention system for exporters was a great catalyst for the upsurge in nontraditional exports. In addition, the removal of consumer subsidies and other fiscal measures considerably reduced the fiscal deficit. All these measures helped to bridge the gap between the international financial institutions and Tanzania on the appropriate adjustment strategy to be pursued in future.

Economic Recovery Program 1984/85–1988/89

The limited success of the three-year Structural Adjustment Program, coupled with the need to encourage external financial assistance and the positive results of the liberalization measures enacted in 1984/85, sensitized the Government to formulate a far-reaching adjustment program that would not only stabilize the economy but also ensure the resurgence of growth performance. At the same time, the negotiations with the IMF and the World Bank to have a program that could be supported by the two institutions were continuing in tandem. Much has been written on our post differences with the IMF, and it is not my intention to dwell in detail on these issues. It may suffice to indicate that our differences were basically on three issues: the speed of adjustment policies (gradual versus shock treatment); the thrust of main policies (demand management versus structural "de-bottlenecking"); and the time frame for attaining the objectives of the program.

After various exchanges of view with these institutions, the Government launched a three-year Economic Recovery Program (ERP) in 1986/87. The ERP aimed at achieving a positive growth rate in real per capita income, reducing the rate of inflation, and restoring a sustainable balance of payments position. Its main thrust was to reduce distortions and encourage more efficient resource allocation while exercising fiscal and monetary restraint. The measures proposed included significant increases in producer prices, depreciation of the local currency, institutional changes in the marketing of agricultural produce, price decontrol, and tight fiscal and monetary policies.

Unlike the NESP and SAP, the ERP contained specific macroeconomic and sectoral policies and measures that were extensively discussed with the World Bank and the IMF. The objectives, goals, and policy stances of the ERP were the main springboard for the agreement with the IMF for an initial 18-month stand-by arrangement starting in July 1986, and with the World Bank for a program loan to support multisector rehabilitation, notably in the agricultural, industrial, and transportation sectors. For the first time ever, the Government presented its recovery program at a consultative group meeting of donors in Paris, in June 1986, and received wide support from the international community. Also for the first time, the Government sought debt relief under the auspices of the Paris Club and received an encouraging response.

In this program, the IMF and the World Bank had particularly close collaboration in the diagnosis of Tanzania's economic problems, and in the recommendations of adjustment policies. There was, therefore, for the first time, an agreement between the Fund and the Bank on the conditionalities that were imposed. The measures demanded for implementation included liberal price policies in the form of exchange rate depreciation, upward adjustment of interest rates, enhanced retail price liberalization, and liberalization of trade and payments. In particular, the domestic currency was devalued by 57.5 percent in U.S. dollar terms, or by 135 percent in terms of local currency, with the Government being urged to establish an "equilibrium exchange rate" within one year. The exchange rate policy was to be accompanied by a substantial real increase in producer prices, a 50 percent increase in interest rates, and restrained fiscal and credit policies. As is the practice with Fund-supported programs, quantitative ceilings and performance criteria were established for the duration of the stand-by arrangement. These included reduction of external arrears, limitations on the levels of new external borrowing, domestic credit (both to government and specified parastatals), and overall central government deficit.

Review of Performance of ERP Policies and Lessons

At this point, it may be useful to review the performance of ERP policies and their effects on the main economic parameters. This review also helps to identify some of the lessons derived from the successes and failures of the program. For ease of presentation, the review will be based on both the program targets and the pre-program period of 1980–85.

During the period of the program, 1986–89, the overall economic performance recorded an upturn in growth performance. GDP rose, on average, by 3.9 percent compared with 1 percent during 1980–85 but less than the target growth rate of 5 percent. The productive sectors of the economy showed marked increases: agriculture rose by 4.8 percent (against 3.2 percent during 1980–85) and manufacturing rose by 2.7 percent (against a recorded decline of about 5 percent during 1980–85). This growth performance was facilitated by improved weather, higher producer prices (thanks to the depreciation of the currency), incentives (thanks to liberalization measures enacted in 1984/85), and increased inflow of external funds. There was no major improvement, however, in export volumes; this was due principally to institutional marketing problems, lack of adequate processing facilities, and transportation problems.

Against earlier expectations and worries, the rate of inflation, despite the depreciation of the local currency and price decontrol measures, declined from an average of 30 percent during 1980–85 to 26 percent by 1989. This unconventional result was partly due to bumper food production, liberalization measures of 1984/85 in which consumer prices were effectively priced at market clearing levels, and to the success in reducing fiscal deficit. Some disquieting features emerged nonetheless. During the program period, the rate of capital formation declined by 0.3 percent against an increase of 4 percent during 1980–85. This disinvestment cast serious doubts on the objective of the government to continue the developmental momentum. Also, the serious deterioration of social overhead capital—schools, hospitals—and the apparent widening of income inequalities created tensions in the society with regard to the appropriateness of the adjustment program.

Lessons

Having briefly reviewed the performance of the ERP, I shall summarize under eight broad themes some of the lessons from the Tanzanian experience with structural adjustment programs.

Timeliness of Action

Delays in undertaking appropriate adjustment (structural or stabilization) policies exacerbate the problems that underlie an economic crisis, thereby entailing larger doses of action in future adjustment policies.

It is necessary to give cognizance to the interactions, and probably the vicious cycle, that exist between the real sector and misaligned financial variables. High inflation, for example, works in favor of nontradables and against export sectors, so that if sustained over a long period of time, it may wipe out the export capacity of a country, especially when exchange rate policy is rigid. This is what happened in Tanzania, necessitating large exchange rate depreciations and a very tight credit policy that made the recovery of the real sector even more difficult.

Identification of the "Lead" Sector

Given the limited financial resources, it is often necessary to concentrate resources first and foremost in the sectors that may lead economic recovery. It is critical that one be able to identify those lead sectors and balance the distribution of available resources among them. In Tanzania, there were probably some problems in balancing resources between the agricultural sector (which was identified as the lead sector in the program that began in 1986) and transport. As a consequence, increased agricultural output in 1986/87 could not be translated into increased exports and lower food prices in urban centers because infrastructural bottlenecks, especially transportation, hampered purchases from farmers and movement of the crops from production to consuming centers at home and abroad. With large amounts of crops left in the hands of farmers and some rotting in unsheltered godowns of the Cooperative Unions, the impact of increased output on exports and domestic inflation was less than envisaged. One may therefore tend to think that, in circumstances like ours, *transportation* is probably the lead sector in an economy where it was dislocated by protracted economic crisis.

Supply Bottlenecks

Apart from transportation, other factors, including availability of processing capacity and efficient marketing arrangements, impinge on supply and on the translation of increased output into export proceeds. It has become evident that price incentives notwithstanding, the key determinants of export supply are efficient processing and marketing arrangements, as well as extension services and farm inputs. These were the main bottlenecks that set in motion the crisis in agricultural export production from 1979 or so.

Real Versus Financial Sector Adjustment

Savings mobilization and their efficient investment and allocation are best undertaken by an efficient financial system and constitute the main ingredients to economic growth. The question that arises in an economy where both the financial and the real sectors have been inefficient is one relating to the sequencing of the adjustment measures in the two sectors so as to permit maximum possible growth in the adjustment period without jeopardizing medium- and long-run growth prospects. Tanzania, and other developing countries have tended to emphasize reforms in the real sector, while financial reforms came on only slowly. The case of Tanzania has shown that this approach was a little misdirected and has had disastrous consequences on savings, investment, and long-term growth. It is imperative that adjustments in the real sector are taken in tandem with financial sector reforms, so that regulated real and financial sectors are turned competitive simultaneously. Divorcing the adjustments tends to perpetuate difficulties in the control of money supply and inflation, entailing more protraction of adjustment efforts than would have otherwise been required.

Overloading the Exchange Rate as a Policy Instrument

The stance of exchange rate policy, as discussed earlier, has been one of the major issues of disagreement between the IMF and the Tanzanian authorities. The Tanzanian authorities, while recognizing the importance of the instrument in arresting the deterioration of the external balance, argued that its implementation should take cognizance of the actual situation obtained in the economy, in particular, the inadequacies of the other supporting structures—the transportation system, availability and adequacy of processing facilities, and the marketing system. These issues were not adequately taken into account during the implementation of exchange rate policies during ERP-I and, as a result, the export performance and the overall balance of payments position did not improve as envisaged. True, overall output of exportables increased, but this could not be translated into actual exports because of the weaknesses of the other supporting factors, for example, transportation. This has shown once again that exchange rate policy alone, unaccompanied by appropriate infrastructure, may not result in the intended objective of increased export earnings. Nor is this all. The overloading of exchange rate policy has also created serious problems, at the enterprise level, especially for those institutions—both private and public—that borrowed externally. Exchange rate changes, coupled with high interest rates, have made many of these enterprises insolvent. In turn, these changes have created major problems for banks and other financial institutions, as the borrowers are unable to meet their debt payments on schedule. The inability of borrowers to pay their due obligations, in turn, has increased the amount of nonperforming loans to the banking system, which is now insolvent and is to be restructured and reformed. Clearly, these problems could have been reduced to a more manageable level if the exchange rate stance had been conducted in more staggered manner.

Enforcement of Credit Ceilings

The existence of a multichannel, competitive marketing arrangement seems to be a prerequisite for effective control over domestic credit. This is especially so in an economy where credit developments are dominated by crop financing. Under such conditions, monopolistic and inefficient marketing institutions tempted protection from the government lest farmers be discouraged by crop pileups in the absence of alternative outlets. The results were unduly large operational losses that had to be met by government subsidies, implicitly or explicitly. In the Tanzanian case, the losses were transferred to the banking system through government guarantees; an action that fueled monetary expansion and inflation.

Social Dimensions of Stabilization Program

The stabilization program of 1986/87 to 1988/89, that is, ERP-I, was mainly aimed at arresting the downturn of the overall economic performance. To attain this objective, a greater proportion of government expenditures was allocated to the directly productive sectors of the economy, which resulted in a reduced share for the social sectors—for example, education, health, and rural water supply. This redirection of government priorities coupled with other adjustment measures undertaken during the recovery program increased hardships experienced by the most vulnerable groups of the economy—the poor, children, and women. In order to rectify this omission, the Government has launched a second three-year structural adjustment program—ERP-II—covering the period 1989/90 to 1991/92—with the twin objectives of promoting economic growth and taking account of the social dimensions of the adjustment measures. In this regard, government outlays will be redirected to social as well as economic activities. In particular, government expenditures allocated to education and health sectors will be significantly increased in real terms in order to arrest the deterioration in investment in human capital. The reorientation of the structural adjustment program was deemed to be necessary and essential, given the long-term social economic objectives of the government, as well as to ensure that the greater majority of the population would in fact benefit from the measures undertaken by the Government.

The Role of State, Private Sector, and Market Forces

The severity of the economic crisis and the financial requirements needed for the rehabilitation of the physical infrastructure of the economy, as well as for the parastatal sector, has also brought to the fore the need to redefine clearly the role of the government, or the state, in economic management. During the 1970s, it was government policy to control and own large sections of the productive sectors of the economy. Economic policy was mainly conducted by purely direct administrative measures. Now, however, government policy, because of the crisis and the limited resources available to the government, is to allow greater participation of the private sector—both domestic and foreign—in the economy. This redirection of policy also affects the crop-purchasing policy in which further liberalization has been implemented by making the marketing boards one of the agents of the cooperative sector. Through these changes, government policy is mainly directed to providing the social overhead capital and the necessary environment for the private, as well as public, sector to operate efficiently. This is a major change in the management of economic policy that will help accelerate economic performance, given the limited administrative capacity to effectively direct and control the economy.

Concluding Remarks

Since 1986, the Government of Tanzania has adopted a far-reaching macroeconomic adjustment program, the objectives of which have been to restrain the downturn of economic performance and to restore both internal and external imbalances. Various economic policies were adopted to attain these main policy objectives. These, among others, included currency adjustments, monetary contraction, marketing reforms, price decontrol, fiscal retrenchment, and tariff reforms. Although the macroeconomic and structural objectives were not fully realized, progress was made in implementing various measures. Real GDP growth surpassed population growth; inflation decelerated substantially from 30 percent to 19 percent; and exports, particularly of nontraditional crops, increased.

Despite these reforms and improvements in the major macroeconomic indicators, Tanzania continues to face serious structural and financial problems. Growth is still inhibited by infrastructural bottlenecks, low domestic savings and investments, and inadequate banking and financial services. The external environment, epitomized by weaknesses in commodity prices, is still unfavorable. While the Government of Tanzania will continue, and indeed, intensify the pace of economic and social reforms, adequate external financing is needed to underpin the adjustment effects. The adequacy of external financing is crucial in view of the persisting debt problem and continued weak markets for primary commodities.

II
Africa's Adjustment and the External Debt Problem
Issues and Options

A View from the African Development Bank

A. Sangowawa

The theme of this year's symposium is Structural Adjustment, External Debt, and Growth in Africa. Within that broad theme, this brief paper focuses on Africa's adjustment and external debt problem, with particular reference to the issues and options at stake. To set the stage for the main body of remarks, the paper begins by briefly surveying some of the principal factors underlying the related problems of adjustment and external debt in Africa. It then provides an overview of the structural adjustment programs adopted in most African countries. Finally, some issues and options facing the African countries in the immediate future are given.

Recent Economic Crisis: Origin and Evolution

The decade of the 1970s saw the emergence of persistent and unsustainable balance of payments disequilibria in many African countries—disequilibria that had their origins in various external and internal factors. To focus our thoughts more sharply on the current options and the challenges faced by policymakers, it may be useful to pinpoint some of the critical elements linked to these factors.

On the external side, mention is usually made of the oil price hikes of 1975 and 1979, which represented large real income losses for many countries and also marked the emergence of steadily worsening current account deficits. In the uncertain environment that prevailed at the time, responses varied from country to country. Indeed, while a few countries undertook various policy measures to adjust to the significantly altered global economic environment and absorb, as smoothly as possible, the impact of the price increase, most African countries simply resorted to foreign borrowing as a means of financing the resulting payments disequilibria. This, as it turned out, was an easy option, facilitated, in part, by the perceived need of various international financial houses to recycle the huge payments surpluses of the oil exporting countries and by the favorable terms under which the associated credit was extended.

Beyond the oil price increases, another major external shock to the African economies was the sharp declines in non-oil commodity prices. Although one can point to phases of commodity boom in the 1970s, the decade of the 1980s witnessed a pervasive downward trend in non-oil commodity prices. For instance, in 1986 alone, non-oil commodity prices fell by 10 percent in real terms, and in the 1980–86 period, as a whole, by as much as 30 percent. For a region with as high a degree of commodity export dependence as Africa, export price declines of this magnitude did nothing to improve an already precarious external payments situation—what with the known low demand elasticities for commodities and with technology-induced shifts to substitutes, in some instances.

Closely related to all this was the decline in Africa's terms of trade. In fact, during the 1980s, while the terms of trade for all developing countries declined at an average annual rate of about 2 percent, for Africa, the corresponding figure was almost 4 percent. And although there is some controversy about the impact of adverse terms of trade movements on economic growth, there is little disagreement that they represent real income losses that can have a negative impact on the current account situation.

Beyond this, the performance of the world economy, in particular that of the developed market economies, also contributed to the worsening external payments position in Africa during the period. In the 1980s, as we all know, the industrial market economies grew at an annual average rate that was a full percentage point less than in the 1970s. If one simply recalls that these economies represent the largest markets for Africa's exports, it is not difficult to conclude that the decline in Africa's export earnings and the corresponding payments disequilibria are partly traceable to the slower growth of the industrial countries and the simultaneous decline in import demand.

While external factors have clearly contributed to Africa's difficulties, the policies chosen in Africa are not without blame. Indeed, inappropriate domestic policies, ranging from overly expansionary fiscal and monetary policies, to price and other market distortions, to disincentives to the export sector, to weak public and private investment programs and incentives, and to an often cumbersome administrative machinery have also been important contributors to the present crisis.

This is, of course, all quite familiar territory, but the point can further be illustrated with one example. Overly expansionary monetary policy, partly to finance fiscal deficits, had, during this period, as a natural consequence, higher rates of inflation. But as we know, higher rates of inflation, relative to one's trading partners, lead to real appreciation of the domestic currency, particularly under the fixed exchange rate regimes that prevailed in most African countries in the decade of the 1970s, and reduce international competitiveness. Similarly, overly expansionary monetary policy in a situation of stagnant or slow-growing gross domestic product (GDP), as occurred during the period, is ultimately reflected in attempts to increase real import demand, thus further worsening the current account situation.

The combined result of all these developments—external shocks and domestic policy failures—was the emergence of an untenable balance of payments position; slower economic growth; fiscal crisis; and even a heightening of social and political tensions.

Policy Response

As is well known, the initial policy response in several countries was to view the disequilibria that arose as a short-run phenomenon that could be readily corrected by the application of narrow demand management measures. But it soon became apparent that the observed disequilibria were not amenable to short-run policies of this type and that a more gradual, growth-oriented set of policies—in the form of structural and sectoral adjustment programs—was called for.

The decade of the 1980s, the so-called adjustment decade, thus witnessed the introduction of various adjustment and reform programs in several African countries—broadly speaking, to correct policy shortcomings wherever they may exist, to reduce external disequilibria, and to launch these economies on the path of recovery and growth. The rationale underlying these programs was simply that since the observed disequilibria were neither temporary nor self-correcting, merely financing them would not in any way represent a long-term solution. There was simply no alternative, since a policy of financing without adjustment quickly results in larger and larger external debt, and the further erosion of a country's creditworthiness. Adjustment was therefore inescapable, and those countries that acted more swiftly and effectively were more likely to reverse the economic decline that had set in.

It is now more than a decade since the first structural adjustment program was introduced into Africa. And it has now become a feature of most economies on the continent, though the results of these adjustment programs have been, at best, mixed. Some progress has undoubtedly been achieved in the areas of policy and institutional reforms. But, in a paradoxical sense, going hand-in-hand with these efforts are a rising debt burden, relatively reduced capital inflows, declining per capita incomes, and increasing poverty. Indeed, the adjustment decade saw the emergence of rapidly rising external debt and increasingly burdensome debt-servicing difficulties. From a level of about $109 billion in 1980, Africa's external debt is now estimated at a level of $250 billion, about 70 percent of which is owed to official creditors. Debt service, as a percentage of exports of goods and services, now stands at 30 percent, compared with 13 percent in 1980. Thus, while Africa's external debt is relatively small, compared with other developing regions, its burden and the toll it exerts in terms of human suffering, reduced per capita incomes, and income forgone, is no less great—and is indeed higher. Africa's external indebtedness has evolved to impede economic recovery and growth—particularly in the low-income countries where it is now estimated to be about 100 percent of gross national product (GNP) and represents close to 600 percent of exports.

Options and Constraints in the Future

Given these clearly unacceptable developments, and while readily acknowledging the individual exceptions to this aggregate picture, two questions readily come to mind. For how long and at what cost will the present situation continue? What are the issues and options before Africa and the international community, as the continent tries to cope with its economic difficulties?

It is not easy to predict how long the present situation will last, nor to estimate the associated costs. What is certain, however, is that the time has long passed for Africa to examine, as dispassionately as possible, the feasible set of options available in dealing with the issues of economic adjustment and external indebtedness. In what follows, I will attempt to sketch the broad outlines of a few of these issues and options, in the areas of public policy management, trade policy and economic integration, and debt alleviation.

If one starts from the generally accepted premise that there is no substitute for sound economic management, then it is not difficult to urge African countries to persevere with those policy reforms and adjustment measures that are necessary for economic recovery and sustained development. They should continue to examine, and re-examine, existing policies and to take measures to correct macroeconomic and sectoral distortions, and institutional weaknesses, where they arise. The point needs to be made, however, that, realistically, in the current situation of heavy external indebtedness, adjustment of the extent required can be achieved only over a period of several years and must, therefore, become part of the broader development effort.

Indeed, while it is widely acknowledged that macroeconomic and sectoral problem identification and policy formulation are essential points of departure for the transformation of these economies, they are still no guarantee for sustained economic recovery and growth, as recent experience clearly demonstrates. The road from problem identification and policy formulation to recovery and growth is fraught with far too many difficulties, risks, and uncertainties. For instance, we still know very little about supply responses to producer price changes, or about the response of key macroeconomic variables to policy stimuli. Similarly, we have no firm and reliable estimates about the size of exchange rate elasticities and their short- and long-run profiles. In designing adjustment programs, therefore, it is essential that these uncertainties be recognized, and that programs be made correspondingly accommodating.

One major uncertainty facing adjustment programming relates to financing, as even the best formulated program could easily be derailed by inadequate funding. Adequate and predictable external financial support is thus essential, in order to give policies time to run their course and to insulate economies from the vagaries of temporary shocks, external or domestic, over which they have no control. It is then of utmost importance that reform efforts be reliably supported by the international community, including the multilateral agencies, so that these efforts can be resolutely pursued to their ultimate objective. It is because of this that the African Development Bank (ADB) stepped up efforts to increase finance to the African countries. In particular, the ADB has started policy-based lending.

ADB's Structural Adjustment Lending

The ADB has a relatively short history in policy-based lending. Until recently, project loans and lines of credit constituted virtually all of ADB group lendings. The onset of the current economic crisis in most countries and the subsequent changing needs of regional member countries entailed diversification of the lending instruments. Since the early 1980s, the bank group has started extending rehabilitation and sector loans alongside traditional project lendings. Sensing needs for quick-disbursing funding to support policy reforms, the ADB recently instituted structural adjustment lending.

In 1987, total sectoral and structural adjustment loans amounted to $763 million—constituting over a third of total lending. Of this amount, structural adjustment loans totaled $374 million. In 1988, structural adjustment lending dropped sharply to less than half of the 1987 level. Sectoral adjustment lending increased marginally in the same year. In 1989, the proportions of sectoral and structural adjustment loans changed significantly. Structural adjustment lending increased to $495 million, while sectoral lending dropped to $82 million. An increase in the number of loans approved and the large size of loans to Cameroon, Morocco, and Tunisia explain the high level of structural adjustment lending in that year. In 1990, structural adjustment lending fell by one third, while sectoral adjustment lending increased sharply. Policy-based lending constituted about one fifth of total lending—broadly in conformity with the targets set in the Five-Year Operational Program of the ADB for the years 1987-91. The objective of the ADB's structural adjustment lending is to assist regional member countries in creating a firm foundation for sustained self-reliant growth. The loans provide quick-disbursing balance of payments support that encourages and facilitates policy adjustment. In particular, they are intended to ease the foreign exchange constraint on the importation of foreign inputs.

This increasing role of ADB as a source of policy-based support makes it necessary that it have a broader view of the macroeconomic and structural problems of the regional member countries. To do this, it needs to considerably improve and expand its research and analytical capacities. Lacking the latitude for imposing stiff conditionalities on regional member countries, the ADB approach is to encourage the internalization of policy formulation and policy dialogue. Where the institutional mechanisms for policymaking and implementation are inadequate, the ADB provides technical and institutional support. Although it has yet to make a comprehensive assessment of policy-based lending, its internal reports reflect some satisfaction that the venture is worthwhile, despite its perceived risk. The reason for the satisfaction is that the financial support provided encourages countries to undertake policy reforms. By easing foreign exchange constraint, structural adjustment lending enhances the utilization of idle capacity, promotes growth, and further encourages countries to undertake policy reforms.

Human Dimension of Adjustment

A word of caution needs to be made. Policy reforms, with their emphasis on the alignment of domestic expenditure to domestic revenues, reduction of price and cost distortions, and various institutional changes, usually impose painful costs on the poor, in particular, and on the vulnerable segments of society. Thus, in pursuing the policies of adjustment and reform, it is important to bear in mind the fundamental point that the betterment of mankind is the ultimate purpose of development. Therefore, human resource development, in all its dimensions, should be given priority as a means of enhancing human welfare and, hence, of promoting development. The strategy requires greater support for poverty alleviation programs, such as the provision of minimum food requirements, basic education, primary health care, job opportunities, and so on. Indeed, one of the more deleterious consequences of the current adjustment efforts has been the decline in human welfare, as expenditures on social programs are reduced to meet fiscal, monetary, and other program objectives.

In order to unleash and harness human resource potential for the promotion of economic development, it is essential that greater attention be paid to the social costs of adjustment. In this regard, mention should be made of the Social Dimensions of Adjustment Program, launched jointly in 1987 by the ADB, the UNDP, and the World Bank, which is designed to address the adverse consequences of adjustment. For maximum results, this program too will need to be adequately funded.

The Global Economic Environment and Adjustment

Beyond the broad policy setting and taking into consideration the related issues of financing and the social dimensions of policy reform and adjustment, a crucial determinant of Africa's success will be what occurs with regard to its own trade policy in the context of the global trading environment.

Since the 1980s, most African currencies have undergone significant real devaluations, one rationale for this being the potential contribution to greater export earnings and hence an easing of the external debt burden. Unfortunately, these policies have not been rewarded with significant export renewal. Major nonprice constraints continue to limit the supplies of traditional exports, while their international prices continue to fall. At the same time, nontraditional exports have taken a much longer time to develop than originally expected—a situation that cannot be entirely divorced from the policies of voluntary export restraints, quotas, licensing, and so on that effectively restrict entry of developing country exports to the industrial country markets.

It follows that one of the critical issues that needs to be addressed in the current recovery effort is the export-earning capacity of Africa. In the short run, the dependence of Africa on commodity export earnings would need to continue. But the adverse effects of declining and fluctuating commodity prices must be mitigated through improved funding of schemes established for that purpose, such as the European Community's STABEX (system of stabilization of export earnings), the IMF's compensatory and contingency financing facility, and UNCTAD's (United Nations Conference on Trade and Development) Integrated Program for Commodities. In a longer-term context, the way out of the current dependence on primary commodities is the diversification of the production base through, among other things, local processing. But for this policy to succeed, not only must the broader domestic policy framework be appropriate, but the restraints to global trade we have seen emerge in the 1980s must be quickly dismantled.

And beyond what assistance is offered in the international context, African countries need to move aggressively toward a policy of effective economic integration, in all its dimensions, if they are to nurture and exploit trading opportunities within the continent itself. This strategy closely integrated with broad policy reform efforts, and encompassing all corners of the continent—from the Mediterranean to the South Atlantic—will, perhaps, provide a more lasting solution to the current problems of weak export earnings, mounting external debt, and the associated debt-servicing difficulties.

With regard to the issue of debt alleviation, since the inception of the debt crisis, as is known, many proposals have been advanced to address this problem. Some, such as the Venice and Toronto initiatives, are targeted toward the low-income countries, and others, such as the Baker and Brady proposals, are aimed at the middle-income, highly indebted countries. While many low-income African countries have benefitted from initiatives such as those made in Venice and Toronto, the same cannot be said of the Baker and Brady initiatives. The debt problems of the middle-income countries thus remain largely unaddressed.

To date, African countries have relied on a combination of debt forgiveness, debt reduction, and reschedulings to address the issue. While some progress has been made, the debt problem still remains stubbornly difficult. From the nature of the problem, it is obvious that there can be no lasting solution until there is significant debt and debt-service reduction, and until economic growth resumes on the continent. Without significant debt relief, in whatever form, available resources would continue to be diverted to debt servicing. But we must simultaneously bear in mind that, without growth, even if all of Africa's current debt were forgiven and the slate wiped clean, it would not be long before a new debt crisis emerged, as countries would be required to incur additional debt if the challenges of economic and social development are to be addressed in an effective manner. The resumption of growth, however, is not automatic; it has several elements.

One such critical element is the continuation of policy reforms, as I have just discussed. And adjustment, as noted, must be adequately supported by external financing, to tide a country over the interim period and to provide a breathing space during which necessary policies can be executed to their ultimate conclusion. Needless to say, without adequate external financing, the reform efforts themselves could be undermined by political and social unrest. A further element in the recovery process, as noted earlier, is that the international trading environment must be sufficiently open to permit African countries to earn their way out of the present crisis. Indeed, it is for this reason that it is important that the present deadlock over the Uruguay Round of multilateral trade negotiations be resolved quickly and in a way that guarantees a fair and open world-trading system.

Concluding Remarks

To conclude these brief remarks, it should be emphasized that the restoration of economic health to the economies of the continent will take time and will require bold measures by all concerned. It will also call for continued sacrifice on the part of Africa in terms of the burden of adjustment. But for the adjustment efforts not to be undermined, there must be reasonable hope that, before long, economic growth will resume again. This resumption of growth itself calls for bold measures in the area of international trade and trading arrangements, external capital flows, and the resolution of the current debt crisis. In other words, the domestic efforts of Africa must be complemented by those of the international community; if they are not, the sacrifices that Africa is required to make will be in vain.

A View from the Paris Club

Denis Samuel-Lajeunesse

The question I would like to broach this morning concerns the Paris Club's handling of the debts of African countries, in terms of present status as well as on a more forward-looking level. This, indeed, is a very important issue for these countries, which are often indebted primarily to the governments of donor countries represented in this group of creditors that makes up the Paris Club.

I must add that the topic of this morning's session, "Adjustment in Africa and the External Debt Problem: Issues and Options," seems to involve a great deal of consistency: the external debt of debtor countries can only be handled effectively after they have adopted adjustment policies that take them down a path of lasting growth; and debt handling and adjustment require a dual approach—the settlement of balance of payments problems combined with a more structural, medium-term improvement in the reaction capability of currently indebted economies.

What is known as the debt strategy, in other words, the pragmatic, evolving approach taken by the international community to ensure that these countries, within the context of an acute external payment crisis in many countries, receive adequate financial flows, is based on these briefly summarized principles. The International Monetary Fund (IMF) and World Bank have a central role to play in clarifying these different concerns.

First of all, I would like to review the status in the Paris Club of the application of the Toronto terms to the poorest and most indebted countries, which are the majority in Africa. To date, they have already been applied to 19 countries, including 17 in sub-Saharan Africa and two in Latin America. Accordingly, $5.7 billion in debt has been rescheduled, including $1.5 billion under the partial write-off option, $1.7 billion using the extended repayment period option, and $2.5 billion under the concessional rate option. Mali was the first country to benefit, in October 1988. Subsequent beneficiaries have been Benin, Central African Republic, Chad, Equatorial Guinea, Guinea, Guinea-Bissau, Madagascar, Mauritania, Mozambique, Niger, Senegal, Tanzania, Togo, Uganda, and Zaïre. Some of these countries have already been granted loans under the Toronto terms twice, that is, in two successive debt tranches. This group of beneficiaries comprises the Central African Republic, Madagascar, Mali, Niger, Senegal, Tanzania, and Togo.

The approach involving extension of the rescheduling period also evolved considerably over the past year—in some cases (Mali, Mozambique, and Niger) to the point of actual multiyear agreements. This practice, however, cannot be used systematically. Indeed, we are still wedded to the link between agreements with the IMF and rescheduling agreements that make the efforts of the creditor countries consistent with the adjustment program pursued by the debtor country. Consequently, immediate coverage of maturities over several years can only be considered when the debt is rescheduled at the onset of an agreement with the IMF that covers several years.

The financing needs of the country in question must also be sufficiently visible. In several cases, the debtor country quite legitimately wished to limit the period covered by the consolidation to one year, so that it could adjust its liabilities to official creditors as effectively as possible from year to year. In other cases, the period covered by the consolidation has been limited, owing to the prospect that the debtor country could free itself of successive reschedulings.

The sharp reduction in the rescheduling need for some countries has, indeed, been a significant accomplishment. Much of it results from the writing off of development aid debts, which a variety of creditor countries have elected to do over the past few years, often involving large amounts of money.

The combined effects of these write-offs, aid granted primarily under the special program for Africa, and the adjustment efforts made by debtor countries makes the Paris Club's contribution to the financing of some countries sometimes seem so marginal that we are led to wonder whether it is worthwhile to call a meeting to reschedule such small amounts. In my opinion, we can only be pleased with this phenomenon of countries freeing themselves from the rescheduling process and regret that it is still limited to so few of them. For too many countries, however, the need to reschedule debts is still very great—indeed, it is increasing. Consideration of ways to improve the treatment of these countries must thus be continued.

I will now briefly report on this thinking, which is still in a very preliminary stage. As you know, some creditor countries have announced fairly radical proposals for relieving the bilateral debt of the poorest countries. A Dutch proposal, presented at the Paris Conference on the Least-Developed Countries in September 1990, calls for writing off all debt of the poorest and most indebted countries to governments of developed countries. This very generous proposal runs the risk of presenting considerable problems for many creditor governments. The United Kingdom has formulated a less radical proposal, known as the Trinidad terms. It consists essentially of writing off two thirds of the outstanding bilateral debt balance, rescheduling the rest at market rates over a 25-year period, including a 5-year grace period, and capitalizing all or part of the interest on overdue payments during the grace period. Beneficiary countries should have an agreement with the IMF. Eligibility decisions would be taken by the Paris Club, as is the case for the Toronto terms.

In comparison with the Toronto terms, the Trinidad terms would thus represent considerable progress in at least two ways: quantitatively, by moving from the write-off of one third by only part of the creditors to the write-off of two thirds by all creditors, and methodologically, because this approach would immediately apply to the stock of debt, rather than to successive tranches.

The Paris Club is examining these proposals along with others that have not been announced publicly. The main questions they raise can be summarized as follows: (1) Can all creditor countries accept one approach, or must a system of options be maintained so that each country can respect its internal constraints? (2) Is it possible to deal with the stock of debt all at once while still maintaining sufficiently strong conditionality and allowing a sufficiently flexible response to fluctuations in the payment ability of debtor countries? The answer is complex and merits thorough examination.

In its deliberations, the Paris Club must also be very sensitive to the efforts of other creditors. Of course, I have in mind creditor countries that do not participate in Paris Club meetings. We are making every effort to inform them of our practices and to encourage them to respect the principle of comparable treatment. I am also thinking of banks, which, of course, have lent very little to the poorest countries. But we are concerned to see that some of the agreements between these countries and their bank creditors only provide for conventional rescheduling, with no debt-reduction option. This underscores the urgent need for the prompt use of the $100 million that the International Development Association (IDA) has earmarked for support of operations to reduce bank debt. In this respect, I am pleased with the agreement being negotiated between Niger and its creditor banks, which is the first case in which this IDA facility has been used.

Finally, as you are aware, the Paris Club is also involved in detailed consideration of another category of countries, that is, middle-income countries, and primarily those in the lower range of this category. The outcome of these studies will surely affect how the poorest countries are treated. For this reason, it would be useful for me to describe how the Paris Club treats middle-income countries.

Last July, the heads of state and government of the seven major industrial nations who met at the Houston summit encouraged the Paris Club to continue to examine further options for handling the debt burden and to begin extending repayment periods for the lower middle-income countries. In line with these guidelines, the Paris Club last September approved a set of new measures that could be applied to the lower middle-income countries on a case-by-case basis. This essentially involves extending the rescheduling period for commercial loans to 15 years, including an eight-year grace period, and for official development credit to 20 years, including a ten-year grace period.

Creditor countries also agreed to give interested creditor countries the option to undertake the conversion of debt into local currency for purposes of in-country investments, financing for development projects or environmental protection. This option applies to the entire debt stock in the case of official development aid and direct government credits, and to 10 percent of commercial credit balances. The Paris Club has already applied these measures to three African countries: Morocco, Congo, and Nigeria.

It must be emphasized that the possibility of debt conversion is the first example of concessional treatment in the Paris Club for countries in this category. These operations are clearly of value to debtors in part because they are executed at a discount from the transfer price. They consequently involve a partial write-off of the debt.

Several creditor countries have already expressed the desire to go further. One of them is France, which, at the Houston summit, proposed a menu of options for dealing with the bilateral debt of these countries, including debt reduction, debt-service reduction, and the granting of new money combined with rescheduling of old debt.

All of the above requires exhaustive discussion among creditor countries. Our examination of the matter in the Paris Club is still in progress, and it is still difficult to predict when it will be concluded.

Finally, to conclude these brief remarks, I will point out that, as you can see, the treatment of debt by the Paris Club is a process that has been evolving for a number of years. World economic conditions require these adjustments. Of course, the Paris Club does not claim that it alone holds the key to economic recovery for African countries, and the effort of all parties involved, including commercial banks, as well as the active participation of multilateral institutions, are needed now more than ever. This, quite obviously, is the meaning of the principles underlying the debt strategy, and gives particular pertinence to the topic of our session this morning.

An Unofficial View

G. K. Helleiner*

The most important element in the emerging consensus on the requirements for economic development for sub-Saharan Africa is the adoption by policymakers of a much longer time horizon than is implicit in current structural adjustment programs and many current evaluations.[1] Many of the most important investments and policy changes have very long gestation periods. The costs of pursuing too short-term and, therefore, in the absence of alternative possibilities, too demand-oriented an approach to adjustment in Africa have been severe. The forced adjustment necessitated by short-term balance of payments arithmetic and the concomitant "import strangulation" not only rendered the investment required for recovery impossible but also damaged the limited and painfully accumulated existing capital stock. Worse still, it resulted in unnecessary output losses, as a consequence of the underutilization of partially import-dependent productive capacity, and in unnecessarily severe and extended human suffering.

Agreement is also widespread on the need for restructuring production toward efficient exporting and import-substituting activities and on the typical main elements of previous supply-side policy error—on the relative neglect of agriculture, overambitious aspirations for the role of the state in the productive sector, inappropriate or ineffective pricing policies, the neglect of maintenance and recurrent costs relative to the further expansion of capital stock, and inappropriate technology in all sectors.

Particularly worth noting, in light of the prodding of the Economic Commission for Africa (ECA) and the United Nations Children's Fund (UNICEF), is the fact that the impact of adjustment programs upon

---

*I am grateful for the comments of Roy Culpeper, Mike Faber, Just Faaland, Susan Horton, Philip Ndegwa, Frances Stewart, Rolph van der Hoeven, and the participants in the AACB/IMF symposium in Botswana, none of whom is to be implicated in the contents of this paper.

[1] World Bank (1989); United Nations (1989); Maastricht (1990).

poverty is now receiving much more attention in Africa and elsewhere. Policies for the relief of absolute poverty seem at last to have been added as an eleventh item to the so-called Washington consensus on ten kinds of appropriate policy reform.[2] Still, relatively little effort has been made to monitor absolute poverty levels, assess the implementation of antipoverty policies, or build antipoverty objectives into ex ante design of adjustment programs.[3]

External Resource Requirements and Debt Relief

The overall resource requirements for sustained African development in the 1990s, as estimated by virtually all sources, imply significant increases in transfers from external official sources. (Indeed, the World Bank has consistently understated Africa's medium-term requirements so as to generate aid targets that the major industrial countries would consider within the range they consider to be politically possible.)

The highest immediate returns from expanded official flows to import-strangled economies are typically reaped from the provision of increased inputs for the rehabilitation and full utilization of existing capital stock rather than from the creation of new capital. Increased supplies of "free" foreign exchange in situations of foreign exchange constraint can yield extraordinarily high returns. (They could also, in some circumstances, simply finance increased rents for those controlling mismanaged economies or increased capital outflow, or both.) At the same time, they can render many more potential investments remunerative. Growth-oriented adjustment requires investment for the restructuring of production of tradable goods and services. There are obviously also continuing needs for the expansion of social infrastructure and the directly productive capital stock for steady longer-run development. There can be neither private nor public incentives for such investments without assurances of adequate provision of inputs for their effective operation.

Concern over the "absorptive capacity" of recipient African governments for increased external assistance may in some circumstances, particularly where there is war, civil strife, or gross mismanagement in

---

[2] The others, originally derived from approaches to Latin America, are fiscal discipline, public expenditure priorities, tax reform, financial liberalization, appropriate exchange rates, trade liberalization, foreign direct investment, privatization, deregulation, and securing property rights (Williamson (1990), pages 9–33).

[3] Stewart (1990); see also Mosley (1990), and Sahn (1990).

government, be appropriate. In the main, however, such concerns are inappropriate, in light of the sharp reduction in African imports (and, even more, imports per capita), the virtually universal phenomenon of import-related underutilization of both social[4] and directly productive capital, and the continuing increases in population that will expand import needs. Where absorptive capacity problems do seem to arise, they are frequently the product of donor administrative and other constraints, which it must be a matter of high priority to ease.

The evident need for increased official resource transfers for African development is directly related to the problem of Africa's external debt, most of which is owed to official creditors. If newly acquired external resources have to be employed to service external debt, they obviously cannot contribute to African social or economic development. Official flows and debt problems therefore must be considered in an integrated and consistent fashion. In recent years, the problems created by Africa's external debt have been worsening.[5]

The overhang of African debt now constitutes a significant extra drag upon the prospects for Africa's development. The constant pressure of debt-related financial negotiations deflects decision makers from the necessary and more socially productive activities of development-oriented economic decision making. It thus both detracts from effective economic governance and reduces absorptive capacity for utilization of further public resources, whether locally or externally mobilized, for development. African governments' absorptive capacity for further debt negotiations and extensive consultations with external sources of advice is a much greater problem than their absorptive capacity for further resources. No less important are heavy external debt-servicing obligations that discourage private investors and government reformers alike by imposing a major "tax" upon successful adjustment efforts.

Reducing the current external cash flow obligations and payments on debt account will thus probably be the most cost-effective form of official external resource transfer to Africa in the 1990s. Debt reduction must be a major element of any serious internationally supported effort to restart African development. Of the $43.5 billion of external finance deployed in support of 23 African SPA (Special Program of Assistance) countries between 1988 and 1990, $11.6 billion, or 27 percent, was already in the form of debt relief (capitalization of scheduled interest payments,

---

[4]For example, dispensaries without medicine, schools without textbooks or paper, etc.
[5]Mistry (1988); Humphreys and Underwood (1989); and World Bank (1990b).

postponed scheduled principal payments, and rescheduled arrears). With the anticipated modest potential for further increases in gross official development assistance (ODA) flows to Africa in the 1990s, the role of further debt relief in *marginal* expansion of external support is potentially much larger (as it was in the SPA effort, where it accounted for over 60 percent of the "new" money).[6]

Since a high proportion of Africa's debt, particularly high in the lowest-income countries, is owed to governments and official institutions rather than private creditors, there is high potential for direct political solutions. There have already been many official initiatives in the sphere of African external debt. So far, however, they have had only minor effects upon the transfer of resources to Africa. Cancellation of debt associated with official development assistance programs has mattered little, since the debt was originally on very soft terms.

The so-called Toronto terms for Paris Club debt rescheduling are now widely recognized as far from adequate. Some creditors have consistently availed themselves of the agreed option to extend maturities rather than reduce principal or interest rates (Belgium, the Netherlands, Spain, and the United States). The terms of debt reductions, where they occur, are too modest (averaging about 20 percent),[7] too slow to take effect (because they apply only to servicing obligations during the "consolidation period" rather than to the entire stock of debt), and too costly in terms of negotiators' time. The World Bank estimates that their application in the first 17 African countries (since October 1988) has resulted in a cash flow saving of only about $100 million annually, of which Zaïre and Mozambique together make up over half. Between 1990 and 2000, the introduction of the Toronto terms to those eligible for them will save at most 5 percent of 1989 debt-servicing obligations.[8] Current Toronto terms may be roughly appropriate for other debt-distressed African countries, those not categorized as low-income or least developed.

Debt forgiveness on previously concessional debt (official development assistance) is estimated to have reduced annual debt servicing for Africans by another $100 million in 1990.[9] There is some potential for further gains for debt-distressed African countries as more donors write off their ODA loans; but these possibilities are, by their nature, fairly limited.

---

[6] World Bank (1990b), page 93.
[7] Ibid., page 29.
[8] Ibid., pages 100–104.
[9] Ibid., page 93.

Among the non-African proposals recently floated for improving Paris Club treatment of low-income African countries' debt are: (1) a one-off reduction of the total eligible debt stock (rather than continuing to reschedule only one-year maturities each year) by two thirds, with an initial five-year period of interest capitalization and an extension of the repayment period from 14 to 24 years for the remaining debt; (2) total forgiveness of bilateral official debt to the poorest of the severely debt-distressed countries (the "least developed" and other low-income countries); (3) a three- to ten-year moratorium on all bilateral official debt servicing with all rescheduling on Interntional Development Association (IDA) terms. All of these are to be conditional on the existence of an agreed adjustment program and to be additional to current or anticipated resource flow commitments.

A high-level political agreement is required among creditor governments to ease significantly the current terms of Paris Club rescheduling agreements. This must involve reducing a much larger proportion of the debt "at one go" and reducing payments obligations by much greater proportions. The speed with which the Group of Seven[10] were recently able to agree to better-than-Toronto terms of debt forgiveness for Egypt and Poland illustrates the possibility of effective early action.

Low-income debt-distressed countries' obligations to multilateral institutions are, by common agreement, best handled by refinancing at highly concessional terms; and most of the World Bank's and the IMF's credit to these countries has already been treated in this manner. The problem of arrears to the international financial institutions, however, is a much more difficult issue. Arrears in African countries' IMF repayment obligations are unlikely to be successfully addressed in existing or newly agreed arrangements for dealing with them, all of which require major "up-front" policy change, without the prospect of supportive external resource transfers until much later. Such punitive approaches risk aborting recovery. The World Bank should continue and complete its program for the conversion of Bank loans to IDA terms for currently IDA-eligible borrowers. Other "hard" creditors should do likewise.

Although in most sub-Saharan African countries (Nigeria is a major exception) private creditors account for a relatively small proportion of external debt, failure to deal with them—through clearing arrears, re-

---

[10] The Group of Seven comprises Canada, France, Germany, Italy, Japan, the United Kingdom, and the United States.

scheduling, and writedowns—can be very costly in terms of more expensive or unavailable trade credit and higher-priced imports.

As far as commercial debt is concerned, there is no reason, in principle, for African debtors to be treated in any way less favorably or less quickly than those already benefitting from debt-reduction initiatives under the Brady initiative, or its successor arrangements. There is every reason to expect case-by-case IMF and World Bank initiatives in support of debt-distressed African countries with significant commercial debt outstanding, as in the case of Morocco. The $100 million fund provided to IDA out of the World Bank's profits for this purpose is much too small. Under its rules, each beneficiary country may receive up to $10 million in grants, but there are already 15 countries with upward of $2 billion of commercial debt that have applied for its use.

Developed country governments that are themselves writing down their own African debt should also be expected to insist that their private creditors offer no less favorable arrangements to the beneficiary debtors. Thus far, they have largely, and inappropriately, stood aside from these negotiations.

Conditionality and Local "Ownership"

A great deal of energy has been devoted to the assessment, by the IMF and the World Bank, as well as by others, of the effects of their stabilization and adjustment lending activity and, by implication, of the efficacy of their conditions.[11] Granting all the methodological problems, notably the difficulty of establishing appropriate counterfactuals, there is evidence of modest improvement in overall economic performance in countries with IMF or World Bank programs. The IMF's studies also now indicate that there *are* initially negative growth experiences associated with typical IMF programs.[12] But it remains difficult to disentangle the positive results of increased resource flows from those of policy reform; a lot of uncertainty about the effects of particular components of reforms remains; and the evidence is, in any case, much less persuasive in Africa than anywhere else.

It is important that any generalizations from these studies not be translated into universally identical policy prescriptions. Not only do different kinds of countries and different kinds of problems require different solu-

---

[11] World Bank (1988) and (1990a); Khan (1990); and Mosley, Harrigan, and Toye (1991).

[12] Khan (1990).

tions but apparently fairly similar circumstances may, in fact, cover widely varying underlying constraints.[13]

One way in which prescription for most African countries probably should differ from current generalizations is in the sequencing of adjustment policy. The current "conventional wisdom" posits that macroeconomic stabilization, especially in the realm of inflation, should come first; followed by the restructuring of incentives, addressing the most severe distortions first; and only then expanded investment and growth.[14] In today's Africa, where critical early investments must be undertaken by government (in education, health, and infrastructure), where confidence in government has been shattered, and where much of the relevant private decision making is done by peasant farmers, the *first* step has normally been to restore some public investment, generate some early growth, and restore some government credibility.

Most African countries can be described as different from the developing country norm, if indeed there is such a thing at all, in their very low income, very limited base of human, physical, and institutional capital, heavy dependence upon primary production and exports, limited flexibility of production structure, "soft" administrative systems, and small economic size. At the same time, most are both extremely susceptible to external shocks and extremely limited in their capacity to respond rapidly to them via appropriate borrowing and adjustment. They are uniquely fragile in economic terms (as well as, frequently, in ecological ones). Policy prescriptions for them must take these special characteristics fully into account. Ultimately, however, there is no substitute for full *country*-specificity in adjustment programs.

It is particularly difficult to generalize about the development consequences of more micro-level policy reforms. It would be a very brave analyst who could conclude that there have so far been unambiguously positive effects from African efforts at financial liberalization, import quota and tariff reform, privatization of public enterprises, or tax reforms, to name some of the principal areas of policy pressure. As experience accumulates, there will undoubtedly be scope for improved policies and results in these spheres.

The principal shortcomings of African stabilization and structural adjustment programs in the 1980s are obviously controversial, but many would find some fault with their

---

[13] Taylor (1988), especially pages 69–74.
[14] World Bank (1990a).

- continued overreliance upon demand restraint;
- overoptimism concerning the market prospects for traditional exports and the short-run possibilities for expanding nontraditional ones;
- relative neglect of the provision of crucial public goods, especially agricultural infrastructure;
- relative neglect of the maintenance of human capital, particularly health expenditures, and failure to minimize the impact upon absolute poverty;
- failure to grasp the nature of required changes in the financial system, and overestimation of the efficacy of financial "liberalization" and interest rate increases;
- overestimation of the efficacy of privatization, especially in agricultural marketing and input distribution;
- inadequate appreciation of the fiscal implications of reform packages incorporating sharp devaluations and interest rate increases;
- exaggerated expectations of the role of foreign direct investment, and the prospect of returning flight capital;
- inadequate consideration of the potential gains from regional and subregional cooperation; and
- underfunding, and frequently inappropriate forms of external assistance.

On the other hand, as far as more immediate prospects are concerned, one lesson of recent experience is quite clear. Whereas it has been very difficult to prove unambiguously that policy reform itself has improved development performance, either in Africa or anywhere else, it is beyond dispute in econometric investigations that there is a positive and statistically significant correlation in recent years between increased imports and improved growth.[15] Increased external resources, evidently, can be highly productive in periods of foreign exchange stringency in the short to medium term, probably primarily through their effects upon capacity utilization.[16]

Among the most important other thrusts in development and adjustment thinking in recent years, derived in large part from these same studies, is the increased emphasis now placed upon stability, policy cred-

---

[15] Notably those within the World Bank, see Faini, and others (1989) and also Mosley, Harrigan, and Toye (1991).

[16] Faini and others (1989); and Ndulu (1990).

ibility, and sustained government effort.[17] More important than achieving policy "perfection" at each point in time, whatever that might mean, is the creation and maintenance of a stable overall policy environment, and the creation and preservation of credibility for and confidence in an announced adjustment and development program. Stable incentives and politics can compensate for quite a lot of policy "imperfection." Only with the resulting reduction in overall uncertainty will private decision makers and public servants be able to act rationally, consistently, and in the longer-run social interest. This new perception of the prime prerequisites of success has created a fresh interest in "critical thresholds" in policy change, below which very little will happen but above which much more is possible. Once this threshold is crossed, and, provided that relapse does not occur, there may be considerably lower marginal returns to further "fine-tuning" of policies. Once the most grotesque distortions, particularly, in Africa, those related to the real exchange rate and the fiscal deficit, are repaired, further "improvements" of prices and policies may not be nearly so productive. Adjusting African governments, in fact, have achieved significant real currency devaluation and other major price reforms in the 1980s. Insistence upon too many further policy reforms, which are often disputed, risks disruption of the stable investment flows on which development depends.

Among the key elements in securing policy credibility are the adequacy of finance and assurance of its continuation. It makes little sense to strain over optimal policies if all can see that adjustment possibilities are so tightly constrained by resources as to throttle the best of reform efforts.

More debate is required not only on the conditions for external support of low-income countries' adjustment and development programs but also on the process for monitoring and enforcing them. Current arrangements provide for a very short leash on African governments. Arrangements under the IMF's structural adjustment and enhanced structural adjustment facilities are between one and three years in duration, and performance is assessed every six months. Within the World Bank, there is active discussion of the possibility of shortening the leash on adjustment lending still further. Some suggest that, where reforms take a long time either to implement or to take effect, loan disbursements should be geared to the continuation of appropriate policy or policy change in order to reduce the prospect of "policy slippage."[18]

---

[17] World Bank (1990a).
[18] Ibid.

While this recommended "short-leash" approach may be defended on the basis of the incentives (against policy slippage) that it creates, it makes little sense in terms of broader adjustment objectives. If there are balance of payments problems associated with adjustment efforts, increased external finance should be made available; the amounts to be provided should relate to the objective need for both quick-disbursing and steady program support, not fairly subjective assessments of whether programs of uncertain outcome in the longer-run are being adhered to. The stability of incentives and expectations, and the credibility of development programs, both of which are critical to success, are hardly enhanced by "stop-go" approaches to the commitment or provision of external finance.

Much more persuasive than the calls for shorter-leash financing is the call for improved contingency financing—what used to be called "supplementary finance"—to adjustment programs supported by the World Bank to stay on track in the face of unexpected events, such as terms of trade deterioration.[19] The new evidence that investment rates vary directly with the stability of overall output lends extra support to this advice.[20] It is striking that the existing contingency financing arrangements with the IMF, introduced in 1988 with considerable fanfare, have not been utilized.

Among the most critical issues in the development of appropriate adjustment programs in small low-income countries is the time and energy of the relevant skilled personnel, which are available for dealing with foreign sources of finance. The "transactions costs" of endless dealings with individual bilateral donors, the World Bank, the IMF, and, in the case of the debt-distressed countries, the Paris Club are enormous when expressed in terms of their domestic opportunity costs. It is inconsistent for external sources of finance to demand simultaneously both that local programs be developed by national governments and be fully "owned" by them and that they devote the amount of effort required to service the informational and other requirements of the external creditors. Short-term, short-leash finance implies, for these countries, that there will be little time left for the relatively small numbers of key economists and administrators to develop their own programs and policies for development.

While the rhetoric of the IMF and the World Bank clearly admits the need for local "ownership" of programs and policies, the practice of "leaning" fairly hard on the weaker members, notably those in Africa, has been resistant to change. Yes, the IMF and the World Bank have experienced

---

[19] Ibid.
[20] Serven and Solimano (1990).

professionals and access to the best support systems, but their combined resources cannot completely substitute for local understanding. Even if it could, policies and programs will come to naught when those who implement them do not believe in them, or do not regard them as their own. As I emphasized earlier, the African countries have limited absorptive capacity, either in administrative or political terms, for external reformist advice during any given period.

African development is likely to be best served when (1) no single foreign source of ideas and finance has disproportionate power, and (2) African indigenous technical capacity is built to the point where genuine policy dialogue, based upon mutual respect, takes place between external donors and African policymakers, and where Africa's development programs are fully and unambiguously locally constructed.

At present, there is a fairly general professional, governmental, and popular consensus within Africa that the relative influence of the IMF and the World Bank, particularly the latter, has grown too large. There is little consensus as to what should or can be done about it: for example, Seek to strengthen the African Development Bank or the ECA, or both? Press for more diversified sources of external assistance (while somehow still seeking to minimize transactions costs and improve aid coordination)? Improve various forms of South-South exchange and cooperation? Or what?

On one longer-term response, there is a firm African consensus: that technical capacity-building is a matter of very high priority. For obvious reasons, there is widespread nervousness in African economists' circles about too great a Washington influence upon technical and economics capacity-building as well as everything else. For the present, the IMF and the World Bank will continue to perform their most useful roles when they provide, upon request, specific technical assistance and advice, and contribute to the quality of ongoing, primarily domestic, policy debate.

The Roles of the IMF and World Bank

Table 1 shows the net international transfers to (and from) sub-Saharan Africa by the IMF, the World Bank, and others in the 1980s. Most striking are the IMF's negative net transfers from 1984 onward, totaling over $4 billion over the 1984–90 period. Sub-Saharan African use of IMF

Table 1. The IMF, the World Bank, and the External Transfers to Sub-Saharan Africa, 1980–90
(In millions of U.S. dollars)

	1980	1983	1984	1985	1986	1987	1988	1989	1990[1]
IMF									
Gross disbursements[2]	1217	1618	952	738	735	678	1033	865	733
Repayments and interest[3]	487	739	993	1172	1689	1541	1495	1593	1265
Net transfer	730	879	–41	–434	–954	–863	–462	–728	–532
IDA									
Disbursements	424	637	778	881	1400	1681	1697	1700	—
Repayments and interest	21	44	56	79	94	111	128	126	—
Net transfer	403	593	722	802	1306	1570	1569	1574	—
IBRD									
Disbursements	400	708	832	647	898	998	581	835	—
Repayments and interest	328	438	527	616	865	1073	1306	1226	—
Net transfer	72	270	305	31	33	–75	–725	–391	—
IMF, IDA, IBRD, Total net transfers	1205	1742	986	399	385	632	382	455	—
Other net transfers									
Multilateral[4]	707	664	442	487	650	709	672	607	—
Bilateral[4]	1657	2295	1925	472	1210	1194	630	945	430
Private[5]	2818	270	–1667	–2648	–1132	–213	–434	–428	–1818
Total long-term debt Related net transfers	5657	4092	1727	–856	2067	3185	1712	2307	657
Grants[6]	3057	2844	3422	4514	4823	5030	6567	6570	—
Direct foreign investment	20	882	494	1059	460	1167	687	2301	—
Total net transfers	6573	7485	4419	2779	5209	6763	7511	8692	—

Source: Derived from World Bank, *World Debt Tables, 1990–91* (Washington, 1990), Vol. 1, pp. 130–33.
Note: IMF = International Monetary Fund; IDA = International Development Association; IBRD = International Bank for Reconstruction and Development.
[1] Projected.
[2] Purchases.
[3] Repurchases and charges.
[4] Excluding grants.
[5] Publicly guaranteed and unguaranteed, excluding direct foreign investment.
[6] Excluding technical assistance.

credit peaked in 1987 and has fallen by about 15 percent since.[21] Table 1 also shows sharply rising IDA disbursements until 1987 and a negative World Bank transfer beginning in the same year. The total net transfers to sub-Saharan Africa from the Washington international financial institu-

---

[21] World Bank (1990b), page 130.

tions in the late 1980s were positive but small, only about one third to one fourth the size of those transfers early in the decade, and far less than the transfers from other official sources. A significant proportion of sub-Saharan Africa's actual debt service, 32 percent in 1989, is paid to the IMF and the World Bank.[22] The net transfers to the IMF alone have exceeded those to private creditors in 1987, 1988, and 1989.

Table 2 shows net IMF credit flows at the country level in 1988–90 (exclusive of charges, because the data are not publicly available). In the year ended April 30, 1990, about half of Africa's countries were, on balance, transferring resources to the IMF. Of the 39 African countries (35 sub-Saharan) that have had IMF programs in recent years, only 21 (19 sub-Saharan) still had them outstanding at the end of November 1990. The IMF's enhanced structural adjustment facility (ESAF) has not extended nearly as much credit to Africa as originally anticipated. The reasons for this come down to controversy over conditionality. During 1990, the structural adjustment facilities for Chad, Guinea-Bissau, and Tanzania expired. None was immediately renewed. Major further tests will arise in 1991 and 1992 as eight structural adjustment and seven enhanced structural adjustment facilities formally expire.

The IMF has long since shifted from its previous proclaimed purity as a (short-term) financial institution, treating all members equally, to a new role in which development assistance is also provided as a matter of course. The subsidized interest rates and longer terms within its Trust Fund, the structural adjustment facility, and the enhanced structural adjustment facility have, willy-nilly, converted the IMF into an aid agency, at least in part. Having "lost its virginity" in this realm, the IMF can no longer easily defend its failure to act more vigorously in the provision of expanded resources to developing countries on the ground that its role is "monetary" rather than "developmental." At a bare minimum, the IMF should now be acting so as *not* to generate a net transfer of resources from countries that are at present in desperate circumstances in consequence of terms of trade deterioration, heavy levels of external debt, and other factors.

Surely the time has come for a reconsideration of the usefulness of holding roughly 103 million ounces of gold with a market value of $40 billion in the coffers of the IMF. The low-income developing countries have an unprecedented need for increased financial assistance, some of it directly associated with payments obligations to the IMF that were inappropriately offered and incurred. Article V, Section 12(*f*)(ii) of the Articles

---

[22]Calculated from World Bank (1990b), pages 130–32.

Table 2. Net Flows of IMF Credit to African Countries, 1988–90[1]
(In millions of SDRs)

	Year Ended April 30		
	1988	1989	1990
Sub-Saharan Africa			
Angola	—	—	33.06
Benin	—	—	6.26
Burundi	0.00	12.81	8.54
Cameroon	—	69.53	15.45
Central African Republic	4.08	1.46	−8.66
Chad	6.12	−1.75	5.68
Congo	—	—	−2.38
Côte d'Ivoire	−19.25	−125.06	−87.46
Equatorial Guinea	—	2.43	−2.31
Ethiopia	−8.80	−6.47	−18.45
Gabon	20.12	51.16	8.22
Gambia, The	4.73	0.04	3.88
Ghana	−21.37	−41.37	23.39
Guinea	7.28	17.37	−6.01
Guinea–Bissau	1.00	−0.94	1.78
Kenya	−27.35	9.79	−14.03
Lesotho	—	3.02	4.53
Liberia	—	−1.29	−2.36
Madagascar	3.48	−28.04	−12.26
Malawi	−15.15	−0.25	0.30
Mali	−15.20	−1.24	7.79
Mauritania	16.97	−5.14	8.66
Mauritius	−22.80	−32.27	−31.19
Mozambique	30.50	12.20	0.00
Niger	−0.60	−7.54	−3.32
Sao Tome and Principe	0.01	—	0.80
Senegal	11.11	23.32	1.23
Sierra Leone	−0.70	−0.01	−2.42
Somalia	−1.63	−8.50	−1.22
Swaziland	−4.50	−1.10	—
Tanzania	31.88	32.10	13.93
Togo	−3.23	−6.88	0.06
Uganda	−3.18	17.21	−6.13
Zaïre	−26.50	−71.98	−98.52
Zimbabwe	−90.40	−41.77	−25.11
Subtotal	123.38	−129.16	−178.27
North Africa			
Algeria	—	72.05	470.90
Egypt	103.50	−6.25	—
Morocco	−28.10	−121.24	−35.94
Tunisia	47.00	—	−18.71
Subtotal	122.40	−55.44	416.25
Total	−0.98	−184.60	237.98

Source: International Monetary Fund, *Annual Report of the Executive Board for the Financial Year Ended April 30, 19–* (Washington, various issues).

[1] Excludes arrears.

of Agreement of the IMF specifies that proceeds of gold sales, held in a Special Disbursement Account, may be used for

> balance of payments assistance . . . on special terms to developing countries in difficult circumstances, and for this purpose the Fund shall take into account the level of per capita income.

Can it be realistically argued that anything significant in respect of the IMF's potentially important international operations would be altered if, say, 30 million ounces of gold were sold over the course of the next few years in the interest of providing expanded resources to the IMF's debt-distressed low-income members? The resulting profits could be utilized by the IMF in such a way as to improve its own balance sheet and increase the prospects of some of its most distressed members returning to "normal" relations with the Fund, by financing arrears or interest on arrears and other credit.

In the words of the recent Fraser Report to the United Nations:

> The gold is not essential to IMF operations and serves no socially useful function at present. By selling a relatively small portion of the gold [20 percent is suggested], the IMF could raise enough profits to rectify the arrears of poor countries with the IMF through new low-interest loans, and to contribute additional resources to the IMF Trust Fund for subsidizing interest rates on other advances to poor countries.[23]

It is no longer realistic, at least under current IMF arrangements, to consider the use of SDRs (special drawing rights) to achieve a "link" with aid requirements. When the link proposals were originally formulated, SDRs carried a highly concessional interest rate and therefore constituted a potentially very valuable source of external finance for low-income countries. As subsequently developed, however, the SDRs carry a market rate of interest. That increased credit to low-income countries at market interest rates is not considered appropriate under present circumstances is evident in the highly concessional terms of SAF, ESAF, and IDA lending. It *would* be possible, however, to provide interest rate relief on SDR issues to low-income countries either by special Trust Fund contributions (perhaps financed by gold sales, among other sources) or by willing suspension by creditor nations of the interest earnings on SDR accumulations to which they would otherwise be entitled. In short, the IMF still has considerable underutilized capacity to perform an important further role as a source of development finance if it chooses to employ it.

---

[23] United Nations (1990), page 94.

Is it not, at last, time to reconsider seriously the appropriate means for the provision of international finance to very low-income countries? Not only has the IMF been unable, despite contrary statements of intent, to prevent net aggregate repayments from sub-Saharan Africa for the past half decade, but its contingency financing facility has failed to play any role in the stabilization of those low-income countries' adjustment and development programs that it has supported. The overwhelming need in these countries is for grants and long-term finance in support of long-term development programs. Might it not be preferable, in the case of very low-income (or "least developed") countries, to build new (and workable) contingency financing arrangements into the longer-term financing programs put together by the World Bank and other aid donors in World Bank consortia, United Nations Development Program (UNDP) roundtables, and the like, and allow the IMF to retreat to a relatively smaller role as a source of technical advice on monetary matters.

The IMF would thereby be relieved of an "aid" role with which it is not totally comfortable,[24] the "bad press" associated with its steady *negative net transfer* out of Africa, and its inappropriate role as "gatekeeper" for access to debt relief and external finance. The IMF's existing claims on very low-income countries could either be frozen at existing levels or eliminated by using the proceeds from limited sales of IMF gold. Others, notably the World Bank Group, would then take over primary, though certainly not exclusive, responsibility for assessing these countries' needs for external finance, and the formulation and monitoring of country-specific conditions for its provision. To perform this role effectively they would be required both to encourage efforts to expand the role of independent advisors and further to develop cooperation among national and international development agencies, including those of the United Nations and, in Africa's case, the African Development Bank and the ECA. "Graduation" from very low-income (least-developed? IDA-eligible?) status would thereafter involve a return to "normal" IMF membership.

To some degree the international financial system has already been edging in that direction. Is it not now time to shift in a more direct and visible manner? In any new dispensation it will be important, above all, to avoid the creation of any one overpowering arbiter of Africa's development requirements. The object must be, rather, to assist Africans to reach their own development decisions through the provision of multifaceted and

---

[24]See, for instance, Polak (1989), pages 48–52.

sustained external assistance—in the context of genuine policy dialogue and consistent and sustained domestic effort.

Bibliography

Faini, Ricardo, and others, "Growth-Oriented Adjustment Programs: A Statistical Analysis", Development Studies Working Papers, No. 14 (Torino and Oxford: Centro Studi Luca d'Agliano—Queen Elizabeth House, 1989).

Helleiner, G. K., ed., "The Question of Conditionality" in *African Debt and Financing*, ed. by Carol Lancaster and John Williamson (Washington: Institute for International Economics, Special Reports 5, 1986), pp. 63–91.

Humphreys, Charles, and John Underwood, "The External Debt Difficulties of Low-Income Africa," in *Dealing With the Debt Crisis*, ed. by Ishrat Husain and Ishac Diwan (Washington: The World Bank, 1989), pp. 45–68.

Khan, M. S., "The Macroeconomic Effects of Fund-Supported Adjustment Programs", *Staff Papers*, International Monetary Fund (Washington), Vol. 37 (June 1990), pp. 195–231.

Maastricht Conference on Africa, *Issues Paper* (Maastricht, 1990).

Mistry, Percy S., *African Debt: The Case for Relief for Sub-Saharan Africa* (Oxford, England: Oxford International Associates, 1988).

Mosley, Paul, "Increased Aid Flows and Human Resource Development in Africa," Innocenti Occasional Papers, No. 5 (Florence: UNICEF, International Child Development Centre, 1990).

―――, Jane Harrigan, and John Toye, *Aid and Power: The World Bank and Policy-Based Lending in the 1980s* (London; New York; Routledge, 1991).

Polak, Jacques J., "Strengthening the Role of the IMF in the International Monetary System" in *Pulling Together: The International Monetary Fund in a Multipolar World*, by Catherine Gwin, Richard Feinberg, and others (New Brunswick, New Jersey; and Oxford, England: Transaction Books, 1989), pp. 45–68.

Ranis, Gustav, "Debt, Adjustment and Development: The Lingering Crisis," in *The Lingering Debt Crisis*, ed. by Khadija Haq (Islamabad: North-South Roundtable, 1985), pp. 207–216.

Sahn, David E., *Fiscal and Exchange Rate Reforms in Africa: Considering the Impact Upon the Poor*, Cornell Food and Nutrition Policy Program, Monograph 4 (1990).

Serven, Luis and Andres Solimano, "Private Investment and Macroeconomic Adjustment in LDCs: Theory, Country Experiences and Policy Implications" (mimeograph, Washington: The World Bank, Country Economics Department, 1990).

Stewart, Frances, "The Many Faces of Adjustment," paper presented to International Conference on Policy-Based Lending, University of Manchester, September 1990.

Taylor, Lance, and World Institute for Development Economics Research, *Varieties of Stabilization Experience: Towards Sensible Macroeconomics in the Third World* (Oxford: Clarendon Press, 1988).

United Nations, Economic Commission for Africa, *African Alternative to Structural Adjustment Programmes: A Framework for Transformation and Recovery* (Addis Ababa, 1989).

———, *Africa's Commodity Problems, Towards a Solution* (1990).

Williamson, John, *The Progress of Policy Reform in Latin America*, Policy Analyses in International Economics, No. 28 (Washington: Institute for International Economics, 1990).

World Bank, *Adjustment Lending: An Evaluation of Ten Years of Experience*, Policy and Research Series, No. 1 (Washington: Country Economics Department, 1988).

———, *Sub-Saharan Africa: From Crisis to Sustainable Growth* (Washington, 1989).

——— (1990a), *Adjustment Lending Policies for Sustainable Growth*, Policy and Research Series, No. 14 (Washington: Country Economics Department, 1990).

——— (1990b), *World Debt Tables 1990–91* (Washington, 1990).

Discussants

Africa's Adjustment and the External Debt Problem

Percy S. Mistry

A View of African Adjustment and Development as a Point of Departure

Judging by the volume of literature from various sources on the subject, it is clear that few endeavors in modern development economics have attracted as much effort on the part of (recipient and donor) governments, central banks, multilateral financial institutions, and academia, as comprehending the experience of structural adjustment programs in sub-Saharan Africa. It was recognized from the outset that the structure and characteristics of the region's low-income economies posed special challenges: how to formulate policy prescriptions and recommendations on structural measures that would revive development and growth after nearly two decades of sustained retrogression in per capita incomes. That has not, however, prevented a "sameness" in analysis and approach to adjustment prescriptions and the design of programs that belies the differences these economies are acknowledged to have.

Structural adjustment programs for Africa have clearly had their theoretical roots in stabilization prescriptions evolved over time by the International Monetary Fund (IMF). Invariably, they have emphasized (a) the management of demand, usually through austerity, by means of tightly controlled fiscal and monetary policies; (b) economic, financial, and trade liberalization measures; and (c) decontrolled pricing aimed at reflecting market-clearing outcomes. Specific conceptual attention to reconstructing and diversifying the fragile supply side of low-income African economies has, until very recently, been lacking in the institutional thinking of the Bretton Woods twins (the IMF and the World Bank); although the

United Nation's Economic Commission for Africa (ECA) has pointed out that shortcoming on different occasions. A study by the World Bank,[1] which appeared toward the end of 1989, represents perhaps the most thoughtful (though belated) attempt so far to recognize and correct that deficiency. Until then, the assumption on the part of the IMF and the World Bank seems to have been that, if correct macroeconomic and pricing policies were pursued, the supply side would automatically take care of itself. That this assumption has not been borne out after a decade of adjustment experience underlines the difference between low-income African economies, whose switching responses are extremely weak, and other developing economies whose characteristics might make that assumption more tenable.

Quite understandably, strenuous efforts continue to be made by the World Bank and the IMF to look for conclusive signs of adjustment success.[2] Those signs remain ephemeral. The more realistic conclusion from a survey of the available evidence might be that some African economies have succeeded in achieving macroeconomic stabilization at a low level of output. Between 1987 and 1990, agricultural production certainly seems to have revived, but for reasons in which variables (especially the weather) other than price reforms may have played a significant part. Genuine "structural" adjustment—that is, resulting in (a) more efficient, diverse, and flexible structures of production, which would induce desired supply responses across all sectors of economic activity in response to appropriate market-price signals, and (b) a revival of domestic savings and investment, which would permit a degree of self-sustainability of the adjustment effort and the growth process—does not yet appear to have taken place anywhere in Africa. At the end of a decade of adjustment,

---

[1] World Bank, *Sub-Saharan Africa: From Crisis to Sustainable Growth* (Washington, 1989).

[2] A particularly egregious example of overinterpreting the evidence available (which was itself thin and contentious) was a report entitled *Africa's Adjustment and Growth in the 1980s*, by the World Bank and the United Nations Development Program (UNDP) (Washington, 1989). That report engendered considerable controversy in Africa and in the international academic community with the Bank being accused of intellectual legerdemain and attracting a particularly sharp rebuttal from the ECA (*African Alternative to Structural Adjustment Programmes: A Framework for Transformation and Recovery*). More neutral and sober reflections on the adjustment experience, (though still biased toward somewhat more adjustment success) are contained in the two successive reviews of "Adjustment Lending Policies for Sustainable Growth" carried out by the World Bank in 1988 and 1990 respectively and "The Macroeconomic Effects of Fund-Supported Adjustment Programs," by Mohsin Khan in *Staff Papers*, International Monetary Fund (Washington), Vol. 37 (June 1990), pages 195–231.

African economies have become more burdened with debt, more dependent on continuing flows of official aid resources at unsustainable levels, and less attractive as long-term investment propositions for the private sector. Many are trapped in a devaluation-inflation vortex from which they find it difficult to exit.

It is not even clear that the more cautious assessments of recent months, that is, that *adjustment* in Africa will take much more time than earlier thought, is the right one.[3] Such a view implies that the adjustment prescriptions made are basically correct and that efforts of the past decade have resulted in laying the proper foundations for a period of renewed and sustainable growth based increasingly on internal resource generation. The evidence in support of that view is not conclusive. It may well be that the macroeconomic policy reforms that have been undertaken have been *necessary* for future progress. It is quite clear, however, that they have by no means been *sufficient*. The unfortunate reality seems to be that neither the World Bank nor the IMF (nor indeed the African governments concerned or the academic and UN communities) as yet have a coherent conception of an exhaustive set of interventions, policies, programs, or investments that might represent sufficiency in this context. Obviously, none of the evidence suggests that countries should be encouraged to persist with the wrong policies on exchange rates, interest rates, price controls, support for loss-making parastatals, and loose monetary and fiscal policies. But neither does it suggest that simply correcting these policies provides a panacea for achieving a quick turnaround and sustained growth thereafter.

The debate about whether the right kind of structural adjustment for low-income Africa is indeed likely to be achieved with neo-liberal prescriptions has been continuing for some time. Essential arguments on each side have been made in various documents issued by the World Bank and the IMF, on one side, and by the ECA, the United Nations Conference on Trade and Development (UNCTAD), and large parts of the African and international academic communities, on the other (footnoted below). Those arguments leave much to be desired from both empirical and conceptual perspectives. What is now perceptible is that the conceptual underpinning for structural adjustment in Africa seems to be shifting toward precepts concerned more with long-term development and away from

---

[3] For example, in The World Bank's long-term perspective study, *Sub-Saharan Africa: From Crisis to Sustained Growth,* and in various speeches made by senior World Bank representatives at several conferences on the region's situation, most notable the one held in Maastricht, the Netherlands, in July 1990.

those aimed at immediate stabilization. The notion (which has taken hold with confusing repetitiveness in obscure World Bank-IMF jargon)—that structural adjustment is a unique medium-term "in-between" phenomenon marking a sort of chronological midpoint between short-term stabilization and long-term development—is a peculiarly untidy, if all too convenient, one. It now needs to be abandoned.

In substance, where low-income Africa is concerned, there seems to be no conceptual, practical, or programmatic difference between what the Bank and Fund now refer to as "adjustment over the long term" and what previously used to be known more simply as "development." It may well be that a long, roundabout route has been taken to recognizing an elementary point—that is, that the process of development involves more than making a series of efficient investments to improve physical and social infrastructure and to expand and diversify productive capacity for increasing output, employment, and incomes. It also involves making continual policy and institutional adaptations to changes in internal and external circumstances, which are now occurring at a much faster pace than before. That is what adjustment quite literally means. It is, in that sense, a process without end, not one that has some finite temporal dimension that can be stretched like elastic to suit the convenience of either the World Bank or the IMF when it comes to fund-raising (or one's intellectual shortcomings when one is pressed to prove that what one is doing is working!). Continuous adjustment is inescapably an integral part of long-term development; it does not end when macroeconomic stability is achieved.

Low-income Africa may have the capacity to make physical and social investments in a static environment, if development were that easy. It lacks the capacity to make such investments in a dynamic environment because its weak structural endowments—which have been further eroded throughout the 1970s and 1980s—render it incapable of adapting as readily as external circumstances warrant. That rather simple view, though made in a painfully laborious way, provides the point of departure for assessing the implications of the way in which Africa's external finance and debt relief needs have been managed over the last decade.

Debt Management and Its Implications for Adjustment

The view taken here is that the annual financial programming exercises that form the basis for financial gap plugging and for consequent debt relief—which today constitutes by far the largest component of external "financing" for Africa—are fundamentally flawed in two ways. *First*, they have an inherent bias toward underestimating the extent of transitional financing that is really needed for successful adjustment to occur and take hold in any given time period. *Second*, because these exercises are excessively sensitive to the practices and protocols of institutions offering debt relief—in particular, the Paris Club—they are biased toward providing finance on the wrong terms, for too short a time.[4] If one accepts the view expressed earlier—that structural adjustment and development in Africa are, for all intents and purposes, synonymous—then it becomes immediately obvious that focusing on new financing and debt relief on a short-leash basis for 18 months at a time is entirely inappropriate. Apart from making the trajectory of long-term resource flows for development financing highly uncertain, such an approach has resulted in the embedding of a mentality of continuing crisis management in African governments. Apex level policymakers have become so absorbed with allocating the next week's foreign exchange availabilities that they have little time to focus on or manage the execution of programs intended to address intermediate and longer-term priorities. Moreover, the rituals and procedures involved in negotiating debt relief, again especially with the Paris Club,[5] have become so involved, arduous, and repetitive that they absorb far more time, energy, and are far more wasteful of scarce administrative resources than can possibly be justified by the gains that have so far accrued.

The Record of Debt Management in Africa

What is the record of debt management in low-income Africa between 1980–90? On the evidence, fairly dismal. Table 1 provides a summary view of what has happened over that period of time.

The picture that emerges is clear. On an outstanding debt stock of just over $70 billion at the end of 1982, sub-Saharan Africa serviced nearly $85 billion in principal and interest payments between then and December 31, 1990. Official grant flows to the region increased from around $5 billion in 1982 to over $12 billion in 1990. Yet, its debt burden is

---

[4] This hypothesis is being rigorously tested in a research project being undertaken by Percy S. Mistry and Mathew Martin (with the full involvement of research teams from Ghana, Mozambique, Senegal, Tanzania, and Zambia) on "External Finance for Structural Adjustment in Africa" at the International Development Center, Queen Elizabeth House, University of Oxford. The preliminary findings of that research support the view expressed above. The findings of the research project are expected to be published in mid-1992.

[5] See the companion paper in this volume by Mathew Martin.

Table 1. Evolution of the Debt Situation in Sub-Saharan Africa, 1980–90
(In billions of U.S. dollars, except where otherwise specified)

	1980	1982	1989	1990[1]
Total debt stocks outstanding	56.20	70.25	146.99	160.79
Of which				
Bilateral creditors	16.49	19.79	56.09	64.04
Multilateral creditors	7.55	10.39	31.31	36.41
Use of IMF credit	3.03	4.93	6.38	6.42
Total official debt	27.07	35.11	93.78	106.87
As percent of total debt	48.17	49.98	63.80	66.47
Private long-term	19.42	25.88	37.19	38.63
Private short-term	9.70	9.26	16.01	15.30
Debt stocks as percent of GNP	27.4	37.4	98.3	111.9
Actual annual debt service	6.30	7.44	8.82	11.18
Debt service as percent of exports	10.9	19.3	22.2	24.4
Debt service as percent of GNP	3.1	4.0	5.9	7.8
Interest arrears	0.22	0.63	7.23	6.67
Actual debt service as percent of scheduled debt service	89.0	72.0	39.0	37.0[2]
Total debt service between 1982–90				84.55
Of which				
Interest				29.28
Principal				55.27

Source: World Bank, *World Debt Tables, 1990–91* (Washington, 1991).
[1] Projections.
[2] Estimate.

estimated to exceed $160 billion in 1990 after eight years of crisis "management." Worst of all, Africa's debt profile has changed, with a larger proportion of debt due to preferred multilateral creditors (up from 18 percent in 1980 to 27 percent in 1990) to whom service obligations are nearly impossible to reschedule, and the costs of running arrears are far higher, than in the case of official bilateral or private creditors.

It is also clear that despite repeated bilateral reschedulings for almost all severely indebted countries in Africa, Africa's ability to meet its rescheduled payment obligations (after adjustment measures have been instituted) continues to deteriorate, not improve. And this is after significant amounts of official development assistance (ODA) debt cancellations (amounting to over $6 billion by the end of 1989) and attempts at other forms of commercial debt reduction, such as buy-backs and swaps, The export of real resources from Africa by way of debt service has increased from about 3 percent in 1980 to 6 percent in 1989 and a projected 8 percent in 1990. That is indefensible in a continent where per capita incomes are still declining from levels that are already abysmally low.

These aggregates—which although they must be broken down by country for appropriately sensitive treatment of the debt problem— suggest quite clearly that, despite repeated measures to liberalize the terms of official debt relief and the efforts being exerted to reduce the burdens of private debt service, something is still wrong with the present debt management approach and its results. Those directly involved in the progressive softening of Paris Club rescheduling terms with the Venice Agreement in 1988, the Toronto Terms in 1989, and the wider application of Trinidad (or even better Pronk) Terms in 1991[6] have applauded themselves for the "progress" made, pointing to seemingly insuperable technical difficulties and political objections that have finally been surmounted. And perhaps they are to be congratulated for their Herculean efforts. But the stark reality remains that for Africa, and particularly for its poor, what has been achieved still amounts to marginal trimming of the remote outer branches of the problem and not hacking away at its roots. Debt relief, though much to be appreciated and further encouraged, is still being provided to Africa on a "too-little, too-late" basis. It is not sufficient to help the adjustment efforts being made to take hold, nor to ameliorate Africa's trade credit problems, or the related 30–40 percent premiums in import prices that Africa has to pay on the open market. The economic instability created in large part by the debt overhang also continues to pose a continuing threat of interminable devaluations and accompanying inflations. Together, these make it nearly impossible to regenerate domestic or foreign private investment to any significant degree. That, however, is not the only pernicious effect being experienced.

Research being done at Oxford University on domestic resource mobilization difficulties[7] in Africa suggests that the effects of adjustment failure are resulting in significant financial dissavings and disintermediation

---

[6]For explanations and elaborations of these progressively liberalized terms and their application in particular cases, see the introductory text chapters in the summary volumes of the *World Debt Tables* (particularly for 1988–89, 1989–90, and 1990–91), which are published annually by the World Bank.

[7]Under a research project entitled "Domestic Resource Mobilization in Africa: Examination of the Effects of Adjustment Policies," by Percy S. Mistry and Machiko Nissanke (with the involvement of local research teams from Ghana, Kenya, Malawi, Tanzania, and Zambia) at the International Development Center, Queen Elizabeth House, University of Oxford. Preliminary findings are available and a final report is due to be published.

by households that are now exercising their preference to hold net wealth in nonmoney forms. Paradoxically, this phenomenon is accompanied by an illusory liquidity balloon in many African economies caused by the buildup of effectively unusable parastatal deposits in the commercial banking system. Overall, the signals being sent by the joint, but related, failure of both debt management and adjustment efforts are feeding back to discourage rather than encourage domestic savings and investments—two forces that must be revived if Africa is to have any serious hope for climbing out of its predicament.

Where Does Africa Go from Here?

Many gatherings (such as this symposium) have been held over the past four years on the subjects of structural adjustment, debt, and growth in Africa. At those meetings, much the same things seem to have been said and much the same reactions elicited. Proponents of radical change have been tarred as unrealistic academics who have little appreciation of how the real world works. The only gratification that experience provides is that radical changes have indeed occurred in the system; unfortunately, they have not been radical enough! Hence, the effort to achieve further change must be renewed vigorously.

On the *bilateral* debt front, it is now quite clear that Toronto terms, generous though they seem in relation to the past, are not sufficient for the future. The proposals for more generous rescheduling treatment, involving the entire stock of official bilateral debt, made by (now) British Prime Minister John Major at the meeting of Commonwealth finance ministers in Trinidad (in September 1990) seem more realistic. But even they can only be a way station to the ultimate goal enunciated by Minister (for Development Cooperation) Jan Pronk of the Netherlands—the cancellation of all official outstanding bilateral claims for all debt-distressed, low-income African countries. If it is indeed necessary to go through the intermediate step offered by the Major proposal, and it may be, then consensus should be reached sooner rather than later on universal adoption of these proposals by the Organization for Economic Cooperation and Development (OECD), the Organization of Petroleum Exporting Countries (OPEC), and former Council for Mutual Economic Assistance (CMEA) creditors.

For *multilateral* bank debt, the steps being taken by the World Bank to cover interest payments on outstanding World Bank debt through its interest subsidy facility extended on International Development Association (IDA) terms is a step in the right direction, but it does not go far enough. To begin with, the facility is not large enough to cover all interest obligations for all low-income African countries with such debt stocks outstanding. At present, it only covers 60 percent of annual interest obligations due to the World Bank, although in recent months steps have been taken to expand coverage to 90 percent of interest due. Second, it still leaves the residual obligation of clearing about $2 billion in outstanding principal, most of which will fall due for amortization within the next five years. Refinancing at the outset those residual principal obligations on IDA or grant terms (if bilateral donors were to contribute) would be a far superior option to exercise at the present time. For countries that have ongoing programs financed by the Bank, this is in effect what happens as the Bank attempts to maintain positive net transfers with IDA financing taking into account repayments of interest and principal on World Bank loans. But the way in which it is done still imposes larger debt-service obligations over time than would arise if there was a clean-out up front. Moreover, similar treatment needs to be extended to the African Development Bank (AfDB) loans, which continue to be disbursed to low-income recipients who are patently uncreditworthy to receive funding on such terms. The same applies to other multilaterals (such as those in the Arab-OPEC world), which have extended hard-window facilities. Though outstanding debt stocks due to multilateral banks accounted for about 20–22 percent of total African debt stocks, debt-service payments to these creditors at present account for 30–35 percent of total debt-service payments.

Debt to the *IMF* poses a similar problem to that of the multilateral banks. And the steps that the IMF has taken to refinance upper tranche obligations on concessional terms through use of its structural adjustment and enhanced structural adjustment facilities have not been effective enough to significantly reduce debt-service obligations to the IMF. Though outstanding obligations to the IMF amount to less than 4 percent of total outstanding debt stocks, debt service to the IMF in 1989 and 1990 by low-income African countries accounted for nearly 20 percent of total debt service. The IMF is now a significant net taker of resources from Africa at a time when the opposite should clearly be the case. Much more needs to be done by the IMF to contribute to more equitable sharing of the debt relief burden, although that is not an argument that the IMF has ever been prepared to accept. However, in Africa, as a large part of the problem of very rapid debt accretion between 1982–90 has been due, directly or indirectly, to the Fund's previous actions, there is a powerful case to be made that the Fund ought to be doing much more to alleviate the present burden.

Yet as Volume 1 of the *World Debt Tables* for 1990–91 reports,

> [t]he total resources available to all eligible countries under these two facilities [SAF and ESAF] amount to SDR 8.7 billion. . . . After four years of SAF operation, by the end of July 1990, SAF arrangements had been approved for 20 countries in sub-Saharan Africa. The total amount committed for these countries was SDR 1.1 billion of which SDR 661 million was disbursed. As of the end of September 1990, 11 ESAF arrangements had been approved for African countries. The total ESAF resources committed to these countries for the three-year period amounted to SDR 1.3 billion, of which SDR 770 million has so far been disbursed [page 92].

The arguments that the IMF would make to defend such performance are well known by now; but the fact remains that the IMF is not doing enough to contribute to the relief burden. It is undoubtedly true that many constraints operate on the IMF that do not afflict other creditors. But these constraints are not as absolutely binding as one is often led to believe. In that connection, it should also be said that the maturities and grace periods of the structural adjustment and enhanced structural adjustment facilities, while generous in comparison with the IMF's nonconcessional facilities, are inappropriate for African countries. Refinancing of upper tranche Fund obligations should be done on IDA terms, or at the very least, on the terms proposed by Mr. Major in Trinidad for the uncancelled portion of official bilateral debt.

In 1990, a mechanism was created to deal with the problem of a few countries (such as Zambia, Sierra Leone, Sudan) that had built up large and chronic arrears in their payments to the IMF. This has commonly come to be known as the "rights approach" and involves freezing IMF arrears as of a certain date while reinstituting normal operational relationships between the IMF and the country concerned but without the IMF disbursing any new money. During a three- to four-year period of time the country services all current obligations to the IMF (including the interest payments on frozen arrears) and adheres to a Fund-monitored program. Each year the country builds up "rights" to accessing the IMF's concessional facilities until at the end of the period the IMF disburses a sufficient quantum of funds from the enhanced structural adjustment facility to clear the frozen arrears. This approach has broken the impasse that formerly existed in the IMF's dealings with deeply debt-distressed countries, such as Zambia, which were in large arrears. But it has the major disadvantage of such countries bearing the burden of unaffordable annual interest service charges to the IMF on large arrears balances. It results in other financiers effectively financing the IMF's debt service rather than in increasing net resource flows to the country. To make the rights approach more effective something more needs to be done about the interest on arrears that involves both a reduction in the amount of interest charged on arrears and its capitalization.

Finally, the world community has eschewed, without sufficiently careful consideration, the prospect of a small, noninflationary special SDR emission for the specific purpose of writing off World Bank and IMF debts owed by low-income African countries. This is perhaps not the forum to go into all the pros and cons of this proposal, which has been made before (by the author and others), but the opportunity is taken of raising it again.

Progress in reducing obligations owed to *private creditors* on any significant scale has simply not been made. Private debt is priced in secondary markets at a substantial discount but progress toward executing officially supported debt buy-back schemes, or in executing debt-equity swaps, is abysmally slow. That reflects both the obduracy of commercial bankers who are in no hurry to negotiate appropriately priced debt-reduction deals and the bureaucratic incompetence of agencies entrusted with the task of designing and negotiating buy-backs. There is a strong case to be made for creditor governments, especially those that have provided tax relief to banks at the time of their making provisions, to consider drawing back such relief if provisions are not translated into write-offs within a conscionable time period (not more than two years from now). Except for Nigeria, most commercial bank assets representing claims on African countries have now been fully provided for. Write-offs would do no damage to the balance sheets of banks. The amounts involved are trivial from the banks' point of view but not from the viewpoint of debtor countries. Arrears and reschedulings of commercial claims are raising the cost of trade credit and of import prices to Africa.

The specific suggestions embedded in the foregoing would, taken individually or as a whole, make a significant difference to providing further, and necessary, debt relief to Africa and facilitate prospects for returning to a trajectory of sustainable long-term development. It is often argued that even with greater debt relief, the development problems of Africa are not going to be solved. That counterargument to the case for debt relief misses the point and sidesteps the issue. No one has ever argued that debt relief is or can be a panacea for curing all of Africa's ills. What is being argued is that, in most of the region's low-income countries, significantly greater debt relief than has been offered in the past is crucial to (indeed may even be a sine qua non for) any accompanying attempts at successful adjustment and recovery in those countries.

Issues and Options

Jack Boorman and Ajai Chopra

The sluggish economic growth and declining per capita income in Africa during the last decade are the combined result of adverse institutional and natural circumstances, depressed commodity prices, and, in some cases, poor economic policies. This disappointing economic performance has been accompanied by rapid growth in Africa's external debt. At the same time, stagnant export earnings have been stagnant and the balance of payments position of most African countries has deteriorated. External arrears have grown sharply, and large amounts of those arrears and scheduled debt-service payments have been restructured. Arrears on debt service have interrupted some aid flows and new loans from commercial sources have dried up. Against these trends, however, overseas development assistance (ODA) and grants to African countries have risen.

The above broad brush treatment of the aggregate economic situation of the region, and of sub-Saharan Africa in particular,[1] masks the considerable diversity among the individual country situations. As the adjustment and financing experiences and the prospects of African countries are not the same, a case-by-case approach is essential in dealing with the debt situation.

Three themes relating to the debt situation in Africa are discussed in this paper. The first relates to the various country circumstances, and, for illustrative purposes, three broad country categories based on financing situations are distinguished: countries that have avoided rescheduling, countries with temporary debt-service difficulties, and countries with unsustainable debt situations. The second theme concerns the distinction between actual and scheduled debt service, and it is noted that actual

---

[1] In this paper, sub-Saharan Africa comprises all African countries, except Algeria, Morocco, Nigeria, South Africa, and Tunisia. All data are taken from International Monetary Fund, *World Economic Outlook: A Survey by the Staff of the International Monetary Fund*, World Economic and Financial Surveys (Washington, October 1990), unless noted otherwise.

debt-service payments (relative to exports) have been broadly unchanged since 1983. In view of the cash-flow relief obtained, the third theme relates to the impact of the outstanding stock of debt burden on the economic performance and prospects of African countries. Although an excessive stock of debt may harm growth prospects, there is little evidence that it is the immediate factor underlying the poor investment levels and economic performance in Africa.

Finally, some issues relating to the heavily indebted African countries are examined. For them, the debt situation appears to be unsustainable even with the adoption of policies to transform the economy and raise payments ability in the future; the poor prospects for honoring loan contracts and normalizing relations with creditors within a reasonable time frame suggest that fundamental debt relief may be required. A combination of appropriate debt relief, efforts to promote exports, and adequate flow of resources in support of growth-oriented reform programs would go a long way toward achieving a sustainable economic situation in such cases.

Country Circumstances

Several African countries have had repeated reschedulings with official and commercial creditors over the last decade; others have been able to service their debts in full through prudent economic and debt management policies and other forms of assistance. Some countries are indebted almost exclusively to official creditors, and their debt is mainly on concessional terms, whereas others have substantial debts to commercial creditors.

For illustrative purposes, three broad categories of countries in terms of financing situations may be distinguished. The first group has been able to maintain full debt-service payments and avoid rescheduling. It includes some countries that have heavy debt burdens in terms of conventional debt ratios. Confronted with external and domestic shocks, many of these countries have implemented significant policy adjustments to help retain access to capital markets and official credits. Preserving access to external financing is crucial, and the experience of the last decade has underlined that the costs of rescheduling and loss of access are high and often long lasting. For these countries, the level of debt may not be a problem, but debt management is. When they face temporary difficulties, prompt official assistance can help support sound economic policies that give confidence to domestic and foreign savers and investors. In the future, it would be hoped that they could rely to a greater extent on private flows, including in particular non-debt-creating equity flows.

The second group of countries has been temporarily unable to meet external obligations in full and may not yet have normalized relations with creditors. These countries have obtained support mainly in the form of the rescheduling of debt-service obligations—in some cases based on concessional options—and the provision of new credits. This support has been provided in conjunction with domestic policy efforts to adjust to external shocks and to reorient the growth strategy. With the sustained implementation of appropriate adjustment and reform policies, countries in this group could be expected to service their debts fully in the foreseeable future. Indeed, some have already graduated from debt rescheduling to normal debtor-creditor relations. For this intermediate group, when commercial bank debt stands at a significant discount, market-based debt buy-backs and exchanges would be beneficial for attaining a viable balance of payments position but are not essential. The opportunity cost of undertaking such operations would need to be carefully weighed.

The third group of countries has very high debt burdens, based on conventional indicators. Their debts are mainly to official creditors, but, in some cases, those to private creditors are not negligible. The rescheduling of debt on conventional terms with the capitalization of interest payments has resulted in an increase in the debt stock. This would be sustainable only if the debtor is undergoing a transformation that will raise its payments ability in the future.[2] The experience, however, of many of these countries during the last decade suggests that this is not happening and that they may have passed the point where they are able to reduce consumption or increase production sufficiently to create the necessary surplus for full debt service. This group of countries, most of which are in sub-Saharan Africa, tends to get the most attention in the discussion of the debt problem in Africa, and is hence the focus of much of the remainder of this paper.

Scheduled and Actual Debt Service and Net Resource Flows

At the end of 1989, the estimated debt of all African countries was about $210 billion, or some $80 billion higher than at the end of 1983.

---

[2]For sustainability, the stock of external debt (expressed, for example, in terms of U.S. dollars) must grow more slowly than nominal GDP (expressed in the same currency as the stock of debt). If the average nominal interest rate on the external debt is lower than the growth of nominal GDP, sustainability would allow for a deficit on the current account (excluding interest payments and including official transfers), but with a limit on its size.

Total debt was equivalent to over half of their gross domestic product (GDP) and nearly two and a half times their exports.[3] For sub-Saharan African countries, these ratios are higher still and are considerably above those of developing countries in other regions of the world—total debt is equivalent to about three fourths of their GDP and nearly three and a half times their exports.

Much of the outstanding debt of sub-Saharan African countries is owed to official creditors, often on concessional terms. As a result, although debt has increased sharply (in both absolute and relative terms), scheduled debt service as a percentage of exports has increased less dramatically, by only 12 percentage points since 1983 to around 44 percent in 1989 (Table 1). The ratio of actual debt-service payments to exports, however, has remained roughly constant at around 21 percent of exports, because of reschedulings and the accumulation of arrears (which were often subsequently rescheduled).[4] In 1983, sub-Saharan African countries had paid two thirds of scheduled debt-service payments; by 1989, this ratio of actual to scheduled debt service had declined to less than half.[5] The actual debt-service payments, measured against exports, have thus remained broadly unchanged as countries have obtained cash-flow relief from their creditors. By postponing governments' external debt-service payments, reschedulings have permitted higher public sector savings and freeing of resources for domestic expenditures. Of course, as the debt reschedulings have usually involved the capitalization of interest, the stock of debt has increased thus increasing future scheduled payments.

There is, however, marked dispersion around these aggregate figures. For example, in 1989 the scheduled debt-service ratio in Mozambique was 178 percent, but actual payments amounted to 32 percent of exports. Scheduled debt-service payments in Madagascar also exceeded annual exports in 1989, but after debt relief actual payments amounted to 59 percent, around half the scheduled amount—though still high by any standard. In Tanzania, actual debt-service payments in fiscal year 1988/89

---

[3] In the context of debt ratios in this discussion paper, the term exports applies to exports of goods and services. When relevant, workers' remittances are included as a part of service receipts.

[4] Between 1980 and 1983—a period of declining exports, rising trade deficits, and, consequently, high external borrowing by sub-Saharan Africa—both scheduled and actual debt service as a percentage of exports rose by about 5 percentage points.

[5] As a number of countries continued to service their debts as scheduled, the decline in payments actually made by countries that rescheduled is therefore substantially larger than the average.

Table 1. Sub-Saharan Africa: External Debt and Debt Service, 1983–89[1]

	1983	1984	1985	1986	1987	1988	1989
	(In billions of U.S. dollars; unless otherwise noted)						
Stock of external debt	56.2	58.4	69.1	80.8	95.8	100.1	105.5
Short-term	6.6	6.1	7.5	8.5	11.0	12.1	13.1
Medium- and long-term	49.6	52.3	61.6	72.3	84.8	88.1	92.4
Scheduled debt service	7.9	9.3	9.7	10.2	11.3	13.1	13.6
Interest	3.2	3.8	4.1	4.4	5.1	5.6	5.8
Amortization	4.7	5.5	5.6	5.8	6.2	7.5	7.8
Actual payments	5.2	6.2	5.8	5.9	5.7	6.5	6.5
Interest	2.4	2.7	2.7	2.7	2.6	3.0	3.1
Amortization	2.8	3.5	3.1	3.2	3.0	3.6	3.4
Payments not made[2]	2.7	3.1	3.9	4.3	5.6	6.6	7.1
Interest	0.8	1.1	1.4	1.7	2.5	2.6	2.7
Amortization	1.9	2.0	2.5	2.6	3.1	4.0	4.4
Actual and scheduled payments	66.0	66.8	59.9	57.8	50.3	49.7	47.9
Interest	76.0	72.3	65.3	61.7	51.6	52.9	53.8
Amortization	59.2	63.0	55.9	54.8	49.2	47.3	43.5
	(In percent of exports of goods and services)						
Stock of external debt	226.6	221.2	271.0	303.8	331.5	338.2	341.4
Short-term	26.6	23.1	29.4	32.0	38.1	40.9	42.4
Medium- and long-term	200.0	198.1	241.6	271.8	293.4	297.6	299.0
Scheduled debt service	32.0	35.3	38.1	38.3	39.0	44.3	44.1
Interest	12.9	14.4	16.1	16.5	17.6	18.9	18.8
Amortization	19.1	20.9	22.0	21.7	21.3	25.4	25.3

Actual payments	21.1	23.6	22.8	22.1	19.6	22.0	21.1
Interest	9.8	10.4	10.5	10.2	9.1	10.0	10.1
Amortization	11.3	13.2	12.3	11.9	10.5	12.0	11.0
Payments not made	10.9	11.7	15.3	16.2	19.4	22.3	23.0
Interest	3.1	4.0	5.6	6.3	8.5	8.9	8.7
Amortization	7.8	7.7	9.7	9.8	10.8	13.4	14.3
Memorandum item							
Export of goods and services	24.8	26.4	25.5	26.6	28.9	29.6	30.9

Source: International Monetary Fund, *World Economic Outlook: A Survey by the Staff of the International Monetary Fund*, World Economic and Financial Surveys (Washington, October 1990).

[1] Excluding Nigeria and South Africa.
[2] Debt-service payments rescheduled and net accumulation of external debt arrears.

amounted to less than 5 percent of exports, while scheduled debt-service payments were some 56 percent of exports. Similarly, in Zambia scheduled debt service amounted to 57 percent of exports in 1989, but only the equivalent of 15 percent was actually paid.

For sub-Saharan Africa, the aggregate current account deficit excluding official grants was $13.4 billion in 1989, nearly double the nominal amount in 1984 (Table 2). About one third of this increase was accounted for by the rise in scheduled interest payments; the remaining two thirds was essentially the result of increasing trade deficits as imports increased faster than exports. New financing was provided through two main channels: grants from official sources and external borrowing (net of scheduled amortization payments), also mainly from official sources. In addition, countries have obtained exceptional financing in the form of debt reschedulings, which provided cash-flow relief on interest and amortization payments, and have accumulated arrears on debt-service payments.

The net resource flow to sub-Saharan African countries has increased sharply from an average of $4 billion in 1983–85 to over $8 billion in 1988–89.[6] Data reported in the World Bank's debt tables lead to a similar conclusion: net transfers increased from an average of $4.8 billion in 1983–85 to $8.7 billion in 1988–89.[7] These figures are in contrast to the assertions sometimes made that the international community has been withdrawing resources from Africa. Often, such assertions are based on the export of real resources from Africa by way of debt service; they do not take into account the import of resources through grants and soft loans.

In view of the cash-flow relief on interest and amortization payments obtained through debt reschedulings, it is worthwhile to examine how excessive external debt affects economic performance. This is taken up in the next two sections.

Debt and Economic Performance

The poor investment and growth performance of highly indebted developing countries in the past few years has often been attributed to the

---

[6] The concept of net resource flows, as used in the IMF's *World Economic Outlook*, is the sum of the deficit on goods, services (excluding scheduled interest payments), private transfers, and the net accumulation of reserves.

[7] The World Bank, *World Debt Tables, 1990–91*, Vol. 1 (Washington, 1990), page 130. In this case, net transfers (excluding IMF transactions) are calculated as loan disbursements plus official grants and foreign direct investment, minus total debt-service payments (interest and amortization).

large stock of their foreign debt. It is argued that when a debtor country is not fully performing on its external obligations, an increase in production and exports may be used at least partly for payments to foreign creditors, which gives rise to a disincentive effect for foreign and domestic investors. This disincentive problem, which has been referred to as the "debt overhang," arises mainly when the debtor is unable to meet its scheduled debt-service obligations and the amounts actually paid are subject to uncertainty. This uncertainty arises in part due to the need to renegotiate frequently the terms of the debt. In brief, the debt overhang hypothesis states that the accumulated debt acts as a tax on future income and discourages productive investment plans of the private sector. Based on this hypothesis, it has been argued that if the amount of debt burden is excessive, reschedulings that provide only cash-flow relief and do not reduce the outstanding debt will not be sufficient to restore investor confidence.

Although a substantial body of theoretical literature on the effects of excessive debt on investment exists, little empirical work is available on the subject, which itself is symptomatic of the difficulties implicit in attempting such an evaluation.[8] In practice, an evaluation of the impact of either market-based debt reduction or outright debt forgiveness on countries' investment and growth performance must be preliminary and extremely tentative, because they are recent events and experience is thus limited; also expectations are notoriously difficult to measure. Moreover, the scale and timing of the effects of debt reduction will depend importantly on the domestic policy environment and the other policy reforms taking place at the same time.

In the 1980s, investment rates in Africa were among the lowest in the developing world. While gross capital formation in Africa ranged between 19 percent and 21 percent of GDP during 1983–89, the corresponding

---

[8]One contribution in this area is an econometric study on the Philippines, which discerns a debt effect as a factor depressing private investment after 1982 (see Eduardo Borensztein, "Will Debt Reduction Increase Investment?" *Finance and Development* (Washington), Vol. 28 (March 1991), pages 25–27). Some evidence of a link between debt restructuring and economic performance is also provided by the case of Mexico, where domestic interest rates declined by over 20 percentage points to a 33 percent nominal annual rate following the announcement in July 1989 of the preliminary agreement with banks on a comprehensive debt- and debt-service reduction package. This was accompanied by large inflows of private capital contributing to a 5 percent real increase in domestic investment in 1989, and the acceleration of real output growth to 3 percent, twice its level in preceding years.

Table 2. Sub-Saharan Africa: Balance of Payments and Net Resource Flow, 1983–89[1]
(In billions of U.S. dollars)

	1983	1984	1985	1986	1987	1988	1989
Exports	19.7	21.5	20.8	21.1	22.4	23.0	23.7
Imports	−21.2	−20.4	−20.0	−22.0	−24.4	−26.3	−27.6
Trade balance	−1.5	1.1	0.8	−0.9	−2.0	−3.3	−3.9
Services and private transfers (net)	−7.6	−7.6	−7.9	−9.2	−9.4	−10.1	−9.5
Of which: scheduled interest payments	−3.2	−3.8	−4.1	−4.4	−5.1	−5.6	−5.8
Deficit on goods, services and private transfers	−9.1	−6.5	−7.1	−10.1	−11.4	−13.4	−13.4
Financing							
Official grants	3.3	3.4	3.6	4.4	4.9	5.4	5.6
Other non-debt-creating flows	0.4	0.6	0.7	0.8	0.5	0.6	0.8
Net external borrowing	2.9	0.4	−0.1	2.2	0.9	1.6	1.1
Disbursements	7.6	5.9	5.5	8.0	7.1	9.1	8.9
Scheduled amortization	−4.7	−5.5	−5.6	−5.8	−6.2	−7.5	−7.8
Other net flows and net errors and omissions	−1.5	−1.1	−0.6	−0.3	−0.1	−0.3	0.0
Reserves (net)	1.3	0.1	−0.4	−1.3	−0.4	−0.5	−1.2
Exceptional financing[2]	2.7	3.1	3.9	4.3	5.6	6.6	7.1
Memorandum items							
Net resource flow[3]	6.2	2.9	3.4	6.4	6.2	8.3	8.4

ISSUES AND OPTIONS

Outflows	-6.7	-7.3	-6.4	-6.2	-5.8	-6.8	-6.5
Actual debt service	-5.2	-6.2	-5.8	-5.9	-5.7	-6.5	-6.5
Other net outflows and net errors and omissions	-1.5	-1.1	-0.6	-0.3	-0.1	-0.3	—
Inflows	12.9	10.2	9.8	12.6	12.0	15.1	14.9
Official grants	3.3	3.4	3.6	4.4	4.9	5.4	5.6
Non-debt-creating flows	0.4	0.6	0.7	0.8	0.5	0.6	0.8
Disbursement from loans	7.6	5.9	5.5	8.0	7.1	9.1	8.9
Reserve-related liabilities[4]	1.6	0.3	—	-0.6	-0.5	—	-0.4

Source: International Monetary Fund, *World Economic Outlook: A Survey by the Staff of the International Monetary Fund*, World Economic and Financial Surveys (Washington, October 1990).

[1] Excluding Nigeria and South Africa.
[2] Debt reschedulings and net arrears accumulation.
[3] Deficit on goods, services, and private transfers (excluding scheduled interest payments) plus net accumulation of reserves.
[4] Mainly net credit from the IMF.

figures for Asia were 27 percent and 29 percent. The difference is further magnified by the low returns to investment (measured simply as the ratio of the growth of output to the rate of investment in a given year) in many African countries. Comparative figures cited in the World Bank's long-term perspective study on sub-Saharan Africa indicate that the average annual return on investment in sub-Saharan Africa declined from 13 percent in 1973–80 to 2.5 percent in 1980–87, while in South Asia it averaged around 22 percent throughout the two periods. The study concludes that neither drought nor falling world demand is the reason for the low and declining returns to investment in sub-Saharan Africa, nor the debt burden. Instead, in explaining the low productivity, it notes that "Africa's crop yields are smaller, its cropping cycles on irrigated land are fewer, its transport costs are higher, and its utilization rates for factory capacity are lower."[9]

Indeed, for many African countries, the external debt has become a heavy burden because past borrowing—undertaken mainly by the public sector, including public enterprises—has generally not resulted in a commensurate increase in the productive capacity to service the debt. Much of the borrowing, often on inappropriate terms, was incurred to finance investments that yielded little or no return; in such circumstances, even debt on concessional terms can impose a heavy burden. In many cases, external borrowing financed unrealistically high exchange rates and flight capital and was used to maintain domestic consumption—particularly government expenditures, including on the military—at levels which proved to be unsustainable.

In the absence of empirical studies on Africa, it is difficult to arrive at a firm judgment of the impact of debt on investor confidence. For many African countries, it would seem reasonable to postulate that debt is not the immediate factor underlying poor investment levels and the low yield of investment. Misaligned relative prices (exchange rates, interest rates, producer prices, wages), distortionary trade policies, an inadequate financial intermediation system, poor infrastructure, lack of human capital, an unsuitable climate for entrepreneurship, and low levels of domestic and foreign savings are perhaps more important in the African context.

If low investment has primarily been the result of structural impediments and distortions rather than a debt problem, reducing debt without removing other distortions would not be expected to increase investment

---

[9]The World Bank, *Sub-Saharan Africa: From Crisis to Sustainable Growth* (Washington, 1989), pages 26–27.

significantly. That is, policies that discourage domestic investment and inhibit the private sector must be remedied. But, this is not to say that some countries do not have excessive debt. Rather, due to the low productive levels and narrow tax base in some of these economies, there may simply be little that the authorities could hope to further "tax away" to pay its creditors. On this hypothesis, once structural impediments and distortions are removed, the relative importance of the amount of outstanding debt when making investment decisions may increase.

Issues Concerning Countries with Unsustainable Balance of Payments Prospects

The section on country circumstances referred to a group of countries whose debt situation is such that rescheduling debt on conventional terms would unlikely bring about a viable balance of payments position within an acceptable time frame or at a reasonable level of economic growth. For these countries, the future normalization of relations with creditors will remain difficult if debt service falling due is in practice simply capitalized and postponed.

Even if the debt situation is not the immediate factor underlying the poor economic performance of these countries and a variety of structural impediments must also be addressed, the reform efforts of governments may themselves be affected by the existence of a debt problem. For example, frequent reschedulings create an uncertain economic climate and use up the scarce management resources of these countries. In addition, having arrears can dry up new loan commitments and disbursements of existing loans. As a result, the formulation of adjustment programs becomes difficult. Furthermore, the emergence of arrears often leads to substantial increases in effective import prices, as foreign suppliers—unsure of being paid on time or at all—charge premium prices for their goods and services.

The possibility of rescheduling debt may also introduce an element of moral hazard in the relationship between debtors and creditors. If a country adjusts successfully, the resources provided through future reschedulings falls, which may be viewed as a tax on reform efforts. Although creditors attempt to prevent this by requiring debtor countries to adhere to an adjustment program before agreeing to a rescheduling, the incentives to relax the adjustment effort once the debt relief is obtained may still exist. Moreover, the lack of adjustment itself could act as a disincentive to private investment. Under these circumstances, far-reaching debt relief may be required when long-run prospects are particularly bleak.

Conventional rescheduling practices assumed that loan contracts could be rewritten maintaining the contractual value of the debt, but with some "breathing room" before payments needed to be made. It is now increasingly recognized that the payments difficulties of some countries are deep-rooted and their indebtedness is clearly out of line with their export potential. It is unlikely, therefore, that these countries can normalize relations with creditors within an acceptable time frame unless the average terms of their debt are reduced significantly. That is, for some countries, contractual obligations need to be brought into line with what can reasonably be expected to be honored in the future; for these countries, there are strong arguments for fundamental debt relief. As commercial bank claims are only a small portion of these countries' debts, debt relief initiatives by official bilateral creditors will be a key element. Private creditors, however, would clearly need to share the burden of debt relief measures.

Concluding Remarks

The challenge of addressing Africa's imbalances is enormous. Clearly, for some African countries a solution to the external debt problem needs to be found that, at the same time, meets the objectives of recovery and growth.

In this regard, African governments are recognizing that the key for improving the situation is domestic, and a number of countries have embarked on a process of structural and financial adjustment. Sustained economic growth requires greater and more efficient investment and higher domestic and foreign savings to support this investment. Higher foreign savings, in turn, requires confidence on the part of creditors, donors, and investors that the recipient country will pursue economic and financial policies conducive to restoring creditworthiness. Higher savings and investment will only bring about lasting economic growth if investments are productive; this requires structural reforms in a number of areas.

At the same time, the international community has recognized that many African countries cannot turn the corner on their own, even with stronger domestic adjustment efforts. Creditors and donors have shown a willingness to support countries that are undertaking sound growth-oriented adjustment and reform programs. The debt strategy pursued in the last several years has been explicitly based on a cooperative approach between creditors and debtor countries. There has recently been considerable adaptation of the strategy with regard to the rescheduling terms for certain groups of countries. But it is clear that for some African countries more needs to be done on this front.

The IMF and the World Bank can play a role in this process by assisting countries in the design and the implementation of comprehensive macroeconomic and structural reform programs and by supporting such programs with adequate resources. As of the end of August 1991, 23 African countries had IMF arrangements in place: 1 extended arrangement and 4 stand-by arrangements for middle-income countries, and 6 arrangements under the structural adjustment facility and 12 under the enhanced structural adjustment facility, for low-income countries.

The IMF also stands ready to assist member countries in arrears to the IMF to become current again. For the countries with protracted arrears to the IMF, the Executive Board of the IMF has endorsed the concept of a "rights" approach, under which a country could accumulate rights—conditioned on performance during the period of a program monitored by the IMF—toward a disbursement of IMF resources once its arrears have been cleared. In addition, external resources are required to meet the country's financing needs during the program period, such as its import and other direct financing requirements, including obligations falling due to the IMF and the World Bank. To complement the country's own efforts to meet these obligations, the assistance of support and consultative groups, often in the context of the World Bank's Special Program of Assistance for Africa, is envisaged. To enhance the effectiveness of this approach, the IMF has also decided to suspend the application of special charges, which fall mainly on overdue charges, for those members that are actively cooperating with the IMF.

In sum, the active and coordinated participation of creditors and donors is essential in supporting the efforts of the African countries. African countries, however, must themselves come forward with appropriately strong programs that the international community can support. The challenge of achieving economic recovery and a sustainable solution to the external debt problem can be met with strengthened and concerted efforts by all.

Official Debt Reduction: Toronto Terms, Trinidad Terms, and Netherlands Initiative

Francesco Abbate and Anh-Nga Tran-Nguyen*

The Setting

In 1988, Paris Club creditors introduced the "Toronto terms," a major policy advance in the rescheduling of the official bilateral debt owed by low-income countries. The implementation of the Toronto terms has not, however, resulted in debt relief commensurate with the weak debt-servicing capacity of most low-income African countries.

Recognizing the inadequacy of the Toronto measures, the governments of the United Kingdom and the Netherlands have recently put forward proposals for massive debt reduction. The U.K. proposal, known as the "Trinidad terms," consists of reducing the stock of Paris Club debt by two thirds and rescheduling the remaining one third over 25 years, with interest payments capitalized during a five-year grace period; debt service would then grow as a function of the debtor's export capacity.[1] The Dutch proposal calls for full forgiveness of official bilateral debt owed by the least developed and other low-income countries facing severe debt problems, provided they are implementing sound economic policies.

The debt-service profiles resulting from the implementation of the Toronto and the Trinidad terms (the latter with two different rates of

---

*This paper was prepared with the assistance of Anne Miroux, Cape Kasahara, and Lucette Fagedet.

[1] The following repayment formula underlies the Trinidad terms:

Let D_1 be the debt outstanding at the beginning of Period 1 (which follows the the grace period of five years); P_1, the initial debt-service payment, r, the interest rate (and also the discount rate); g, the rate of growth of payments (which can be made equal to the projected rate of growth of export earnings); and N, the repayment period (20 years).

growth of debt-service payments, 5 percent and 8 percent) demonstrate that the debt-service reduction under the Trinidad terms is substantial (Chart 1).² In fact, the Trinidad terms are concessional; the resulting grant element would amount to about 67 percent, while the combined grant element of the three Toronto options is only 20 percent. Moreover, under the Toronto terms, debt-service obligations generally must be rescheduled repeatedly, sometimes every year (the assumption used in the chart). The resulting debt service would increase sharply from Year 9—reaching a level slightly below the debt service due in the absence of debt relief—and would peak in Year 14 at a level almost four times higher than the debt service under the Trinidad terms.

This paper examines the adequacy of the three debt-relief measures in relation to the debt-servicing capacity of beneficiary countries. These are the low-income, debt-distressed countries in sub-Saharan Africa, which are recipients of the World Bank's Special Program of Assistance (SPA).³

If all payments are made at the end of each period, then

$$D_1 = \sum_{t=1}^{N} \frac{P_1 (1+g)^{t-1}}{(1+r)^t}$$

From the above, the value of P_1 is given by

$$P_1 = \frac{D_1 (r-g)}{1 - \left[\frac{1+g}{1+r}\right]^N}$$

²Under the Trinidad terms, the debt-service profile varies with the growth rate of payments (g, as in footnote 1). Chart 1 shows the debt-service profiles on the basis of two hypothetical values of g: 5 percent and 8 percent. Given a constant repayment period of 20 years, the lower the value of g, the higher are the payments during the first few years. If g is equal to the export growth rate, a paradoxical situation might occur: the lower is the export growth rate—that is, the lower the debtor's servicing capacity, the higher are the initial payments. An alternative formula could be used whereby g is higher than the export growth rate, while the repayment period is kept unchanged. This would enable debtor countries with low growth in export earnings to make smaller payments in the earlier part of the repayment period. Another alternative to be appplied in those circumstances would be to lengthen the repayment period while g equals the export growth rate.

³As of February 1991, 23 countries have received SPA support: Benin, Burundi, Chad, Central African Republic, The Gambia, Ghana, Guinea, Guinea-Bissau, Kenya, Madagascar, Mali, Malawi, Mauritania, Mozambique, Niger, Sao Tome and Principe, Senegal, Somalia, Tanzania, Togo, Uganda, Zaïre, and Zambia.

Chart 1. Debt-Service Profiles: Toronto Options and Trinidad Terms[1]

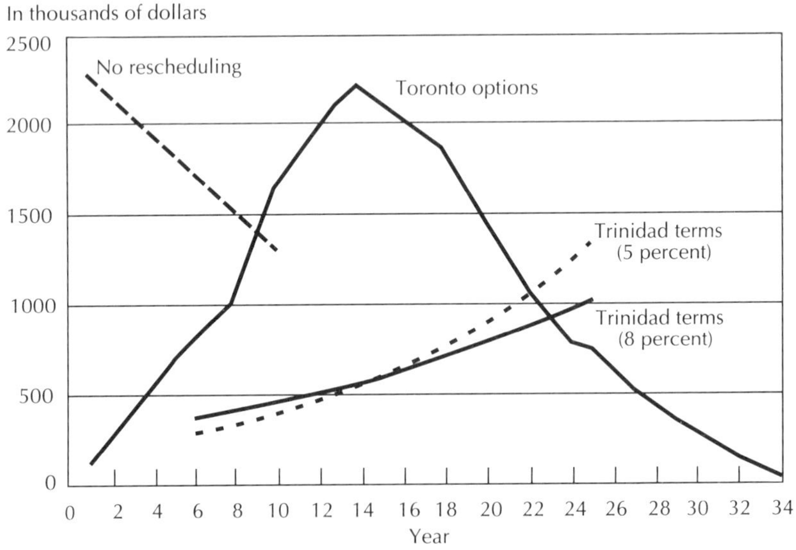

In thousands of dollars

Source: United Nations Conference on Trade and Development (UNCTAD), *Trade and Development Report,* 1991 (Geneva, 1991), p. 54.

[1] Debt-service payments are derived from a hypothetical loan of $12 million, with a maturity of ten years and an interest rate of 9 percent

The schemes are assessed here according to their ability to remove the debt overhang. The analysis is first carried out for the SPA countries as a whole and then for each of these countries.

The Impact of Alternative Debt Relief Measures on SPA Countries as a Whole

To evaluate the impact of the three measures on SPA countries as a group, their overall export earnings have been projected through 1997 on the basis of two different annual average rates of growth, 5 percent and 8 percent both in nominal terms (Table 1). The rate of 5 percent might look quite modest but, in reality, is somewhat optimistic when compared with the negative growth rate of −3 percent registered during the past decade.

To determine the amount of debt service these countries would be able to pay, a "normative" debt service equivalent to 20 percent of projected export has been chosen in light of a number of considerations. During the past decade, actual debt-service payments of severely indebted low-income countries averaged about 25 percent of their exports of goods and services

Table 1. Alternative Debt-Service Obligations of 22 SPA Countries[1]
(In millions of U.S. dollars)

	Year 1 (1990)	Year 8 (1997)	
		Export growth of 5 percent	Export growth of 8 percent
Export of goods and services	12,011	16,901	20,585
Total debt service			
Normative[2]	2,402	3,380	4,117
No scheduling	6,383	4,590	4,590
Toronto terms[3]	4,566	4,442	4,442
Trinidad terms[3]	4,284	3,790	3,734
Dutch proposal[3]	4,284	3,452	3,452
Debt service on eligible Paris Club debt[4]			
No rescheduling	1,855	1,136	1,136
Toronto terms[5]	282	990	990
Trinidad terms	0	338	282
Dutch proposal	0	0	0

Source: Author's calculations based on World Bank, *Special Program of Assistance: Proposal for the Second Phase* (Washington: World Bank, 1990), Annex D.4.

[1] Data exclude Zambia.
[2] 20 percent of exports.
[3] Net of expected rescheduling of non-Paris Club debt on current rules.
[4] Excludes debt contracted after the cutoff date. The stock of eligible Paris Club debt amounted to about $10 billion in 1989.
[5] On the assumption that the debt service is rescheduled each year.

(after reschedulings and accumulation of large arrears). However, despite significant capital inflows, these countries as a group (and especially the SPA countries) experienced negative growth rates of per capita gross domestic product (GDP). A debt-service ratio of 20 percent would release additional resources to finance some per capita GDP growth, especially if the export growth rate is weak and if external capital inflows are not buoyant, as is expected. It should be noted that a debt-service ratio of 20 percent is still quite high relative to the actual debt-service ratio of 12 percent, which the low-income African countries registered in 1980–81.

The normative debt service may be compared with the debt service that debtor countries would have to pay under the Toronto terms, the Trinidad terms, or the Dutch proposal. This "post-relief" debt service is obtained by applying the three measures to scheduled debt service, as projected by the

World Bank on the basis of the existing (end of 1988) stock of debt, disbursements from existing commitments, and new commitments foreseen as of 1990. The World Bank projections might therefore underestimate the debt service due in 1997.

If the post-relief debt service exceeds the normative debt service, then additional debt-relief measures are needed to bring the debt service into line with the servicing capacity of debtor countries. The additional debt-service reduction that would be necessary under the different schemes is show in Table 2.

The Toronto terms appear to be inadequate under both export growth assumptions, because large amounts of additional debt-service reduction are required. The additional reduction would equal about 23 percent of total scheduled debt service (before debt relief of any kind) when the export growth rate is 5 percent, and approximately 7 percent when the export growth rate is 8 percent. When the export growth rate is high, both the Trinidad terms and the Dutch proposal would release enough resources to service the remaining debt; however, when the rate is low, both proposals would require additional debt-service reductions equivalent to about 9 percent of scheduled debt service under the Trinidad terms and some 2 percent under the Dutch proposal.

It should be noted that the three schemes do not cover debt contracted after the cutoff date.[4] For SPA countries as a whole, such debt represents about 11 percent of total nonconcessional bilateral debt owed to Paris Club creditors; but for some individual countries the share is much higher. In the case of Uganda, for example, it is about 50 percent. Moreover, debt owed to non-Paris Club creditors—accounting for 25 percent of total bilateral nonconcessional debt—is not subject to the same debt-relief measures. The amount of required additional reduction under the Trinidad terms could be met—at an aggregate level—by advancing the cutoff date and extending the scheme to debt owed to non-Paris Club creditors.

The maintenance of the cutoff date is central to the Paris Club policy of protecting new export credits from rescheduling. However, the increase in concessional debt relief obtained from bringing forward the cutoff date would far outweigh any possible adverse impact on new export credits. In any case, most low-income African countries will be able to attract and afford only highly concessional flows for many years to come. Alter-

---

[4] In Paris Club reschedulings, the cutoff date usually precedes the first agreement by three to six months and is kept in successive agreements.

Table 2. Debt-Service Ratios and Additional Debt-Service Reduction Requirements in 1997 for 22 SPA Countries
(Values in millions of U.S. dollars; ratios in percent)

	Export Growth			
	5 percent		8 percent	
	Debt-service ratio	Additional debt-service reduction[2]	Debt-service ratio	Additional debt-service reduction[2]
Toronto terms	26.3	1,062	21.6	325
Trinidad terms	22.4	410	18.1	0
Dutch proposal	20.4	72	16.8	0

Source: Table 1.
[1] Data exclude Zambia.
[2] To attain a 20 percent debt-service ratio.

natively, if the cutoff date policy is not changed, even greater aid flows will be required in some cases to compensate for the servicing of post cutoff-date debt.

Impact of the Trinidad Terms on Individual SPA Countries

The results described above do not distinguish between countries; yet, individual countries' debt burden and need for debt relief differ significantly. Estimates of the impact of the Trinidad terms on debt-service ratios of each of the 18 SPA countries highlight the differences (see the appendix).[5] These estimates have been made assuming that the Trinidad terms would have been applied in 1990 on the overall debt (including post cutoff-date debt) owed to Paris Club creditors, after taking into account cancellations of official development assistance (ODA) debt that were granted by donor countries in 1989 and 1990. Exports are projected to grow by 5 percent annually. After five years of grace and interest capitalization, debt-service payments would also increase by 5 percent a year, in line with following the suggestion contained in the Trinidad terms' formula linking payments growth to export growth.

---

[5] Of the 22 SPA countries covered in Table 1, Burundi, The Gamiba, Ghana, and Kenya have not been included in the projections because they are not likely to require Paris Club reschedulings in the foreseeable future.

It is noteworthy that the debt-service ratios have been calculated on the basis of World Bank projections of debt-service payments on the existing (end of 1989) stock of long-term debt. As is the case for SPA countries as a group, these projections tend to underestimate future debt-service obligations, since new commitments, short-term debt, and IMF credit, are not considered.

In examining the impact of the Trinidad terms on debt-service ratios, one can divide the SPA countries into four groups: *Group 1.* For Benin, Central African Republic, Chad, Malawi, and Togo, whose debt-service ratios originally did not exceed 20 percent, the Trinidad terms would result in a reduction in their ratios of a few percentage points. Most of the debt of these countries is on concessional terms. *Group 2.* Guinea, Niger, Senegal, and Zäire would benefit significantly from the Trinidad terms. Their debt-service ratios would be lowered from levels originally ranging from 25 to 35 percent to less than 20 percent by the Year 2. *Group 3.* For Madagascar, Mali, Mauritania, Tanzania, and Uganda, debt-service ratios would decline below 20 percent from Year 6 to Year 8 and beyond. But for the first five to seven years, they would continue to be afflicted by the debt overhang, although for Madagascar and Tanzania, the immediate debt-service reduction would be considerable. In this group, about 40 percent of total debt is owed to Paris Club creditors.

Group 4. Guinea-Bissau, Mozambique, Sao Tome and Principe and Somalia would maintain high, sometimes extremely high, debt-service ratios. While the Trinidad terms would have a significant impact on their ratios, they would remain far above 20 percent. For instance, in Year 8, debt- service ratios would be about 60 percent in Guinea-Bissau and some 30 percent in Mozambique. In Sao Tome and Principe and Somalia, they would be in the 30–40 percent range. All countries in the group owe a large part of their debt to either non-Paris Club bilateral creditors, or multilateral institutions. Guinea-Bissau, for example, owes about three fourths of its official bilateral debt to non-Paris Club creditors and approximately half of its total debt to multilateral institutions.

Conclusion

If the Trinidad terms are applied, almost half of the SPA countries (i.e., the nine countries in Groups 1 and 2) would register debt-service ratios lower than the normative level of 20 percent within two years. But for the remaining countries, saddled with an extremely heavy debt burden, the initiative would not, by itself, remove the debt overhang. This conclusion is reinforced by the fact that debt-service projections do not include debt contracted after 1989 and assume that debt reduction would also apply to post cutoff-date debt, a scenario more favorable to debtors than that which would prevail if the Trinidad terms were adopted. Additional measures, therefore, are needed, such as a higher percentage of debt reduction, as advocated in the Dutch proposal; inclusion of post cutoff-date debt; equivalent measures to be taken by non-Paris Club creditors; rescheduling of multilateral debt; commercial bank debt reduction; and increased ODA flows.

Debt-relief measures must be tailored to the specific needs of debtor countries. For severely indebted, low-income countries, the writing off of two thirds of Paris Club debt, as proposed by the United Kingdom, should be treated as a benchmark. Creditor countries should consider granting additional concessional debt relief, when necessary, in order to contribute to the removal of the debt overhang.

Appendix
Debt-Service Ratios of SPA Countries, Before and

Year	Benin			Central Africa Republic			Chad		
	(1) Before	(2) After	(3) (1)–(2)	(1) Before	(2) After	(3) (1)–(2)	(1) Before	(2) After	(3) (1)–(2)
1991	17.9	14.5	3.4	12.2	8.8	3.4	4.0	3.2	0.8
1991	15.2	11.5	3.7	13.8	9.8	4.0	4.6	3.7	0.9
1992	12.2	8.7	3.5	13.1	9.0	4.1	5.0	3.7	1.3
1993	11.0	7.7	3.3	12.4	9.2	3.2	5.0	4.0	1.0
1994	10.5	7.4	8.1	10.6	8.4	2.2	4.8	4.1	0.7
1995	9.8	7.8	2.0	9.3	8.1	1.2	4.9	4.3	0.6
1996	9.3	7.3	2.0	7.2	7.2	0.0	4.7	4.2	0.5
1997	11.7	7.1	4.6	6.4	6.9	–0.5	5.2	4.1	1.1
1998	11.3	7.1	4.2	5.8	6.2	–0.4	5.4	4.2	1.2
1999	10.4	6.8	3.6	5.3	5.7	–0.4	5.5	4.4	1.1
2000	9.9	6.4	3.5	5.1	5.6	–0.5	5.3	4.2	1.1

Year	Malawi			Mali			Mauritania		
	(1) Before	(2) After	(3) (1)–(2)	(1) Before	(2) After	(3) (1)–(2)	(1) Before	(2) After	(3) (1)–(2)
1990	20.0	14.0	6.0	33.0	30.7	2.3	31.1	27.4	3.7
1991	18.5	13.3	5.2	34.0	31.3	2.7	33.8	26.9	6.9
1992	17.8	13.8	4.0	36.0	31.0	5.0	32.8	26.6	6.2
1993	16.2	13.0	3.2	34.0	29.5	4.5	28.9	23.8	5.1
1994	14.9	12.3	2.6	33.0	28.2	3.8	24.0	19.6	4.4
1995	13.8	12.3	1.5	31.0	27.2	3.8	18.8	16.4	2.4
1996	13.2	11.8	1.4	30.0	24.5	5.5	16.7	15.7	1.0
1997	10.6	9.4	1.2	22.5	18.5	4.0	22.5	21.7	0.8
1998	9.6	9.6	0.0	16.7	13.1	3.6	14.2	12.0	2.2
1999	9.5	8.4	1.1	16.3	12.8	3.5	13.4	11.4	2.0
2000	9.7	8.7	1.0	15.0	10.8	4.4	11.1	9.5	1.6

Year	Senegal			Somalia			Tanzania		
	(1) Before	(2) After	(3) (1)–(2)	(1) Before	(2) After	(3) (1)–(2)	(1) Before	(2) After	(3) (1)–(2)
1990	35.3	22.6	12.7	116.4	74.5	41.9	65.2	43.7	21.5
1991	28.3	17.4	10.9	140.3	73.1	67.2	55.6	34.7	20.9
1992	22.1	12.2	9.9	125.9	60.5	65.4	66.0	31.7	34.3
1993	17.7	10.0	7.7	121.1	52.0	69.1	73.5	28.9	44.6
1994	15.9	8.8	7.1	106.8	43.2	63.6	65.9	25.7	40.2
1995	12.9	9.3	3.6	99.1	47.1	52.0	57.9	27.6	30.3
1996	10.5	7.8	2.7	68.0	43.4	24.6	47.2	18.8	28.4
1997	9.1	7.2	1.9	62.2	43.7	18.5	33.2	16.3	16.9
1998	7.8	6.6	1.2	48.5	39.5	9.0	23.4	14.0	9.4
1999	6.7	5.8	0.9	45.0	37.4	7.6	25.1	13.4	11.7
2000	6.0	5.3	0.7	39.8	33.8	6.0	23.0	12.8	10.2

Source: Author's calculations based on the World Bank Reporting Debtor System.

After Implementation of the U.K. Proposal

Guinea			Guinea-Bissau			Madagascar		
(1) Before	(2) After	(3) (1)–(2)	(1) Before	(2) After	(3) (1)–(2)	(1) Before	(2) After	(3) (1)–(2)
33.2	25.8	7.4	69.7	59.9	9.8	105.9	69.5	36.4
25.5	16.5	9.0	142.9	130.5	12.4	72.2	36.5	35.7
26.4	16.9	9.5	135.8	124.0	11.8	71.0	33.7	37.3
23.2	14.6	8.6	128.1	116.8	11.3	66.3	27.9	38.4
21.0	13.2	7.8	120.0	109.3	10.7	53.1	19.3	33.8
17.0	13.1	3.9	99.5	92.0	17.5	42.3	22.5	19.8
13.0	11.0	2.0	91.8	85.3	6.5	29.6	20.1	9.5
11.0	10.1	0.9	72.9	62.7	10.2	20.0	17.0	3.0
8.7	7.7	1.0	69.2	57.0	12.2	15.4	13.7	1.7
8.2	7.2	1.0	67.5	54.5	13.0	15.8	14.8	1.0
6.2	5.4	0.8	58.9	47.2	11.7	13.3	13.8	−0.5

Mozambique			Niger			Sao Tome and Principe		
(1) Before	(2) After	(3) (1)–(2)	(1) Before	(2) After	(3) (1)–(2)	(1) Before	(2) After	(3) (1)–(2)
207.2	173.6	33.6	25.8	17.5	8.3	93.8	87.7	6.1
171.4	140.1	31.3	25.8	16.7	9.1	84.2	78.3	5.9
144.2	115.5	28.7	25.5	16.1	9.4	73.8	72.2	1.6
116.5	92.3	24.2	24.3	16.1	8.2	67.4	65.9	1.5
97.4	75.2	22.2	21.5	14.9	6.6	60.4	59.0	1.4
83.9	65.9	18.0	18.4	14.6	3.8	39.7	39.0	0.7
49.0	41.1	7.9	14.4	12.5	1.9	34.6	32.7	1.9
37.2	26.6	10.6	10.3	9.5	0.8	31.7	29.8	1.9
38.7	26.1	12.6	8.9	8.4	0.5	25.4	22.5	2.9
48.3	34.1	14.2	8.6	8.0	0.6	23.0	19.7	3.3
42.0	29.3	12.7	7.8	7.4	0.4	20.4	18.3	2.1

Togo			Uganda			Zaïre		
(1) Before	(2) After	(3) (1)–(2)	(1) Before	(2) After	(3) (1)–(2)	(1) Before	(2) After	(3) (1)–(2)
16.6	6.3	10.3	54.3	50.4	3.9	33.5	12.1	21.4
16.8	5.3	11.5	42.9	37.7	5.2	38.3	10.0	28.3
16.1	6.0	10.1	35.6	31.9	3.7	34.9	9.2	25.7
14.8	5.7	9.1	34.2	30.3	3.9	31.2	9.0	22.2
13.2	5.4	7.8	26.1	21.3	4.8	30.3	8.8	21.5
9.7	6.5	3.2	21.7	18.2	3.5	23.5	11.4	12.1
8.1	5.3	2.8	18.7	15.8	2.9	14.4	10.8	3.6
6.2	4.3	1.9	18.4	14.8	3.6	11.2	10.3	0.9
5.9	4.6	1.3	16.9	12.9	4.0	15.3	14.7	0.6
5.5	4.6	0.9	16.2	12.6	3.6	14.0	13.6	0.4
5.1	4.4	0.7	15.1	11.6	3.5	11.9	12.5	−0.6

III
Financing Growth and Development in Africa Outlook and Issues

Estimating the Cost of Financing African Development in the 1990s

Maria Cristina Germany, Charles P. Humphreys, and Stephen O'Brien

This paper discusses the magnitude of external resources that sub-Saharan Africa may require during the 1990s.[1] There can be no firm projections because requirements are affected both by the growth and efficiency targets chosen and by a wide range of factors, internal and external, that often interact to reinforce or offset one another. The specific projections provided by this paper do, however, offer a point of departure for further discussion. To facilitate such discussion, a qualitative framework is given for considering how various factors affect resource requirements.

To achieve the gross domestic product (GDP) growth target of 5 percent a year by 2000 proposed in the World Bank's *Sub-Saharan Africa: From Crisis to Sustainable Growth*, the quantitative scenario in this paper shows that sub-Saharan Africa could require gross external capital of $28–29 billion a year, on average, for the period 1991–2000. About half of those inflows would finance net imports of goods and services (other than interest), needed for *current* and *future* growth; the other half would finance debt-service payments on borrowing that financed expenditures mostly in the *past*.

These financing needs can be met with no increase in nominal gross external inflows. The composition of the gross inflows will change, however: by the end of the decade debt relief will disappear under the debt

---

[1] Based on Culagovski (1991) which explains in more detail issues related to savings, investment, and efficiency of capital; it also describes, in the annex, the general assumptions used in the projections and the sensitivity results to changes in major assumptions. A summary of this PRE working paper, "African Financing Needs in the 1990s: A World Bank Symposium" was also published in October 1991.

relief options *now in effect*, as debt becomes ineligible for further rescheduling; and aid flows would have to almost double over the decade, thus providing over two thirds of the resource transfers, if nonconcessional loans remain stagnant. Even if aid increases this much and net foreign direct investment doubles, a financing gap of $3–4 billion a year, on average, would remain. Achieving this scenario will require appropriate domestic policy reforms, especially those designed to raise investment to a level equivalent to 25 percent of GDP and to achieve a dramatic improvement in the efficiency of capital.

The conceptual framework used in this paper for estimating external resource requirements is based essentially on a two-gap model, in which the gap between domestic savings and gross investment must equal the difference between imports and exports and is financed by external capital or foreign savings. To provide a context for the discussions, the paper starts with a section on the economic history and evolution of sub-Saharan Africa. The main section analyzes the external resource requirements, as projected by the model, and discusses implications for other related economic and financial variables.

Economic Change and Evolution

The Last Thirty Years

About thirty years ago colonialism was ending in Africa. Resources were channeled substantially toward industrialization. Agriculture took second place, basically supplying raw materials and providing tax revenues. The development strategy, fully supported by donors, entailed a dominant role for the government, which spent heavily on the social sector and infrastructure. The region's economies initially performed well after independence, but subsequently deteriorated. GDP grew at 5.9 percent a year during 1965–73, about the same rate as for other developing countries. Strong export demand and high investment, financed from export earnings, commercial borrowing, and aid, boosted the GDP growth rate; however, after the first oil shock in 1973–74[2] Africa's performance started to lag behind that of other developing countries. In the early 1980s, output began to decline. The region has now suffered a decade of falling per capita income and begun to show signs that its land and human

---

[2]The biggest increases in oil prices, here referred to as oil shocks, took place in 1973–74 and 1979–80, and are the basis for the periods selected to average data.

resources are eroding. With many African countries starting reform programs, GDP growth began to recover in the second half of the 1980s, but the aggregate growth rate for the region has remained below that in the rest of the developing world except in 1989 (Table 1).

Table 1. Growth of Aggregate GDP, 1967–89
(In percent a year)

	1967–73	1974–80	1981–84	1985–87	1988	1989
Sub-Saharan Africa	7.0	2.7	–1.1	2.6	2.5	3.6
Less Nigeria	4.4	2.0	1.9	3.1	1.5	2.2
Non-African developing countries	6.5	5.4	3.5	5.4	5.8	3.4

Source: World Bank data files.
Note: Growth rates are calculated using trend line regressions and data in 1980 prices and exchange rates.

Performance has varied greatly from country to country. Average annual GDP growth during 1961–87 ranged from 8.3 percent for Botswana to –2.2 percent for Uganda. Oil exports greatly affected performance, with oil exporters doing well or badly according to fluctuations in the oil prices. Middle-income countries have, in general, fared better than low-income countries and small economies better than large ones. Domestic economic policies have also greatly affected countries' ability to recover from external shocks, their economic performance, and their external financing requirements.

The Crisis

In the 1970s, most African countries expanded public consumption and investment. Instead of raising domestic savings, governments financed much of the expansion with foreign funds, taking advantage of expanded borrowing capacity based on unprecedented high export prices and negative real interest rates in international markets. This quick expansion required rapidly rising imports, which grew faster than during any other period in the past thirty years (7.6 percent annually for the years 1974–80). The increase in imports was largely financed by nonconcessional borrowing, which continued after the second oil shock despite a sudden rise in international interest rates, as borrowers and lenders believed that the high export volumes could be soon restored and that high export prices would continue. These expectations did not materialize, and in 1984 nonconcessional lending was sharply reduced following the global debt crisis; in 1985 there was virtually none.

The large increase in absorption during the 1970s failed to establish a sustainable base for future growth. During most of this decade, GDP growth was lower than population growth and exports stagnated. The poor quality of public investments, financed at the margin by foreign savings, and domestic policies that reduced the region's international competitiveness diminished economic efficiency and undermined the region's ability to cope with the huge reduction in foreign capital. The region ended the decade in crisis.

The crisis was pervasive, affecting all areas of the economies (Table 2). During 1981–84, export and import volumes fell (by 7.5 and 6.8 percent annually, respectively); investment as a percentage of gross national product (GNP) went back to the 1966–73 levels (16.7 percent); gross national savings as a percentage of GNP averaged only 9 percent, or about half their 1974–80 level; foreign direct investment expanded at the lowest rate of the last thirty years; export market shares continued to erode. To make matters worse, net nonconcessional capital flows collapsed, and the negative real interest rates of the past gave way to very high ones. Debt at 45 percent of GNP in 1983–84 was more than double its 1975 level, and the debt-service payments, despite rescheduling, reached 27 percent of exports in 1984, or four times higher than in 1975. Despite the crumbling economies, private consumption continued to grow during 1981–84, albeit at a small and reduced rate (1.1 percent a year), financed by a rapid decline in the gross national savings rate (which reached an all-time low of 7.3 percent of GNP in 1983) and modestly increasing net official development assistance (ODA) flows. This consumption growth, however, was lower than population growth, and per capita consumption declined 2 percent a year.

The drop in output was caused by the very low efficiency of investment. High population growth, oil price and international interest rates shocks, war, and drought have contributed to the crisis in sub-Saharan Africa, but weak economic management—beginning in the 1970s—was also a major cause. Bad investments and inappropriate domestic policies weakened domestic economic productivity, reduced flexibility to respond to shocks, and left a legacy of debt service that began to absorb a growing share of both domestic and foreign resources. Weak policy-implementing capacity also impeded improved economic performance.

**Table 2. Evolution of Key Economic Indicators
for Sub-Saharan Africa, 1967–88**

(Average annual percentage change; unless indicated otherwise)

	1967–73	1974–80	1981–84	1985–87	1988
Gross domestic product (GDP)	7.0	2.7	–1.1	2.6	2.5
Export volume	17.1	0.2	–7.5	2.1	1.2
Import volume	4.3	7.6	–6.8	–0.7	–2.8
Gross domestic investment (percent of GNP)[1]	16.7	22.3	16.7	15.0	16.6
Gross national savings (percent of GNP)[1]	13.0	17.2	9.0	8.8	8.0
Private consumption	4.1	1.8	1.1	1.3	2.2
Gross official development assistance (percent of GNP)[2]	3.2	3.6	4.2	6.6	8.9
Terms of trade index (1980 = 100)[1]	83.9	84.4	101.3	83.0	74.2
Gross national income					
Total	3.9	4.5	–1.1	0.7	2.4
Per capita	1.2	1.7	–4.1	–2.4	–0.9

Source: World Bank data files.
Note: Growth rates are calculated using trend line regressions and data in 1980 prices and exchange rates. GNP = gross national product.
[1] Refers to 1966–73.
[2] Refers to 1970–73.

The Reforms

The case for reforms was too strong to ignore. By the mid-1980s, many sub-Saharan countries had begun the reform process; by 1990, 29 had active World Bank-supported adjustment programs and 27 had IMF-supported programs. Reform programs started first in the area of macroeconomic stabilization; fiscal, monetary, exchange rate, and other macroeconomic reforms were used to bring aggregate expenditures in line with total available resources. The programs that followed, in the later 1980s, focused more on increasing output and reducing the social costs of adjustment. These reform programs increased the emphasis on adjustment policies to improve productivity and increase production and exports. They liberalized external and domestic trade, raised producer prices, strengthened the financial sector, restructured public enterprises, improved public investment programming, reordered public expenditure priorities, and improved performance in key sectors, especially agriculture and industry. In many countries, these reform efforts have depreciated the real exchange rate, raised real interest rates, reduced domestic deficits, liberalized trade and prices, and improved public sector management including public enterprises.

Even though the aggregate results for sub-Saharan Africa as a region are dampened by those countries that have not engaged in reforms, the trends show how output growth has been restored in the region, reaching 3.6 percent in 1989, compared with −1.1 percent in 1981–84. Export performance is beginning to turn around, but import volumes are still declining, albeit at a slower pace than before the reform period. Gross domestic investment and national savings, which reached their lowest point in 1983–85, are no longer declining as a percent of GNP (although the gap between the two remains about the same as in the early 1980s). Private consumption began to recover in 1985–87 and improved in 1988, as stronger output growth was channeled more into consumption than savings (see Table 2).

Response to reforms is more evident when the record for reforming countries is examined separately. Recent data, through 1990, for the countries eligible for the Special Program of Assistance (SPA), which covers most reforming countries, show that during SPA1 (1988–90) output in the 20 core SPA countries grew at 4 percent a year, on average.[3] Exports grew almost as fast, and gross domestic investment (GDI) expanded even faster; gross domestic savings (GDS) continued to grow as a share of GDP; and the decline of real per capita consumption is close to being arrested (Table 3).

In contrast to the expansion that took place in the SPA countries, deterioration, or at best stagnation, characterized countries outside the SPA group. During 1988–90, output growth continued to slow and was only 2.2 percent a year, on average, despite the fact that this group

---

[3] Donors and creditors launched this ongoing program in late 1987 as an extraordinary response to the problems facing low-income, debt-distressed African countries lacking adequate resources to adjust and grow. Twenty-three countries have received assistance from SPA; however, because Somalia and Zaïre received support in 1988 and 1989 but are now inactive, and Zambia became eligible for SPA only in late 1990, only 20 of them are defined as "core" countries.

Data used for the SPA analysis are based on constant 1987 prices and exchange rates, and therefore are not directly comparable to data through 1988 used in Tables 1 and 2 and elsewhere in this paper, which are based on constant 1980 prices and exchange rates. Aggregates are unweighted averages, which characterize the experience of a typical country in each of the groups and avoid the problem of large countries, like Nigeria, dominating the weighted averages.

Table 3. Selected Performance Indicators for Sub-Saharan Africa, 1980–90
(Annual average percentage change; unless specified otherwise)

	1980–84	1985–87	1988–90
GDP			
SPA core countries	1.0	3.2	4.0
Other countries	3.3	3.2	2.2
Export volume			
SPA core countries	–0.6	3.0	3.7
Other countries	1.3	2.0	2.4
GDI (*percent of GDP*)			
SPA core countries	18.4	16.7	19.3
Other countries	23.9	21.2	19.6
GDS (*percent of GDP*)			
SPA core countries	2.9	4.0	4.9
Other countries	8.9	9.3	8.8
Terms of trade index (1987 = 1)			
SPA core countries	1.05	1.06	0.94
Other countries	1.21	1.06	1.02

Source: World Bank data files.
Note: GDI = gross domestic investment; GDS = gross domestic savings; SPA = Special Program of Assistance. Other countries include Somalia, Zaïre, and Zambia; and exclude Angola, Comoros, Djibouti, Equatorial Guinea, and Swaziland because of incomplete data. GDP, exports, and terms of trade data are on 1987 constant prices and exchange rates. GDI and GDS ratios are based on current price series.

includes some of the fast-growing sub-Saharan countries like Botswana and Mauritius. Export growth was also weaker, expanding only slightly faster than GDP; real investment increased moderately;[4] gross domestic savings fell as a share of GDP; and the decline of real per capita consumption continued.

External Flows and the Investment-Savings Gap in Sub-Saharan Africa

As national savings dwindled and public consumption and investment continued, external resources have been used to finance growing fiscal deficits on both current and capital budgets. The investment-savings gap has increased two and a half times in 22 years, growing from 3.7 percent

---

[4]Because the GDP deflator rose faster than the prices of investment goods, investment continued to decline as a share of GDP.

Table 4. Investment and Savings in Sub-Saharan Africa, 1966–88
(Average annual percentage of gross national product)

	1966–73	1974–80	1981–84	1985–87	1988
Sub-Saharan Africa					
Gross domestic investment	16.7	22.3	16.7	15.0	16.6
Gross national savings	13.0	17.2	9.0	8.8	8.0
Gap[1]	3.7	5.1	7.7	6.2	8.6
Nigeria					
Gross domestic investment	14.8	22.8	13.8	10.3	13.6
Gross national savings	10.3	23.7	8.8	8.4	8.7
Gap[1]	4.5	–0.9	5.0	1.9	4.9
Other IBRD countries[2]					
Gross domestic investment	22.2	29.5	26.4	21.8	19.6
Gross national savings	14.2	12.2	13.7	14.7	11.7
Gap[1]	8.0	17.3	12.7	7.1	7.9
IDA-only countries[3]					
Gross domestic investment	16.1	18.8	16.8	16.1	16.3
Gross national savings	13.8	10.6	7.3	6.9	5.7
Gap[1]	2.3	8.2	9.5	9.2	10.6

Source: World Bank data files.
[1] Defined as investment minus savings.
[2] IBRD = International Bank for Reconstruction and Development.
[3] IDA = International Development Association.

of GNP in 1966–73 to 7.4 percent in 1985–88 (Table 4); for the SPA countries, ODA reached about 14 percent of GDP—or almost three times the share in 1970–73. While in 1966 almost 90 percent of investment was financed by sub-Saharan Africa's savings, in 1988 only 50 percent was. The persistent widening of this gap has occurred mainly in the International Development Association (IDA)-only countries, that is, those countries eligible to borrow IDA credits but not IBRD loans.

The decline in savings in sub-Saharan Africa can be explained by two main factors: (a) declining income, which leaves fewer resources for public and private consumption and savings; and (b) the government's negative savings that resulted from growing recurrent budget deficits.[5]

---

[5] Some misclassification of foreign inflows may make the level of domestic savings look lower than it actually is. This misclassification stems from the possible overreporting of foreign-funded investment and underreporting of foreign-funded consumption. Savings are calculated as the difference between production and consumption. To the extent that part of consumption has actually been financed by foreign funds (and would not occur without this foreign financing), actual domestic savings will be higher than calculated.

Donors and recipients commonly focus on the inadequacy of funds for investment; however, *inadequate demand for investment* is equally, or more, important in explaining low levels of investment in sub-Saharan Africa. Inadequate demand has been caused by the insufficiency of sound public investment projects that are attractive to international or bilateral lenders and donors, and by low and uncertain returns on private domestic assets—caused in part by distorted economic and financial policies, as well as political animosity and uncertainty, which make private investment less attractive than in other countries. The weak demand for domestic investment is demonstrated by large capital flight from the region. While difficult to evaluate, cumulative capital outflow from 36 sub-Saharan African countries may have amounted to as much as $40 billion between 1976 and 1987[6]—an amount equivalent to about half the total official development assistance received by sub-Saharan Africa during the same period. Assuming a linear function between investment and output, this cumulative capital flight would have cost an output loss by 1987 of about 30 percent of GDP. This situation suggests that stagnant investment and output resulted from inadequate demand for investment, as well as inadequate national savings and external financing.

In fact, net external flows to sub-Saharan Africa have almost doubled as a percentage of GNP during the past two decades. Net loan disbursements plus grants and net foreign investment amounted to 6 percent of sub-Saharan Africa's GNP in 1970, but to 10.9 percent in 1988. Moreover, the net flows have become more concessional. In 1970, less than half the net flows were concessional compared with five sixths in 1988.

Past trends show how past borrowing coupled with inefficient public investments and domestic policies that weakened production incentives and competitiveness has increased the region's dependence on foreign resources. The task ahead is to expand reform programs that can gradually reduce this dependence. In the interim, however, foreign savings are still needed to help increase the effects of reforms.

---

[6]See Chang and Cumby (1991). This estimate is based on a broad definition of capital flight, measuring the total increase in the private sector's net foreign assets. An alternative measurement, based on the change in the stock of private claims held abroad, gives an estimate about 20 percent lower. In a different study, Alexander Yeats (1989) calculated that African countries paid considerably more than other developing countries for the same imports; part of these higher payments is a conduit for capital flight.

Estimated Financing Requirements

The Analytical Framework

The basic targets and assumptions used to project financing requirements for sub-Saharan Africa during the 1990s are presented in Table 5. They are similar to those used in *Sub-Saharan Africa: From Crisis to Sustainable Growth* (World Bank (1989a)). For the region as a whole, that report assumed real GDP growth during the 1990s of 4–5 percent a year, annual export volume growth of over 5 percent, an import elasticity falling to about 1.1 by 2000, investment rising to 25 percent of GDP, and an incremental capital output ratio declining from about 7 in 1990 to 5 by

Table 5. Past and Projected Key Economic Indicators for Sub-Saharan Africa, 1985–88, 1995, 2000
(Average annual percentage change; unless indicated otherwise)

	1985–88	1995	2000
Domestic indicators			
Real gross domestic product (GDP)	2.6	4.0	5.0
Real gross domestic investment (GDI)	–6.9	8.7	7.7
GDI (*percent of GDP*)	14.0	20.7	25.0
Gross domestic savings (*percent of GDP*)	11.4	16.6	20.0
Real consumption per capita	–0.7	0.1	1.3
Real gross national income (GNY)	–1.8	4.2	5.4
Real GNY per capita (*1988 U.S. dollars*)	314.0	304.0	334.0
Real effective exchange rate	–4.0[1]	–3.3	–3.4
Incremental capital output ratio (ICOR)			
(at 1988, 1994, 1999 prices, respectively)	6.8	4.9	4.8
Trade indicators and official development assistance			
Import elasticity	–1.6	1.0	1.0
Import volume	–4.0	4.1	5.0
Imports (*percent of GDP*)	22.9	33.1	39.3
Export volume	1.9	3.6	4.3
Exports (*percent of GDP*)	20.3	29.0	34.3
Import prices	6.3	4.6	5.4
Export prices	–4.6	4.8	5.9
Terms of trade index (1988 = 100)	111.5	103.5	107.5
Real gross official development assistance			
(ODA)	13.9	3.3	1.1
Gross ODA (*percent of GDP*)	5.9	8.6	9.0
Debt–service indicators before debt relief			
Debt-service ratio (*percent of exports*)	–	26.5	15.7
Debt-service (*percent of GDP*)	–	7.8	5.4

Sources: World Bank data and projections.
[1] Median for about three fourths of the sub-Saharan countries; 1986–88.

2000. These targets are more optimistic than historical trends for the region overall, but they are consistent with the historical experience of successful countries in and out of Africa and with recent improvements in reforming countries. The key assumption in these projections is a dramatic improvement in savings performance over the decade, to around 20 percent of GDP by 2000. This would reduce the dependence on net external financing by half, from 10 percent of GDP to 5 percent, by the end of the decade.

The requirements are based on "the most likely" scenario presented in the *World Development Report 1990*, which assumes that industrial countries will grow at 3 percent a year during the 1990s. The projections use an import elasticity of one. Reserves are targeted to rise gradually to three months of imports by 2000. Compared with 1988–90, the terms of trade index for the region (excluding Nigeria) is projected to increase slightly during the decade, but to increase substantially for Nigeria; for IDA-only countries, however, the index would remain below its level in 1988–90, declining slightly over the decade. Bilateral ODA flows are assumed to grow in line with nominal GNP in the countries of the Organization for Economic Cooperation and Development (OECD). Multilateral ODA flows in the early 1990s stem from present arrangements, and after 1993 are assumed to grow at the same rate as bilateral aid, except for the IMF. Private transfers are assumed to decline to zero by 2000. The assumptions lead to an increasing openness, in line with assumed trade liberalization measures and continued real currency depreciation.

Projected Gross External Capital Requirements

Sub-Saharan Africa

The gross foreign financing requirements for all of sub-Saharan Africa, before debt relief of any kind or the accumulation of new arrears, are projected to average about $28 billion a year (in nominal prices) between 1991 and 2000, or about $50 per capita annually (see Table 6).[7] These

---

[7] The requirements are the sum of three major components: the trade balance (of goods and services, excluding interest obligations on external debt), all external debt-service obligations, and assumed increases in foreign reserves. The estimate excludes Angola, Botswana, Cape Verde, Comoros, Djibouti, Equatorial Guinea, Gabon, Lesotho, Mauritius, Namibia, Seychelles, and Swaziland. These countries—many with positive current account balances—accounted for less than 10 percent of sub-Saharan GDP in the mid-1980s and are unlikely to have significant on projections of total financing requirements.

Table 6. Past and Projected Financing and Debt Relief for Sub-Saharan Africa, 1985–88, 1995, 2000
(Average annual percent of GDP; unless indicated otherwise)

	1985–88	1995	2000
Total foreign financing required			
In billions of U.S. dollars	14.8	26.5	32.0
In percent of GDP	10.2	14.2	12.7
Gross foreign inflows projected	10.1	11.9	11.9
Of which			
Loan disbursements	6.5	6.2	5.8
Official transfers	3.1	5.0	5.3
Direct foreign investment	0.4	0.7	0.8
Net debt relief[1]	...[2]	1.2	–0.7
Residual financing gap	0.1	1.1	1.5
Memorandum items			
Debt-service indicators *after* debt relief			
Debt-service ratio			
(*as percent of exports*)	31.2	22.5	17.7
Debt service	6.5	6.6	6.1

Sources: World Bank data and projections.
[1] Net of moratorium obligations on consolidated amounts.
[2] Debt relief and accumulation of arrears have already been taken into account in calculating financing requirements because historical debt service is shown as payments, not as obligations.

projected financing requirements compare with estimated gross financing of $27–28 billion in 1988 and $24–25 billion in 1982,[8] implying that the financing needs can be met with no nominal increase in gross external capital. Foreign financing at this level is equivalent to only about 12–14 percent of the total capital flows to the developing world in 1988.

In real terms (deflated by projected import prices), the gross external financing requirements would average about one fourth less than nominal requirements. As African economies continue to grow over the period, gross external financing requirements would also decline as a share of GDP, from about 18 percent in the early 1990s to about 13 percent by 2000. After 2000, gross external financing requirements could continue to rise in nominal terms while declining as a share of GDP. This financing

---

[8] This historical figure includes an estimate for debt-service obligations that were not paid, because they were either rescheduled or allowed to fall into arrears. For example, unpaid debt service was on the order of $10 billion in 1988 (excluding any interest arrears on short-term debt).

comprises what is required both to improve growth and development in the future (the trade gap of goods and nonfactor services) and to deal adequately with the legacy of past borrowing for earlier consumption and investment expenditures (debt-service obligations). The 1990–97 requirement levels mirror the movements of the debt-service obligations: high in the early years, declining in the midyears, and stabilizing after 1997. The requirements rise in the last part of the decade mainly because of the continually widening trade deficit. The trade gap widens during the decade because export growth lags behind import growth in aggregate (owing primarily to the low growth in Nigerian oil exports), the terms of trade decline for oil importing countries, and because the base for projecting import values is about a third larger than export values.

Debt-service obligations—before rescheduling and before the accumulation of any additional arrears—comprise more than half of the gross external financing requirements in the first half of the 1990s, but fall to about 40 percent by the end of the decade. In comparison, debt-service obligations were equivalent to about three fourths of the gross external financing requirements in 1988 but only about a third in 1982. The importance of debt service in total requirements reveals that the external financing problem in Africa is much more than a structural imbalance of imports and exports and indicates the importance of debt relief measures as a source of financing. The most effective to reduce the trade gap will be to achieve growth that is considerably faster than GDP growth. This will be easier if the needed imported capital and intermediate goods have adequate foreign financing.

Changes in underlying assumptions and targets will affect the projections, mostly because of their impact on the trade balance. A few examples illustrate the range of possible effects. If the *GDP growth* target were 1 percentage point higher in each year (which implies that the target proposed in *Sub-Saharan Africa: From Crisis to Sustainable Growth* would be achieved by 1995)—and there were no improvement in import efficiency, gross financing requirements would rise by 20–25 percent, or by $6–7 billion a year on average. If the assumed *export growth* were 1 percentage point higher in each year (bringing it closer in line with that of other developing countries)—and there were no offsetting increases in imports, gross financing requirements would fall by about 15 percent, or some $4 billion a year on average. If the projected *terms of trade index* were 1 percentage point below the base-case scenario in each year (but still resulting in a slight improvement over the period), gross financing requirements would rise by about 15 percent, or $4–5 billion a year on average. And if policy reforms could improve efficiency enough to lower the assumed *import elasticity* by 10 percent (becoming 0.9 instead of 1.0), gross financing requirements would decline by over 5 percent, or almost $2 billion a year.[9]

Projections by Groups of Countries

The aggregate projections for the region mask divergent trends and needs among countries. Some countries—especially the poorest—usually have much more severe financing needs than others—like oil exporters. Moreover, the use of aggregate estimates may underestimate regional needs because it implicitly assumes that surpluses in some countries can offset deficits in other countries, although surpluses are unlikely to be given or loaned to other African countries. In lieu of estimates for each country, the problem caused by divergent trends among countries can be alleviated by grouping countries according to their prospects and needs.

The IDA-only countries account for over 75 percent of the total gross financing required for the region. The financing requirements for these countries are driven by a widening trade deficit, which more than doubles in current terms during the 1990s, rather than by debt service. Therefore, substantially narrowing the requirements cannot be accomplished by short-term solutions. Because exports cover less than $3 out of every $4 of imports in these countries, the export growth rate will have to be a third higher than the import growth rate—or 8–10 percent a year—for a sustained period of time to lower the nominal trade gap. Exports would have to grow even faster if terms of trade decline. Provided that policy reforms are effective, and assuming a favorable trade environment in the industrial countries, the trade gap may begin to narrow after the end of the decade if export growth continues to accelerate. The required rates are optimistic, but they have been achieved by successful developing countries.

---

[9]Changes in *interest rates* would have a small effect on debt-service obligations. A rise in interest rates of 1 percentage point would increase debt-service obligations by only $0.3–0.4 billion a year, or only 1–2 percent of gross financing requirements for the region.

Assuming that higher *oil prices* dampen consumer demand and stimulate increased energy efficiency within Africa, each dollar increase in oil prices will raise financing requirements by about $250 million a year for the oil importing African countries. However, the additional cost to the oil importers would be less than the larger revenues of the five oil exporting countries. At current export levels, each dollar increase in oil prices would raise export revenues by $750 million a year.

For the middle-income countries and Nigeria, the situation during the 1990s contrasts sharply with that of the low-income countries. Middle-income countries[10] account for 20 percent of the total requirements for the region. Their requirements decline during the decade in real terms as well as a percentage of GDP. As opposed to the IDA-only countries, their requirements are not driven by trade (they have a small trade surplus) but by debt service. Debt-service obligations rise during the decade as payments for nonconcessional obligations contracted in the second half of the 1980s become due. Debt relief could fill much of the financing gap of this group. If the creditor community granted more generous debt relief than the Toronto terms of the Paris Club assumed in the model, the need for new financing would be considerably less.

Nigeria needs an average annual gross financing (before debt relief) of $2.4 billion only from 1991 to 1995. From 1996 onward Nigeria would generate a surplus. Nigeria's requirements decrease because of both an increasing trade surplus and declining debt-service obligations over the decade. After debt relief (which includes reduction of commercial bank debt), Nigeria would need an annual average of only $1.1 billion in 1991 and 1992, as it generates surplus after that.

Projected Financing Sources

For illustrative purposes, possible sources of financing for these requirements are also shown in Table 7. The major financing sources, in order of importance, include gross loan disbursements from all lenders, official transfers, debt relief measures (net of additional moratorium debt service), and direct foreign investment. (Private transfers are treated as resources, included in the current account balance.) The composition of the major financing sources is assumed to change over the decade with the share of aid flows increasing but that of debt relief decreasing.

Total gross loan disbursements, net official transfers, and direct foreign investment are assumed to grow at annual average nominal growth rates of 3–4, 7, and 10 percent, respectively. Gross disbursements of nonconcessional loans are assumed to remain constant, in nominal prices, at the 1988 level. As a result, the share of gross loan disbursements and official

---

[10] Projections for this group are based on data for four countries: Cameroon, Congo, Côte d'Ivoire, and Zimbabwe. Other middle-income countries were not considered because they are either too small or are not expected to need special balance of payments support. Their projections are made for the oil sector separately, on the basis of known deposits.

Table 7. Possible Sources of Financing for Sub-Saharan Africa, 1991–2000
(Annual averages in billions of U.S. dollars)

	1991–2000	Of which	
		1991–95	1996–2000
Gross loan disbursements	12.1	10.8	13.3
Of which			
Concessional	7.2	6.1	8.3
Official transfers	10.0	8.4	11.6
Direct foreign investment	1.5	1.1	1.9
Debt relief[1]	1.7	3.9	0.4
Residual gap	2.9	3.3	2.5
Total financing	28.2	27.5	28.9

Source: World Bank projections.
[1] Net of moratorium debt service on rescheduled debt.

transfers in total financing—including debt-service reduction—would rise from 65 percent to 87 percent by the end of the decade. The share of direct foreign investment would double during the decade, although, because the base is very small, its contribution to total requirements remains low (6 percent in 2000). Debt relief of official debt is assumed, for all countries, at the most favorable terms currently allowed under the Paris Club, currently the Toronto Terms.[11] In addition, reduction of commercial debt is assumed through London Club rescheduling and a combination of buybacks at deep discounts, swaps, and other arrangements. However, total debt relief would gradually dwindle and become negative by 1998 as repayment of previous debt consolidations falls due. Two other reasons account for the relatively small contribution of debt relief to total financing resources: about a fourth of Africa's debt is multilateral and currently not eligible for debt relief; and all new borrowing is assumed ineligible for rescheduling, which is in line with the current policy on cutoff dates.

Under this scenario, only about 90 percent of the requirements would be met—implying a residual gap of $3–4 billion a year, on average. This

---

[11] Under these terms all rescheduled concessional debt is to be repaid with a 25-year maturity, including a 14-year grace period. Moratorium interest charges should be at least as low as the rates on the original loans. For nonconcessional debt, the creditor countries can choose repayment conditions from a menu of three options: (a) partial cancellation, (b) extended maturities, and (c) concessional interest rates. The grant element of this scheme is 19 percent, which compares with 81 percent for IDA loans. In addition to the application of the Toronto Terms, most concessional loans are assumed to be written off, in line with current practice.

ESTIMATING THE COST OF FINANCING AFRICAN DEVELOPMENT 169

indicates the need for stronger reforms, export promotion, more efficient use of imports, and additional resources—namely, more favorable debt relief and larger capital inflows, especially from the private sector.

Methodological Summary

The financing requirements of sub-Saharan Africa were projected in nominal U.S. dollars using a macroeconomic accounting framework covering basic relationships among aggregates of the macroeconomy. The target rates of real GDP and export volume growth (about 5 percent a year) were assumed to be achieved gradually during the 1990s, accelerating from the lower levels of the late 1980s. Import volumes were set by an elasticity of one, relative to real GDP growth. While higher-than-aggregate elasticity manifested in the 1980s, when insufficient foreign exchange constrained imports, the future import elasticity, on the other hand, may be expected to exceed one, because of the severe compression of imports during the 1980s (import volume in 1988 was only 76 percent of the level in 1980), because of the need to rebuild critical infrastructure and productive facilities, and because of the need to expand basic social services. Moreover, import intensity normally deepens as economies grow and develop. The assumed international environment would be moderately expansive (3 percent growth in OECD countries during the 1990s). Because of rising real oil prices, terms of trade would be generally favorable for the region overall, but oil importers would face slightly declining terms of trade.

Policy reforms are not explicitly included in the model, although achieving the targets projected for key economic variables assumes the adoption of conducive policies. Real depreciation of domestic currencies is explicitly assumed (about 3 percent a year) because it effects how domestic prices move relative to international prices, and thus affects ratios expressed as a percentage of domestic GDP. Assumed increases in government revenue and decreases in spending would reduce the deficit by 4 percent of GDP during the 1990s, which improves the scope for increasing domestic savings.

The relationship between the amount of investment required and the projected growth rates, generally referred to as the incremental capital-output ratio (ICOR), is assumed to improve during the decade, with the ratio declining from 6.8 in 1985–88 to 4.8 in 2000 for the region as a whole. Substantial improvements in the ratio would be needed for the middle-income countries and Nigeria as the ratio is brought down from its present level to meet the target GDP and investment levels. This change assumes the implementation of policy reform programs that increase the efficiency of capital.

Bibliography

Chang, Kevin P.H., and Cumby, Robert E. "Capital Flights in Sub-Saharan African Countries" (unpublished, Washington: World Bank, 1991).

Culagovski, Jorge, and others, "African Financing Needs in the 1990s," Policy, Planning, and Research Working Papers, WPS 764 (Washington: World Bank, October 1991).

World Bank (1989a), *Sub-Saharan Africa: From Crisis to Sustainable Growth* (Washington, 1989).

―――― (1989b), *World Debt Tables, 1989-90*, Vols. 1 and 2 and underlying data files (Washington, 1989).

―――― (1990a), *Special Program of Assistance. Proposal for the Second Phase* (Washington, 1990)

―――― (1990b), *World Development Report 1990* (Washington, 1990).

Yeats, Alexander J., "Do African Countries Pay More for Imports? Yes," Policy, Planning, and Research Working Papers WPS 265 (Washington, 1989).

A View from the UN Economic Commission for Africa

Owodunni Teriba

In this reflection on the financing of growth and development in Africa, an attempt has been made to underscore the fundamental problems facing African countries in financing economic recovery and development from both domestic and external resources, and to identify the major gaps in existing financing. The focus is on some of the most critical issues in Africa's development financing—issues and questions that, it is believed, must be earnestly addressed in the 1990s and beyond if Africa is to move forward. The paper provides a critical examination of Africa's development financing options and outlook and outlines the policy initiatives and actions required on the part of African governments and the international community for adequate and effective financing of Africa's economic recovery and development.

Some Critical Issues in Africa's Development Financing

The magnitude of Africa's development crisis is well documented in various studies by the Economic Commission for Africa (ECA), the World Bank, and other agencies. At the root of the crisis has been the cruel interplay of internal and external forces. African economies are characterized by weak, inherited colonial structures, and poor management. And, to a large extent, economic performance in many of the countries in the region is determined by exogenous forces and natural phenomena, such as weather, over which they have no control. Also, while African economies are open, and some would say excessively open and fragile, they lack often the capacity to cope with shocks and impulses transmitted from an increasingly unfavorable international economic environment.

In the last decade, a wind of economic change has been blowing through Africa. This is reflected in the increasing acceptance by the region of the need for major economic policy reforms, with as many as 35 African countries currently implementing structural adjustment programs under the prescription and the supervision of the Bretton Woods institutions, even though it is generally now agreed that orthodox structural adjustment programs that focus almost exclusively on short-term macroeconomic and financial balances are not in the least suited to African conditions. Collectively, African countries have also shown their commitment to change by adopting, among others, the Lagos Plan of Action (LPA), Africa's Priority Program for Economic Recovery (APPER), the African Alternative Program to Structural Adjustment for Socio-Economic Transformation (AAF-SAP), and the African Charter for Popular Participation in Development, the primary aim of which is to eliminate the fundamental weaknesses in the African economies and to restore them to the path of rapid and self-sustaining growth and development.

While many African countries have been implementing programs of economic reforms at great social and political costs, the objective of rapid growth and development is far from being achieved. Indeed, the last few years have witnessed a deepening of the region's economic crisis. A major missing link in Africa's adjustment efforts and one that constitutes a serious impediment to the realization of the region's primary objective is the inadequacy of resources for the financing of recovery and socioeconomic transformation. In a real sense, therefore, the African development crisis has become, in part, a financing crisis. By 1987, the financial famine in Africa had assumed such alarming proportions that the distinguished Secretary-General of the United Nations had to establish an Advisory Group on Financial Flows for Africa.[1] This having been said, it is essential to bear constantly in mind that while finance and development have become closely linked—and indeed umbilically linked in the present African context—the availability of finance must properly be viewed and seen for what it is: an instrument for achieving given economic objectives and ends. If the ends and goals are misplaced or wrongly perceived, no matter how generous financial assistance is, all efforts will be of no avail. The experience with the deliberate injection of nonautonomous resource flows into some African countries in the 1980s in support of and as a prop to orthodox structural adjustment programs is a case in point. Not only have such resources failed to induce autonomous private foreign invest-

---

[1] For the report of the Group, see United Nations, *Financing Africa's Recovery: Report and Recommendations of the Advisory Group on Financial Flows for Africa* (New York, 1988).

ment, they have also failed to have any positive impact on domestic savings and investment. Yet, it is the availability of autonomous domestic and foreign financial flows that will ensure that recovery and development proceed in Africa on a sustainable and sustained basis.

Most African countries tend to suffer from the problems of investment-savings gap and foreign exchange inadequacy that arise from the low level of economic development in Africa and the unfavorable nature of the region's participation in the international division of labor. Consequently, one of the orthodoxies of the post–World War II era has been the crucial role assigned to international finance in the development process of Africa. The expectation was that massive external resource inflows would be forthcoming from the developed countries to the region to finance the excess of investment over domestic savings and of imports over exports, and hence for the expansion and diversification of production capacities.

In spite of Africa's urgent need for external resources to augment its import capacity and to help close balance of payments gaps, both of which are crucial aspects of the financing of growth and development, the net inflows of financial resources into the region have, in real terms, been declining since the early 1980s. Over the period from 1980 to 1988, total financial flows to developing Africa from the members of the Development Assistance Committee (DAC), the Organization of Petroleum Exporting Countries (OPEC), and multilateral agencies increased by a mere $2.2 billion, from $21.3 billion to $23.5 billion. The increase becomes insignificant if adjustment is made for inflation and exchange rate fluctuations. And the total net flows of resources were considerably below what is required to compensate for the collapse in the commodity market and the dramatic fall in the prices of African exports. In addition, the reduced control of the international financial institutions over international exchange rates, liquidity creation, and interest rates has, by making financial and monetary systems the world over more asymmetrical and volatile, aggravated the burden of international adjustment and the difficulties faced by developing countries, including those of Africa, in acquiring satisfactory levels of reserves and external financing.

The channeling of external resource flows to African and other Third World countries has been effected through three principal mechanisms: aid, private direct investment, and loans. For a variety of reasons, each of these mechanisms is becoming increasingly inadequate or problematic as a source for the financing of growth and development in Africa.

In the past, aid was the dominant mechanism for transferring resources from the developed industrial countries to Africa. Africa's aid dependence was such that almost all the major development projects in the region were aid driven and were expected to be funded largely externally. But, if anything, it is the failure of aid to finance real development and socioeconomic transformation that the development experience of Africa has amply demonstrated. A major reason for the failure is the form in which foreign aid has been provided. For example, almost a quarter of the official development assistance (ODA) resources is absorbed by technical assistance. It is now increasingly acknowledged, even by donors, that the proportion of aid to Africa in the form of technical assistance is rather excessive, and that reliance on this type of aid may be counterproductive at a time when Africa is undergoing a severe brain drain and gross underutilization of some of its most qualified and experienced personnel. Aid, if it is to be effective in fostering Africa's growth and development, should be provided quickly and efficiently, and targeted more toward raising indigenous African human and institutional capacities.

The other means through which the quality and modality of aid to Africa could be improved includes those recommended in the APPER and the United Nations Program of Action for African Economic Recovery and Development (UN-PAAERD): greater emphasis on program support in the priority areas of the recipient African countries, speedier disbursement of funds, and more consideration of the recurrent and local costs of programs and projects. Unfortunately, there has been a hardening of the terms of concessional flows from the DAC countries thus compounding development financing problems of recipient African countries.

Obviously, the time has come for serious reconsideration of the mentality of aid dependence in Africa, and the whole issue of the role and effectiveness of foreign aid in the region's development process. Clearer thinking as to how best to meet the foreign exchange needs of Africa in the context of development financing is needed. In a situation, such as that in the African region, in which the transformation of domestic savings into domestic investment cannot always proceed without imported inputs of intermediate and capital goods, the savings-investment process is always hostage to the availability of foreign exchange, and the long-term future must consist, in part, in the diversification of production to rectify the structural limitations imposed by lack of an endogenous supply of intermediate and capital goods.

With regard to private direct foreign investment, Africa has not been able to obtain any significant amount of capital flows in this form. Total private direct investment resource flows into the region are estimated at less than $2 billion annually. And the indications are that foreign private investment declined noticeably in all sectors in Africa in the 1980s, except perhaps in a few countries. The general perception of Africa as a continent characterized by political instability and a hostile investment and business environment, coupled with an increasingly unsustainable debt burden, has tended to reduce the attractiveness of the region for this type of capital flow.

The inadequacy of aid and private investment resource flows for the financing of Africa's growth and development has forced the region to depend excessively on external loans which, in turn, has led to a debt crisis. Undoubtedly, the most serious issue now in Africa's development finance is the debt overhang. This phenomenon poses the greatest threat to Africa's economic recovery, and it has become increasingly clear that very little progress can be made without the resolution of the debt crisis. There is no way Africa can service its existing debt and still have resources left for development financing.

Estimated at only $8 billion in 1970, the total external debt of Africa had by 1989 risen to $256.9 billion. In 1989, the debt amounted to roughly 80 percent of the total gross domestic product (GDP) of the region. Measured in current U.S. dollars, total debt at the end of 1989 was nearly thirty-two times its level in 1970. Correspondingly, debt-service payments by African countries grew from less than $1 billion in 1970 to $25.3 billion in 1989, while the average debt-service ratio rose from 8 percent in 1970 to 32.2 percent in 1989. This means that out of total export earnings of $61.4 billion in 1989, only about $41.6 billion remained available for Africa's requirements other than debt services.

Africa's external debt problem had worsened further in 1990. Data available at the ECA indicate that the stock of debt may have grown by about 4.7 percent to reach $271.9 billion in 1990, almost equivalent to the combined GDP of the region and representing about 3.2 times the value of its exports of goods and services. Debt-service obligations have also continued to be high, amounting, on average, to about 34 percent of exports of goods and services in 1990.

The problem with Africa's debt lies not so much in its magnitude as in the maturity profile, the unmanageable debt-service obligations, and the speed with which the debt has been escalating. A high proportion of the debt, particularly that of the middle-income African countries, was contracted short-term at variable rates of interest from the capital markets in the late 1970s and early 1980s. Given the strange notion or concept of underborrowing espoused by the international multilateral development finance institutions at that time, many African nations, such as Nigeria, were induced to extend their indebtedness and borrowing capacity in the belief that they were grossly underborrowed. Awash with OPEC surplus funds, the market was all too willing to lend. The low-income African countries, which had no access to international capital markets owing to lack of creditworthiness, increased their borrowing from official multilateral and bilateral sources. The share of the Bretton Woods institutions in the total debt of Africa now stands at over 25 percent, while about 40 percent of the debt-service payment goes to these institutions. These debts have neither been rescheduled nor written off. The efforts that have so far been made to solve the problem of multilateral debt have been directed, not at reduction of the stock of the debt but at providing additional resources to enable African debtor countries to refinance the interest service charges on the arrears.

As clearly stated by African heads of state and government in the *African Common Position on Africa's External Debt Crisis*, Africa's external debt and excessive debt-service payments are major impediments to the full implementation of the Africa's Priority Program of Economic Recovery. The current reality in Africa, in so far as the debt burden is concerned, is the increasing inability of the continent to service its debt. It is therefore important to get at the root causes of the debt crisis if a just and durable solution is to be found for it.

Among the causes of Africa's debt crisis have been the persistent economic crisis and the dismal economic performance that dogged the region throughout the decade of the 1980s. These were reflected in the consistently low and sometimes negative growth in the productive sectors, and, successive droughts and creeping desertification, leading to increasing degradation of the environment. Added to this is the persistence of inherited colonial economic structures, with a narrow productive base, even decades after independence. Another factor has been inefficient domestic policies, particularly poor debt management. Much of the region's debt was contracted for projects and programs that had little or no capability of enhancing the ability of the debtors to repay. A high proportion actually went into the financing of consumption and "white elephant" projects.

But by far the most significant cause has been adverse changes in the international economic environment. Examples are rising real interest rates, which have increased the burden of debt servicing, and the collapse of commodity prices, which resulted in sharp reductions in export earnings, even in some cases when export volumes increased. Indeed, it was in the face of the collapse of commodity prices that many African countries resorted to heavy external borrowing to sustain existing levels of expenditure. Since the debt crisis is primarily the by-product of the collapse of prices in commodity markets, a long-term resolution must include more serious efforts at addressing the commodity problem. This is the linkage that the ECA has sought to establish over the years.

For too long, undue emphasis has been placed on external resources for financing of Africa's growth and development. The uncertainties and difficulties surrounding external financing would seem to suggest that, in the long run, the primary source of financing for self-sustaining African development will remain the domestic resources. Unfortunately, while the need for domestic financing of development is becoming more pressing, the capacity of African countries to mobilize their resources appears to be weakening and constantly eroding. This is one of the many paradoxes of the 1980s. Thus, the way forward in Africa would depend on whether the lessons of the bitter experience with shortfalls in external financing in the 1980s have been learned, and whether the countries in the region are fully prepared to brace themselves for a return to the objectives and priorities of the Lagos Plan of Action, and for a full and effective implementation of that plan in all its aspects, together with such complementary and supplementary agendas as the AAF-SAP and the African Charter for Popular Participation.

Critical issues in Africa's development financing in the 1990s and beyond are development of the internal capacity and capability to maneuver and to respond to change; to effect quick adjustments to external shocks; and, to master the strategy of managing external economic relations—monetary, trade, and financial—with the rest of the world. All the new elements of the global economic order, ranging from the tendencies toward regional blocs and the changes in Eastern Europe and their possible impact on investment and resource flows to the establishment of a single European market in 1992, pose enormous challenges to African development. One thing is certain, the relatively more attractive investment environment provided by these developments is likely to divert attention away from Africa, thereby further marginalizing it in the world economy amid growing integration and globalization of markets, financial institutions, and services.

Although there is now a general awareness in Africa that domestic resource mobilization should constitute the hub of development financing, the efforts of the region in the mobilization of domestic savings, the development of financial intermediation, and in the effective utilization of resources have been far from encouraging. Domestic savings and investment are essential for transforming the resources of developing countries into real wealth. But, in Africa, the savings ratios have been generally low and have shown only a modest increase in recent years in the vast majority of the countries, from 12.4 percent in 1960 for the region as a whole to the peak of 18.6 percent in 1980, following which it fell to 16.8 percent in 1985 before rising to 17.5 percent in 1988. Even the major oil exporters (Algeria, Gabon, Libyan Arab Jamahiriya, and Nigeria) that were able to raise their savings from about 13.5 percent of GDP in 1960 to 35.1 percent in 1980 have since the mid-1980s experienced a significant diminution in their capacity to save. Both the public and private sectors in Africa have contributed to the dismal performance in resource mobilization, but the fall has been more precipitous for the public sector. The savings rate for the African least-developed countries, after an initial increase from 6.6 percent in 1960 to 10.3 percent in 1970, has declined markedly in the 1980s, falling to about 4.9 percent in 1988.

The capacity for financial intermediation in Africa remains very limited. Well-developed financial institutions (for example, stock exchanges, modern savings and loan associations, commercial and development banks) are still grossly inadequate. African financial institutional structures that were originally designed and conceived essentially for the needs of a colonial economy have, in most cases, still to undergo the fundamental restructuring and reform that would make them effective instruments of national development. The duality of the African financial structures, as exemplified by the demarcation of formal (modern) and informal (traditional) financial sectors, has persisted, to the detriment of domestic resource mobilization and utilization.

Neither has effective mobilization of domestic resources for development been helped by the excessive and continuing foreign exchange leakages characteristic of most African countries. The leakages are effected largely through such trade malpractices as underinvoicing of exports and overinvoicing of imports. At the beginning of the 1980s, the magnitude of resources involved in financial leakages in Africa was about $3.5 billion a year in respect of merchandise trade and $2.5 billion a year in respect of invisible transactions. For the three African countries—Côte d'Ivoire, Morocco, and Nigeria—which are part of the Baker 15 most-indebted countries—capital flight was estimated at $23 billion in 1987. It is easy to imagine the contribution resources of this magnitude could have made to the financing of African economic growth and development had the leakages been plugged. But the level of capital flight and of foreign exchange leakages from Africa has been rising not diminishing over the years. Whatever the reasons, and these could be anything from corruption to business and political uncertainties, the eventual repatriation of funds now lodged by Africans in the developed-country banks or stock markets must be one strong element of any future strategy aimed at revamping the development financing profile of African countries. This emphasizes, in part, the role of an enabling environment in Africa of which effective governance, public accountability, pluralism, the mobilization and empowerment of the people, popular participation in all aspects of the development process, and sound macroeconomic management are only a part.

The allocation and utilization of resources often also leaves much to be desired in many African countries. Available resources—be they financial, physical, or human—are far from being always productively and efficiently utilized in most African countries, and resource allocations do not always match or reflect stated goals and priorities. Military expenditures, for example, loomed large in the African budgets in the 1980s, and more resources went into waging conflicts, civil wars, and internal strifes on the continent than to education and health. There can be little doubt that one of the greatest challenges facing Africa in the 1990s is efficient management of the economy with the highest standards of integrity and efficient use of available resources.

Outlook for Development Financing in Africa

The outlook for development financing in Africa is particularly grim in the short term. Indeed, the prognosis for 1991–92 is for the fiscal situation to get much worse rather than improve, given the emerging global trends and amid the volatilities and uncertainties surrounding the prospects for Africa's exports.

The key determinant of domestic savings, both private and public, is the level of income. For most African countries, the declining trend in output and income that set in since the early 1980s will persist in 1991–92. In the few African countries where modest growth of national output might be achieved, per capita income growth is likely to remain low or negative owing to population pressure.

Under the grave international conditions that are likely to prevail in 1991, the demand for Africa's exports is likely to be further adversely affected, with prices of most primary commodities, including metals and beverages, posting further declines, and thus dampening the growth momentum of the region. With the stockpiling and expansion in oil production that have already taken place following the Gulf crisis, even the petroleum exporting countries of Africa may not be spared the specter of declining export earnings, as the petroleum market is likely to face a market situation of extreme glut, with prices falling even below pre-Gulf crisis levels. Even without the Gulf crisis, the slowdown in economic activity would, in all probability, have continued for the third year in a row in the countries of the Organization for Economic Cooperation and Development (OECD), especially in view of the expected recession in the United States and the almost disappearing Euro-optimism induced by the new economic opportunities presented to Western Europe by the enormous changes taking place in Eastern Europe. Based on the significant slowdown that has already taken place in economic activity in the advanced industrial economies in 1990, the Gulf crisis may very well ensure that these economies enter a full-blown recession in 1991. Thus, it is more likely that the foreign exchange constraint on development, particularly the resource requirements for sustaining higher levels of import, would prove to be tight for the oil exporting African countries in 1991–92, and decidedly even tighter for the non-oil exporting ones unless there are significant improvements in the international economic environment early in the year, including tangible progress on the commodities issue and the problem of debt overhang.

For the medium and long term, the projections of the ECA,[2] based on current trends, indicate that GDP would increase by not more than an annual average of 1.6 percent during the period from 1990 to 2008. Given this projected rate and that of population growth, per capita income would decline by 0.7 percent yearly over the entire period. As in the past, the poor growth performance is expected to have significant implications for the level of savings and the structure of demand. Private consumption and public expenditure are projected to rise at the rates of 0.9 and 3 percent, respectively. Poor economic growth performance has in the past inhibited capital formation. This trend is expected to continue. Investment is projected to decline by 4 percent, as was observed during the period from 1981 to 1987. With an assumed savings ratio of 10 percent, based on the anticipated declining trends in income, the investment-savings gap for Africa under the historical scenario is projected to reach 6 percent by the year 2008.

Prospects are also gloomy with regard to foreign exchange earnings. Since 1989, growth has slowed in the developed industrial countries, with adverse consequences for the growth of world trade, particularly the trade

---

[2]See United Nations, Economic Commission for Africa (ECA), *Beyond Recovery: ECA—Revised Perspectives of Africa's Development, 1988–2008* (Addis Ababa, 1988).

of developing countries. The by-product of the contraction of output in the developed countries has been a generalized decline in the demand for African exports. Demand for African exports is further limited by rapid advances in the technology of synthetics and substitutes.

A worsening of the international environment is projected for African exports, as growth in the developed industrial countries is expected to decline even further in the 1990s and beyond. Increasing protectionism in the OECD countries could worsen the African trade problem as access to markets for African primary and processed goods is curtailed. Already, the limited preferences being enjoyed by the African, Caribbean, and Pacific (ACP) countries in the European Community (EC) under the Lomé Convention have been eroded as a result of concessions made by the Community in General Agreement on Tariffs and Trade (GATT) negotiations. The raising of technical standards in the single European market after 1992 would constitute formidable barriers to African manufactured and some of its traditional export products.

Given the expected deterioration in the international market environment, the historical trend projections of a decline of 3.5 percent a year in the export unit value index is assumed to prevail, bringing down the index to as low as 59.6 by the year 2008 (1980 + 100). The import price index, on the other hand, is expected to be 94.8 (1980 + 100), while the terms of trade index (1980 + 100) will decline to 62.8 by the year 2008. Poor export performance, the deterioration in terms of trade, and debt-service obligations would, as in the past, lead to a compression of imports, the f.o.b. value of which is projected to be $68.9 billion in nominal terms in 2008. With the value of exports estimated at $51.7 billion, the projected trade deficit in the year 2008 is $17.2 billion.

Africa has always had chronic balance of payments difficulties. Since 1985, for example, the current account balance has consistently been in deficit, although the magnitude has fluctuated from year to year. The service account of African countries is unlikely to improve. On the contrary, all the evidence points to a worsening of the deficit on this account, given the increasing debt-service obligations and the known weak capacity of the African region to service its external trade. On the basis of the historical trends scenario, Africa's current account deficit is projected to increase to $41.9 billion in 2008. This is the magnitude of foreign exchange gap that will need to be financed by changes in reserves and inflow of external resources.

At best, and based on past experience, changes in reserves will cover roughly 10 percent of the projected deficit thus leaving still a large proportion to be financed with inflow of external resources. Given the emerging international socioeconomic and geopolitical order and trends, and the increasingly stiff conditionalities—some economic, some political—attached to whatever limited resource flows there are to Africa, the inescapable conclusion is that it will be difficult to mobilize external resources large enough to fill the gap. Past experience does not certainly justify or warrant optimism in this respect, judging from the disappointing low level of performance and assistance with respect to external financing under UN-PAAERD.[3] Already, the main priority interests and preoccupation of the industrial countries of the OECD, the principal source of external resources to Africa, would seem to have shifted to the emerging democracies of Eastern Europe, and there is a growing possibility that some of the external resources that could have been channeled to the flagging economies of Africa will in future years be diverted to Eastern Europe.

Assuming that net foreign direct investment grows in line with the historical rate of 5 percent following the stagnation and decline prevailing in the 1980s, and allowing for the modest financing of current account deficit through depletion of reserves, Africa would still have to contract new loans ranging from $30 billion to $40 billion a year to close the gap between total resource requirements and resource availability. As indicated earlier, not only has the level of resource flows to Africa stagnated, but also the terms under which the resources are made available have tended to worsen. If the same structure and modalities relating to terms and conditions of finance were to continue to the year 2008, Africa, in spite of its diminishing creditworthiness, would be compelled in desperation to make greater recourse to the capital market, thus further deepening its debt and development crisis. By the year 2008, the stock of Africa's debt is projected to reach $362.7 billion, while the debt-service burden is expected to increase to 40–45 percent of export earnings from the ratio of 34 percent in 1990.

The picture that emerges from the historical trends scenario is that of an Africa characterized by slow growth, increasing poverty, and huge investment-savings and foreign exchange gaps. It is a region that will be faced with intractable development financing problems and be trapped in structural indebtedness.

---

[3] For the details, see United Nations, Secretary General, *Mid-Term Review of the Implementation of the United Nations Programme of Action for African Economic Recovery and Development, 1986–1990, Report of the Secretary-General* (New York, August 1988).

But this dismal picture and the ominous outlook for African development financing need not be inevitable under a normative development scenario, the basic underlying assumption of which is that the African countries will in the 1990s and beyond adhere strictly to the guidelines for economic recovery and accelerated development as enunciated in the LPA, AAF-SAP, and the African Charter for Popular Participation in Development. Further, the scenario assumes radical changes and improvements in the structures of production and demand, and in the international economic environment. Under the normative scenario, it is expected that African countries will aim at full utilization of their natural resource base through the development of relevant human capital and institutional infrastructure and the creation of indigenous technological capabilities; that private consumption will be restrained from rising faster than the GDP so that substantial amounts of domestic savings could be generated; that consumption structure will be rationalized in favor of domestic products as against imports; that African markets will be integrated; that adequate and sustainable growth will be generated in the OECD countries to induce substantial increase in the demand for African exports; and, that there will be significant improvements in international economic and monetary systems to make them more mutually beneficial to the developed and developing countries.

It is obvious that the assumptions of the normative development scenario are heroic. The ifs are many and powerful, but they are not unrealizable, and indeed if they are realized, GDP will, according to ECA projections, grow by 5.7 percent a year over the period from 1990 to 2008; investment will rise by 9 percent a year and approach 30 percent of GDP, while the savings ratio will reach between 20 and 25 percent. Under the normative scenario, overall deficit on the current account of the balance of payments is expected to improve significantly with the deficit amounting to only $16.7 billion in 2008 as compared with a level of $41.9 billion projected on the basis of historical trends. The relatively good growth performance of African economies will lead to a sustained increase in resource flows, mainly in the form of direct foreign investment. Finally, debt service will be within manageable proportions and external debt will cease to be a real development burden for Africa.

The wind of political and economic changes blowing through Africa should, if sustained, have a positive impact on its development process in the medium to long term. For example, the implementation of AAF-SAP should engender faster growth through more efficient mobilization and utilization of resources. Also, the ongoing democratization processes and the upsurge of political reforms could lead to greater and more effective harnessing of human and material resources, to greater popular participation and political stability and, hence, a more suitable environment for inflow of foreign investment and the repatriation of flight capital.

Policy Implications and Policy Agenda

From the foregoing analysis, it is obvious that the major challenges of development financing in Africa are how to galvanize the economy and the domestic financial structures so that they can respond more effectively to Africa's resource needs, and how to ensure that economic, trade, and financial relations of the region with the rest of the world serve as a driving force for national, subregional, and regional development and the overriding goal of socioeconomic transformation. What is the necessary policy agenda for meeting these challenges, and for laying the foundations of a genuine process of self-sustaining and self-reliant growth and socioeconomic transformation in Africa as envisaged under a normative development scenario? This is the critical question that this section attempts to answer.

Future orientation in policy must center on the strengthening and building of financial institutions and the designing and implementation of new strategies for effective domestic resource mobilization and utilization. But it must also involve changes in the international economic environment, including a speedy resolution of the debt crisis, as well as more serious attempts to deal with the problems of declining export earnings and stagnating capital flows; all of which have, in the past, combined to reduce drastically the continent's ability to promote recovery, not to talk of pursuing a long-term development strategy.

At the domestic level, there will have to be improvements in fiscal and monetary management, aimed principally at generating larger recurrent budget surpluses, reducing inflationary pressures, and enhancing the quality of investment in the public and private sectors. Greater emphasis will have to be placed on projects that rely more on domestic resources and less on foreign resources. Measures will also have to be undertaken to substantially upgrade the level of financial management, investment planning and administrative capacity, and to strengthen key implementation and monitoring mechanisms. The public enterprise sector, in particular, will have to be improved and reinforced in order to ensure that it contributes significantly to the financing of development rather than being a perpetual drain on the government budget.

The drive for greater public revenue mobilization must however in no way be interpreted to mean piling up of still further taxes on those already overburdened. For most countries, what is required is a significant improvement in existing taxation and tax structures, through wider coverage and more efficient assessment and collection of revenue. Efforts must be intensified to plug all financial leakages and to ensure greater efficiency and honesty in utilizing available resources. The improvements in financial management and domestic resource mobilization must be reflected in a new development ethic, and in new directions in national, subregional, and regional economic and social policies within such contexts as the LPA and AAF-SAP, and the African Charter for Popular Participation in Development. They must also be consonant with new efforts to increase the effectiveness of regional and subregional economic, financial, and monetary cooperation.

To enhance the mobilization of domestic savings for productive investment, extensive reform of the monetary and financial systems to eliminate the structural and institutional deficiencies is needed. This must include the development of a wide range of financial institutions and intermediation processes. For instance, the informal financial sector in Africa has evolved over a long time, deriving its rules and regulations from indigenous customs and traditions. Based largely on trust, it has little formality in its transactions and is free from official regulations and bureaucratic controls. In several respects, therefore, it has developed on its own steam and has turned out, not surprisingly, to be relatively efficient. Therefore, in developing strategies to promote formal and informal savings, it is essential to pay attention to the institutional structures that will effectively link the sources and uses of resources in the formal and informal financial sectors.

With improvements in financial management and domestic resource mobilization, and with greater productivity of investment and more rational and more efficient resource use, African countries may be able to overcome the investment-savings gap. But this will not necessarily eliminate completely their need for external resources. Indeed, given the current high levels of dependence of the economies on foreign technology, capital equipment, and intermediate goods and services, external resources will continue to play a vital role in Africa's development process in the foreseeable future. Hence, external resource availability is likely to remain a major constraint unless there are radical departures in production and consumption structures in Africa, as well as imminent changes in the reverse flow of resources so that Africa ceases to be a net transferor of resources to the rest of the world.

The need to increase the quantity and quality of resource flows to Africa and delink such flows and debt relief measures from the conditionality of orthodox structural adjustment programs is urgent. The rigid adherence to this type of conditionality has made it difficult for African countries to couple adjustment with either growth or equity, and it is sad that additional conditionalities of a political nature—human rights and multiparty democracy—are now being insisted upon by some donors. For years, the international community has turned a deaf ear to Africa's persistent demand for a Marshall-type aid program for the region. Now that a European Bank for Development and Reconstruction has been set up specially for Eastern Europe, in spite of the existence of the World Bank, and a similar bank is being proposed for the Middle East after the Gulf war, the time has come for the international community to examine Africa's claims more positively and to substantially increase resource flows to Africa on a stable, assured, and predictable basis.

As noted earlier, Africa's debt overhang has become the major impediment to the region's economic recovery and development. This problem calls for a comprehensive solution that takes into account the need to reduce the stock of debt and debt-servicing obligations, restore the creditworthiness of African countries, and improve their access to international capital markets. In the past, the debt strategy centered largely on the need to protect the international banking system and the creditor countries; hence the emphasis on rescheduling of matured debt repayments and due debt-service obligations, and limited conversion of International Development Association (IDA) loans to grants, a strategy that appears to have been conceived on the assumption that Africa's external debt crisis was just a "liquidity" problem and was both manageable and temporary. It has now become apparent that increased efforts must be directed at a significant and substantial reduction in the stock of Africa's debt. The cancellation of only 5 percent of Africa's stock of debt that has resulted from recent initiatives of the advanced industrial economies is not only "too late" but "too little" in comparison with Africa's debt relief needs.

Two other measures appear to be desirable. First, donor nations, as well as international lending institutions, should substantially increase quick-disbursing lending to African countries. Second, the eligibility ceiling of IDA lending should be raised to enable more African countries to qualify for such resources, while at the same time ensuring that at least 70 percent of IDA resources are earmarked for assistance to Africa.

Africa's debt and development crises have to a large extent been caused by shocks from the international environment, especially the collapse of commodity prices, and there is an urgent need therefore for improvement in the global trade order[4] and for the designing of new programs to ensure that African countries receive remunerative and fair prices for their commodity exports. Agreements should be reached between producers and consumers to ensure that the prices of key commodities of export interest to Africa, namely, coffee, cocoa, tea, sugar, rubber, etc., do not fall below agreed "floor" levels. In this regard, the establishment of the common fund for the stabilization of prices of major commodity exports is to be welcomed. It must be stressed however that the fund, as presently constituted, is grossly inadequate and may turn out to be difficult and cumbersome to operate. Of equal importance to Africa's economic recovery and self-sustaining growth and development is the need to encourage product diversification and the processing of the region's primary commodities through a guarantee of unrestricted market access for such commodities by the industrial importing countries, and expansion in demand for Africa's exports through pursuit of growth-oriented policies in those countries. These and other measures for stimulating the growth of African exports are as important as the initiatives for reducing the burden of debt and debt servicing, and for encouraging a substantial increase in the flow of resources to Africa.

---

[4] Neither the recent Report of the High-Level Group of Experts on African Commodity Problems under the chairmanship of the former Prime Minister of Australia, the Right Honorable Malcolm Fraser nor the yet inconclusive Uruguay Round of talks have managed to fully address this issue from the perspectives of the African countries. For "Africa's Common Position" on commodity issues and problems, see United Nations, Expert Group on Africa's Commodity Problems, *Africa's Commodity Problems: Towards a Solution* (Geneva, 1990).

Discussants

Resource Gaps and Financing for Growth in Africa

Benno J. Ndulu*

Sustained growth is associated with an economic structure that can respond flexibly to exogenous shocks and with an indigenous capacity that can manage change effectively. In this context, the record of African economies has been mixed over the past three decades. From the 1960s to the early 1970s, emphasis was placed on rapid growth. The external environment was relatively benign, and African economies focused largely on expanding output from primary sectors and developing supportive infrastructure. Industrialization was characterized by import substitution involving simple products and processes.

In the 1970s, greater emphasis was placed on structural transformation. Industrialization, entailing an expanded coverage of products and processes, was pushed strongly, often at the expense of agriculture both in terms of investment and producer incentives. Linked to this attempt at structural transformation were major investments in education, health, and urban development, although these also reflected a concern for basic needs. Sectors characterized by higher rates of growth in productivity were expected to fuel growth in the economy as a whole and also to furnish skills that were in short supply. The 1980s featured major external shocks that threatened to wipe out previous advances in living standards and in the transformation of economic structure. African governments became increasingly aware of the need for active and effective macroeconomic

---

*I am indebted to my colleague, Jeffrey Fine, for incisive comments and suggestions. Any errors are my own.

policies to stabilize economic activity and facilitate adjustment to changes in domestic and external conditions.

In the coming decade, most governments will need to develop realistic approaches to structural transformation and to revive economic growth on a sustainable basis. A central issue therefore is how growth in the capacity to produce will relate to desired changes in structure and the likely availability of finance. Important lessons can be drawn from the experience of the past three decades, and especially the last one, that will condition the prospects for growth and the strategies for financing it.

The first lesson is that a weak economic structure renders African economies vulnerable to exogenous shocks. Of particular note is the import-dependent nature of investment and production. Investment requires capital goods that are not produced domestically. As a result, domestic savings cannot be transformed into investment goods unless there is foreign exchange. Empirical investigation has also shown that imports of intermediate goods are the single most important determinant of capacity utilization. Thus variability in import capacity translates more or less directly into variability in utilization and in the expansion of productive capacity (Helleiner (1986) and Khan and Knight (1988)). Import capacity is thus fundamental to sustaining growth and development. Other attributes of a weak economic structure are rudimentary technology in agriculture, usually the dominant sector, and an institutional setting unable to respond flexibly to rapidly changing conditions.

The second arises not simply from the open nature of African economies but the fact that their ties with the developed world have tended to be procyclical, with the result that the impact of any external shock is amplified rather than dampened. The evidence of the past decade suggests that world recession weakens demand for African primary exports and reduces net resource transfers, thereby exacerbating downturns in domestic economic activity. The rise in real interest on external debt during the first half of the 1980s widened the gap between overall financing needs and resources forthcoming from foreign, as well as domestic, sources. Susceptibility to major shocks, as manifested in the deterioration in external terms of trade, greater volatility in net inflows of external resources, and increased resource transfers through external debt servicing significantly reduced the latitude for measures aimed at sustainable growth and development.

Third, African economies are characterized by a degree of government involvement in the economy that goes beyond the more conventional task of redressing market failure. In most African countries, the state has acted as the principal modernizing agent in the productive sphere as well as the key instrument for income distribution. It follows that fiscal performance is crucial not only for social welfare but also for future growth. Hence, gaps in fiscal resources and in their effective use assume a special significance.

The next section of this paper outlines the principal features of the economic crisis that emerged fully in most African countries toward the end of the 1980s. A summary of the present situation follows, which underscores the fragility of most economies, and hence the importance of pursuing policies that will sustain growth through desirable changes in economic structure. The final section poses a set of issues, in the form of policy choices, that pertain to the financing of economic activity in the coming decade.

The Economic Crisis

Sub-Saharan Africa's rate of growth started to decelerate in the latter half of the 1970s. This rate of decline worsened during the first half of the 1980s (Table 1) and can be attributed to a combination of exogenous shocks and misdirected policies. Here though, we highlight only those aspects bearing on our concern with the financing of and likely constraints to future economic growth.

Key among the exogenous shocks were the deterioration in the external terms of trade, cuts in the net inflow of external resources, and a rise in real interest on foreign debt. The collapse of primary commodity prices and rise in import prices between 1978 and 1980 resulted in a rapid deterioration in the external terms of trade for African countries, with the exception of a few oil exporters. The barter terms of trade for sub-Saharan Africa dropped annually by 4.2 percent between 1980–87. The income terms of trade declined even faster at 5.8 percent annually since the output of exports was dropping each year by 1.6 percent. After 1985, growth of 1 percent in the output of agricultural exports was more than offset by an annual decline in the barter terms of trade, leading a further drop in the income terms of trade of 7.3 percent annually between 1985 and 1988 (Ndulu (1990)).

Foreign savings, defined as the deficit on the current account plus net unrequited transfers, fell drastically as a proportion of gross domestic product (GDP) during the first half of the 1980s. From an average of 11 percent of GDP in 1980/81, it declined to 6.6 percent in 1985, a drop of 40 percent (Table 2). When adjusted for the rise in the real rate of

Table 1. Basic Economic Indicators for Sub-Saharan Africa in Growth Terms
(In percent)

	1965–73	1973–80	1980–87	1980–85	1985–87/88
Gross domestic product					
Total	5.9	2.5	0.5	0.13	1.7
Per capita GNP	3.1	0.5	–2.9	–3.7	–1.5
Total consumption per capita	1.9	0.5	–3.4	–2.6	–7.3
Private consumption					
Total	3.9	2.6	1.1		
Per capita	1.3	–0.2	–2.0		
Public consumption					
Total	9.0	7.0	–0.7		
Investment	9.8	4.0	–8.2		
Exports volume (total)	15.1	0.2	–3.6	–3.9	–2.6
Agricultural exports		–0.8	–1.6	–2.6	1.0
Imports volume	3.7	7.6	–7.1	–7.8	–5.3
Agriculture	2.2	–0.3	1.3	–0.1	1.6
Manufacturing	10.1	8.2	0.6		
Implicit GDP deflator	7.5	6.8	15.2		

Sources: The World Bank, *Sub-Saharan Africa: From Crisis to Sustainable Growth*; and *African Economic and Financial Statistics* (Washington, 1989).

interest on the foreign debt, foreign savings declined even more steeply, from 8.2 percent of GDP in 1980/81 to 3.7 percent in 1985, a cut of 55 percent (Table 2).

Two serious misdirections in policy can be associated with economic stagnation during this period. The first was misguided investment policies, which caused a decline in the return to investment, the reason being that while foreign resources had played a significant role in financing an *expansion* in capacity, the *rate* of capacity *utilization* depended mostly on domestically mobilized resources, which grew much more slowly. The steep decline observed in capacity utilization over the past decade and a half is partly attributable to this mismatch between domestic and external flows of financial resources and largely explains the very disturbing drop in the productivity of investment from an average of 83.8 percent between 1961 and 1973 to only 6.2 percent during 1980–87 (World Bank (1989a)). Thus, respectable rates of investment in sub-Saharan Africa, averaging over 20 percent of GDP between 1973 and 1980, never yielded the anticipated contribution to real growth. The second misdirection per-

Table 2. Resource Gaps Closure in Sub-Saharan Africa, 1980–87
(In percent)

	FORSAV/ GDP	AFORSAV/ GDP	FD/GDP	RIM/GDP	NOTG/ FD	DCR Growth
1980	9.5	7.4	−9.5	26.8	28.9	21.1
1981	11.6	8.9	−10.8	24.7	26.8	21.9
1982	11.5	8.8	−11.6	23.3	23.5	20.9
1983	9.1	6.5	−10.4	20.9	31.1	17.0
1984	6.8	3.8	−10.2	19.8	33.3	12.0
1985	6.6	3.7	−10.9	19.6	31.0	16.2
1986	9.0	—	−11.4	19.8	32.3	15.5
1987	—	—	−11.4	19.3	33.9	—

Sources: The World Bank, *Sub-Saharan Africa: From Crisis to Sustainable Growth*; and *African Economic and Financial Statistics* (Washington, 1989).

Note: FORSAV = Foreign savings = Negative of current account balance plus unrequited net transfers; AFORSAV = FORSAV less interest payment on foreign debt (foreign saving available for current use); FD = Overall fiscal deficit (excluding grants); RIM = Real imports; NOTG = Net official transfers to the government; DCR = Domestic credit.

tains to macroeconomic policy. Although most governments eventually reacted to the crisis with major changes in macroeconomic policy, many of them, at least initially, believed that the shocks their economies were experiencing were temporary. As a result, these governments borrowed heavily from domestic and external sources to maintain real economic activity and consumption and did not meaningfully address underlying distortions in incentives and major rigidities in their economies. In retrospect, these two policy failures aggravated the adverse effects of external shocks to which African economies have been singularly vulnerable.

In terms of resource gaps, the crisis manifested itself in three ways. First, there was a rapid decline in the gross domestic savings rate from 22 percent in 1980 to 12.6 percent in 1985. Coupled with a decline in foreign savings (Table 3), this trend caused a steep cut in domestic investment from 20.2 percent in 1980 to 12.1 percent in 1985. Although investment then recovered to 16 percent of GDP between 1985–87, there was only a negligible rise in domestic savings of 0.4 percent to about 13 percent. As a result, not only growth but even the *maintenance* of economic activity became directly dependent on the vagaries of foreign resource inflows. Although some governments tried to respond through inflation taxation, this strategy proved untenable in political and economical terms.

Second, owing to the import-dependent nature of African economies, the decline in export earnings and the steep fall in foreign resource inflows

Table 3. Evolution of Resource Gaps: Sub-Saharan Africa 1965–87
(In percent)

	1965	1980	1985	1987
Gross domestic investment/GDP	14	20.2	12.1	16
Excluding Nigeria	15	20.0	15.7	16
Gross domestic saving/GDP	14	22.0	12.6	13
Excluding Nigeria	15	14.3	13.8	11
Fiscal deficit (excl. grants)/GDP	—	–9.6	–10.6	–11.4
Excluding Nigeria	—	–9.9	–10.9	–11.8
Import surplus ratio (imports/exports)	106	89	78	111
Excluding Nigeria	106	115	90	112

Sources: The World Bank, *Sub-Saharan Africa: From Crisis to Sustainable Growth*; and *African Economic and Financial Statistics* (Washington, 1989).

during the first half of the 1980s led to a decline in production, investment, and consumption. Import volumes were cut back at an annual rate of 7.8 percent between 1980–85 (Table 1). These cuts were disproportionately larger for consumer and intermediate imports because official foreign assistance was still largely limited to the financing of projects. The resultant steep decline in capacity utilization in import-dependent sectors led to a continuing fall in real output and growth. In the absence of additional external financing, the only means of closing this resource gap was to cut real domestic activity.

Third, the resource balance on the fiscal side deteriorated badly. The tax base shrank because of the decline in the growth in incomes and a rise in tax evasion. The growth in public sector revenues fell drastically behind that of expenditures. Between 1980 and 1982, the fiscal deficit jumped quickly from 9.9 percent of GDP to 11.6 percent. It was financed by continued inflows of foreign resources and by inflation taxation (Table 3). Between 1982 and 1985, the fiscal deficit did contract, but more as a result of massive cuts in expenditure rather than increases in revenue. From an average of 7.4 percent of total expenditure between 1980 and 1984, government interest payments rose to 13.3 percent in 1985–87. The share of expenditures available for real discretionary spending, net of interest payments, dropped between 1980 and 1987, with the steepest decline occurring during 1982–84. In per capita terms, the decline was even steeper (Ndulu (forthcoming)). These cuts translated into a virtual halting of scheduled investment in new infrastructure, a deterioration in the existing stock, and cuts in the delivery of social services. Since 1985, the fiscal deficit, exclusive of external grants, has widened, reflecting some recovery in public expenditures that has been largely financed by foreign grants, which are noninflationary.

Observations Concerning the Present Situation

The past four years have seen African countries shift away from policies aimed at closing resource gaps solely through recessionary measures to those that combine stabilization with growth. Five preliminary observations can be drawn from their experience to date.

(1) The revival in growth over the last four years has been very fragile. Good rains and external resource inflows largely account for the concurrent improvement in growth and reduction in internal and external imbalances that has been observed in some countries.

(2) Although revamped incentive structures have led to modest increases in output, these have been small and slow because of the poor condition of supportive infrastructure, which had deteriorated badly during prolonged economic crisis. Revival of economic activity will take time and its encouragement, through sustained financing of investment in supportive infrastructure and the application of appropriate incentives, will be necessary.

(3) Foreign resources will be needed for two other reasons. First, continued deterioration in the external terms of trade has significantly reduced the benefit forthcoming from adjustment measures. Second, servicing of the foreign debt constitutes a large leakage of resources otherwise available for financing growth and development.

(4) Although an expanded inflow of external resources is essential to initiate economic recovery, growth over the longer term can only be sustained through the effective mobilization of own resources. Furthermore, since economic performance is so sensitive to variations in import capacity, a fundamental improvement in export performance is essential.

(5) The difficulty of financing the external debt through surpluses on the trade account will likely be compounded by the need to transfer such surpluses internally to government, which must service virtually all of the debt. Governments may have to run fiscal surpluses (apart from their interest obligations) to meet these requirements and may therefore end up cutting badly needed programs to rehabilitate supportive and social infrastructure. This outcome would have serious adverse consequences for long-term growth. Although currently confronting only middle-income oil importers in sub-Saharan Africa, this "double transfer" problem would

result in a shift from "real" external constraints to "financial" ones (Taylor (1990)) in other debt-ridden African countries during the 1990s.

Issues for the Nineties

We conclude by examining four issues, posed in the form of policy choices, that will bear directly on efforts of African governments and donors to revive and sustain economic growth in the coming decade.

To What Extent Will Growth Potential Be Constrained by Inadequate Finance or by Its Ineffective Use?

African economies have experienced a precipitous fall in real growth rates in spite of considerable investment and earnest attempts at structural transformation. The mobilization of adequate financial resources, from domestic and foreign sources, will clearly be important. However, our preceding discussion of the African experience has also illustrated the critical importance of using such resources much more efficiently than has been the case hitherto. Governments must pursue macroeconomic policies and apply incentives that raise the effectiveness of financial resources, which will be in short supply (Killick (1990)). Africa simply cannot afford to waste these scarce resources.

Should Financing Policy Give Priority to Expanding Capacity or to Making Better Use of Previous Investments?

Much of the capital stock in African economies lies idle or is seriously underutilized. Foreign exchange will be in short supply. In most cases, countries must choose whether to use foreign exchange to reactivate this idle capacity or expand existing capacity. Recent empirical evidence from five African countries' economies, namely, Nigeria, Tanzania, Uganda, Zambia, and Zimbabwe (Taylor (1990)), suggests that external finance will generate much greater returns if it is used to improve utilization rather than expand capacity.

While caution should be exercised so as not to revive bad projects, available evidence does suggest the desirability of first exploiting the presence of idle capacity over the medium term. Other activities should complement this approach in order to remove operational bottlenecks, so as to first exploit the potential benefits of earlier investment. For donors this strategy implies greater fungibility in their assistance by relaxing stipulations that direct it mainly toward project financing and link import support strictly to those investments financed by them in the past.

Does Emphasis on Sustained Growth Necessarily Imply Sacrificing Redistributive Aims?

The African experience suggests that a redistributive policy that is not founded on the growth of real economic activity cannot be sustained. This contention does not imply the obverse, namely, that growth alone will alleviate poverty through a so-called trickle-down effect. There is in fact strong empirical evidence to the contrary (Kanbur (1987)). The economic crisis of the past decade has, however, clearly illustrated that unless the real resource base is growing, governments will be forced to cut the delivery of essential social services and will eventually lack the capacity to respond to a growing demand for public goods and services over the longer term. Very recent evidence suggests that public expenditure can be restructured so that governments can promote rapid growth and at the same time finance programs targeted toward the poor in order to relieve poverty (United Nations Development Program (1990)). While external resources will clearly be helpful in this regard, the feasibility of pursuing these dual aims will depend on whether scarce financial resources are being used to revive growth in the most efficient way possible.

What, in the Final Analysis, Is Africa's Potential for Growth?

The answer depends in part on the time frame under consideration. The modest projection of 3.2 percent a year set out in a major IBRD study for 1988–95 (World Bank (1989a)) is belied by the actual performance of some countries that are recovering at rates in excess of 6 percent annually over the past two years. Projections of such high growth rates over the medium term, that is, five years may not be unreasonable in light of the considerable latent capacity lying idle in many African economies. While projected rates should be lower over the longer term, because growth in production will depend increasingly on investment in additional capacity, reference to the historical record alone may understate Africa's growth potential. Assuming a more benign international environment and the consistent application of a more coherent set of sound economic policies, African economies should be able to grow at rates comparable to other regions of the developing world.

Bibliography

Helleiner, G.K., "Outward Orientation, Import Instability and African Economic Growth: An Empirical Investigation" in Sanjay Lall and Francis Stewart, *Theory and Reality in Development* (New York: St. Martin's Press, 1986).

Kanbur, S.M. Ravi, "Structural Adjustment, Macroeconomic Adjustment and Poverty: A Methodology for Analysis" *World Development*, Vol. 15, No. 2 (December 1987), pp. 1515–26.

Khan, Mohsin, and Malcolm D. Knight, "Import Compression and Export Performance in Developing Countries" *The Review of Economics and Statistics*, Vol. 70, No. 2 (May 1988), pp. 315–21.

Killick, T., "The Developmental Effectiveness of Aid to Africa" paper prepared for World Bank Symposium on African External Finance in the 1990s (1990).

Ndulu, B., "Growth and Adjustment in Sub-Saharan Africa" paper presented at the IBRD Conference on African Economic Issues, Nairobi, June 1990.

―――, "Income Distribution, Consumption Patterns and the Process of Economic Adjustment: A Reflection on Issues from the Continuing Crisis" in *Adjustment, Stagnant Economic Structures and Human Development in Africa South of the Sahara: Policy Conflicts and Alternatives,* ed. by G. A. Cornia, R. Van der Hoeven, and T. Mkandawire (UNICEF, forthcoming).

Taylor, L., "Foreign Resource Flows and Developing Country Growth" paper prepared for UNU/WIDER Conference on Medium-Term Development Strategy, Stockholm, April, 1990.

United Nations Development Programme, *Human Development Report* (Oxford University Press, 1990).

World Bank (1989a), *Sub-Saharan Africa: From Crisis to Sustainable Growth* (Washington, 1989).

―――― (1989b), *African Economic and Financial Statistics* (Washington, 1989).

Just How Important Is Finance for African Development?

Tony Killick

Evidence for the Unimportance of Finance

The paper by the Economic Commission for Africa (ECA) presents an overtly gloomy view of Africa's economic prospects, seeing difficulties on all fronts and little scope for an easing of present belt-tightening. The World Bank paper strikes a more optimistic note but it too can be read as cautionary, for it is able to arrive at a positive conclusion only on the basis of very optimistic assumptions about improvements within African countries in saving rates and in the productivity of capital. It is only on this basis that it can arrive at a financing gap to be filled through external support that is within the realm of the possible.

The case for finance in support of Africa's adjustment and development efforts can be expressed as follows. (1) There is a need to augment the limited availability of, and capacity for, domestic saving in order to achieve levels of investment necessary to sustain reasonable rates of per capita income growth. (2) External finance is also needed to augment foreign exchange earnings, so as to permit the import volumes necessary to sustain the levels of capital formation, capacity utilization, and consumer incentive goods needed for development. (3) Finance is further needed in support of adjustment programs: to ease the period of transition, reduce the social costs, and reinforce the political sustainability of the process. This case is familiar and needs no elaboration here. But should we take it for granted that finance is commonly the binding constraint on African adjustment and development? There are a number of reasons for doubting so.

First, we all know we should not equate economic growth with development. If we introduce questions about how the benefits of growth are distributed across society (and across generations), and the issues relating to human development recently emphasized by the United Nations Development Program (UNDP), the linkage between what we regard as economic progress and the availability of finance is modified, probably weakened. If we further add environmentalist concerns about the long-term sustainability of the modernization model of development, the connection becomes further attenuated. Additional doubts are generated by the limited success of IMF and World Bank financial backing for stabilization and adjustment programs in sub-Saharan Africa.[1]

Nevertheless, gross domestic product (GDP) growth is an important indicator of the pace of development; so, does the evidence bear out the proposition that finance is the binding constraint on growth in sub-Saharan Africa? On this, see Chart 1, which is a scatter diagram of the relationship in 1980–88 between gross domestic investment (GDI) and GDP growth in 27 sub-Saharan African countries.[2] No connection between the variables is evident there. Investment ratios converged around 15 percent, but the associated GDP growth rates varied from around –1 percent a year to over 5 percent. Three countries (Gabon, Niger, and Togo) maintained investment rates well above 20 percent but had negative or negligible growth. Three countries (Burundi, Cameroon, and Chad) achieved growth rates of around 5 percent on investment ratios of only 15 to 18 percent. This is naive evidence, of course, because so many other factors have an effect on growth, but it is at least suggestive and is consistent with the results of other studies, not confined to sub-Saharan Africa, which throw doubt on the power of investment to generate growth.

Its suggestiveness is reinforced by evidence on the impact of development assistance on Africa's growth and other performance indicators, summarized in Table 1. The figures speak for themselves: comparatively massive levels of aid to sub-Saharan Africa were accompanied by a far worse economic performance than for other developing countries taken as a group. Again, there are many reasons why this might be so (see below), but at the very least one must conclude that the past decade's aid has not

---

[1] Killick, Malick, and Manuel show that of all programs entered into by the IMF and sub-Saharan African governments during 1980–90, and due to be completed by the end of 1990, 48 percent broke down before their intended completion date and could not be fully drawn down.

[2] Based on data in World Bank (1990). The investment data for each country were means of the ratios in 1980 and 1988.

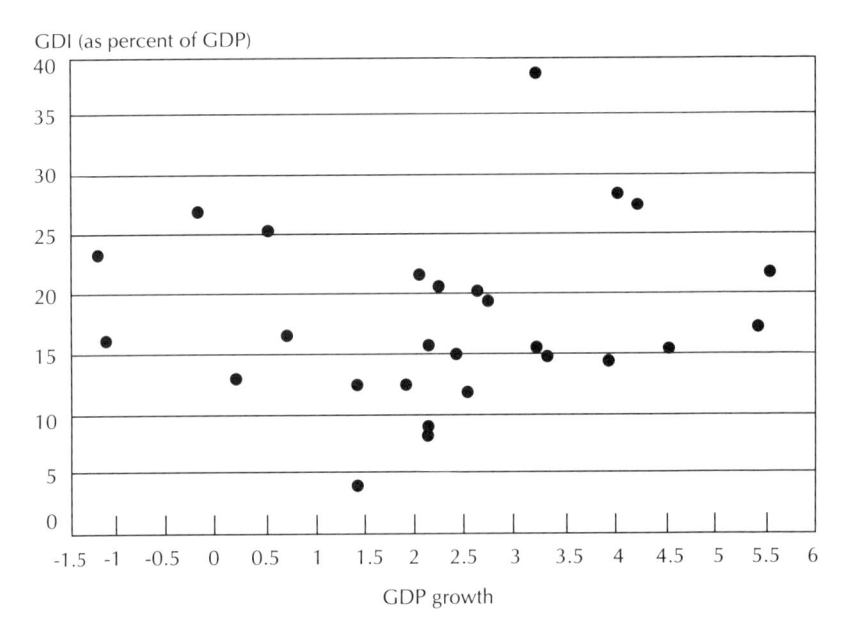

Chart 1. GDP Growth and Gross Domestic Investment, 1980–88

been strikingly effective in economic terms. Other, more sophisticated, tests point to the same conclusion. Why, in this case, might we think that yet higher levels of assistance would produce superior results?

One reason why investment may not be closely correlated with growth in sub-Saharan Africa relates to the difficulties that the very open, import-dependent economies of the region had during the 1980s in sustaining the import volumes necessary for growth, despite the comparatively massive aid inflows. Indeed, we suggested earlier that one of the cases for financial support was to augment import capacity; however, see Chart 2.

We see there that a few countries were able to achieve quite rapid GDP growth with little, if any, expansion in the volume of imports, while a few others managed to sustain quite rapid expansion of imports but achieved only slow economic growth (implying declining per capita incomes). Admittedly there is a little more sign of some correlation here, with most of the regressing economies also experiencing declining imports and most of the more rapidly growing economies achieving at least some positive import growth. Again, this kind of evidence can only be suggestive because of the need to control for the various other influences on economic

Table 1. Comparative Statistics on Aid and Economic Performance, 1980–88

	Sub-Saharan Africa	Other Developing Countries
Aid indicators[1]		
Aid per capita (*in U.S. dollars*)	21.8	5.5
Aid as percent of per capita income	4.9	0.8
Aid as percent of gross domestic investment	33.5	3.3
Aid as percent of imports	25.7	5.2
Performance indicators (annual rates of change)		
Per capita income	–6.4	+0.8
Per capita private consumption	–1.1	+0.8
Daily calorie supply per capita	–0.6	+0.8
Gross investment	–4.1	+1.8
Export volumes	–5.1	+7.3

Source: Killick (1991), based on World Bank data.
[1] Figures relate to net disbursements of overseas development assistance from all sources

growth, but it does at least suggest that the connection is not dominant, which again raises questions about the centrality of finance.[3]

There is, then, a strong conflict between the macroeconomic case for additional financial support for sub-Saharan African economies and the evidence of its past ineffectiveness. If the quantity of neither capital formation nor imports is a prime determinant of economic performance, we are led to focus instead on the *quality*, or productivity, of investment and foreign exchange utilization. This line of thought is consistent with the conclusions arrived at in the literature that investigates the sources of long-term growth in industrial and other economies, which has often found investment per se to have limited explanatory power, leaving a large unexplained residual influence, which has to do with various factors affecting the productivity of resource use. Chart 3 shows evidence of a drastic

---

[3] In a regression in which both gross investment and import growth were included as explanatory variables, neither yielded statistically significant explanatory value for GDP growth, with an R^2 of only 0.23. Note, however, that Khan and Knight (1988) did find a positive and significant correlation between import availability and developing-country export performance.

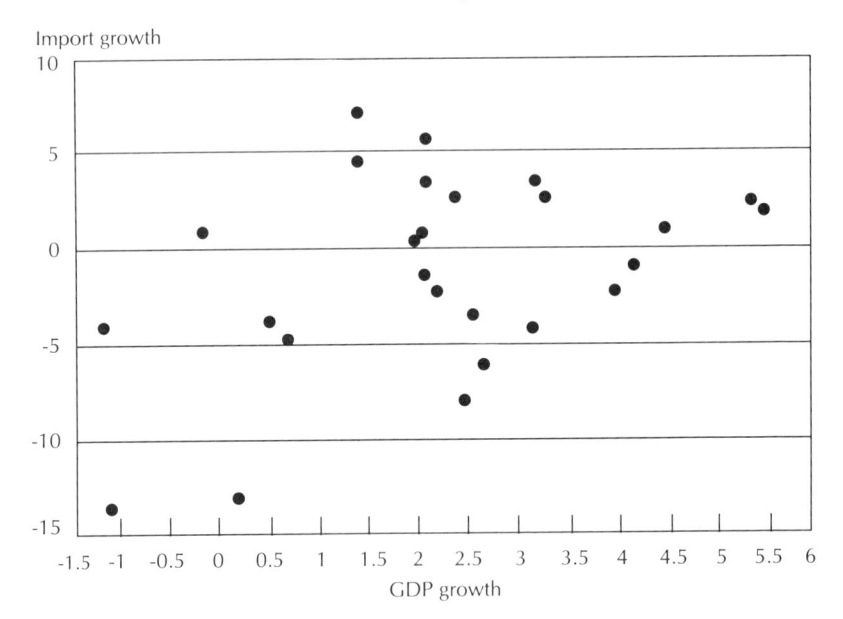

Chart 2. GDP Growth and Import Growth, 1980–88

long-term decline in the productivity of investment in sub-Saharan Africa, which is why the World Bank paper looks for a sharp reversal of this trend. So the question arises, what are the determinants of this productivity?

Influences on Resource Productivity

What might we identify as the chief influences on the productivity of investment and foreign exchange in sub-Saharan Africa? To respond to this question we draw on the results of a recent study I undertook of the developmental effectiveness of aid to that region (Killick (1991)). The discussion was organized around a distinction between factors primarily located within recipient countries, which were broken down into (1) the policy environment and (2) institutional, or absorptive capacity, questions; and those relating primarily to conditions and policies in donor countries, classifying these into (i) questions concerning the world economic environment and (ii) the policies and practices of aid agencies.

The *policy environment* was identified as having had especially strong influence on aid effectiveness. There is now rather general acceptance—reflected in the debates during this symposium—that past policy environ-

Chart 3. Comparative Rates of Return on Investment

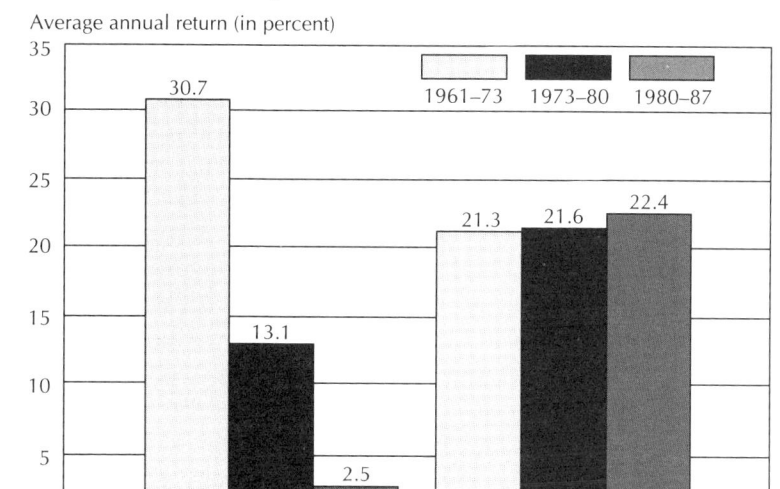

Average annual return (in percent)

Sub-Saharan Africa: 1961-73: 30.7; 1973-80: 13.1; 1980-87: 2.5
South Asia: 1961-73: 21.3; 1973-80: 21.6; 1980-87: 22.4

Source: World Bank, *Sub-Saharan Africa: From Crisis to Sustainable Growth* (Washington, 1989), p.26.

ments in sub-Saharan Africa have often not encouraged good economic performance and, therefore, aid effectiveness, even though there has been major progress in some countries in recent years. Instead of presenting familiar donor views on this, we can quote an important African voice, in a document endorsed by a meeting of African ministers of finance and planning and development: "Government interventions in Africa have so far become discredited, not because there is an effective alternative in the form of an efficient market mechanism but because of inefficient management, poor results and misallocation of resources,"[4] or Ndulu (1986, p. 102):

> The current economic deterioration in sub-Saharan Africa has partly been caused by internal economic mismanagement. Wide state intervention in the productive spheres and in markets for resources and products has led to an inefficient use of scarce resources not only in the "Pareto efficiency" sense, but also in relation to the development goals adopted by those countries. Serious biases against the development of the export and agricultural sectors have produced stagnant economic growth, arrested social development, increased

---

[4] United Nations (1989), page 47.

dependence on food imports, and debt burdens requiring frequent reschedulings.

In its most recent report on sub-Saharan Africa, the World Bank compared the rate of return on investment in sub-Saharan Africa with that in South Asia (Chart 3). Among the chief reasons it identified for the low and deteriorating productivity of investment in Africa were poor public sector management; price distortions, often created by policy interventions; and high cost structures, also much influenced by government policies. It also stressed the heavy costs imposed by Africa's loss of export market shares, which it suggests are considerably larger than losses caused by deteriorating terms of trade and which can also be linked to past policy mistakes, most notably on exchange rates. In this connection, the current weaknesses of the Franc zone arrangements, leaving several Francophone African countries with seriously overvalued real exchange rates that it is impossible to adequately correct without a change in those arrangements, can be seen as a continuing obstacle to effective resource utilization in the affected countries.

The parlous state of public finances in many sub-Saharan African countries is a further illustration. Budgets are often heavily in deficit, so much so that governments have to borrow to finance part of their *current* expenditures, as well as for the capital budget. One consequence is that the public sector has become a large dissaver and the chief reason for the serious decline in overall saving rates that has occurred, absorbing resources that could otherwise be devoted to productive investment and partly offsetting the benefits of capital inflows. There is also evidence that the large claims of the public sector on bank credit to finance budget deficits further competes with the private sector, by crowding out the latter's needs for credit; and that the expansionary effects of deficit financing are an important source of inflationary and balance of payments pressures.

As concerns *institutional and absorptive capacity*, defined as the ability of the economic system to put additional aid to productive use, there are various well-known proximate sources of difficulty: skill shortages; institutional weaknesses; budget constraints; and "the recurrent costs problem." These, however, do not go to the heart of the matter. Of more fundamental importance are the basic structural weaknesses of sub-Saharan African economies and the adverse characteristics of some political systems and processes. The reference to structural deficiencies is noncontroversial, relating to the weak industrial base, poorly functioning factor and product markets, limited saving and tax capacities, dependence on commodity exports and vulnerability to external shocks, small economy size and undiversified output, and the weak policy instruments available to governments.

Identification of political weaknesses within sub-Saharan Africa as a second fundamental source of limited absorptive capacity is, of course, more controversial, but even here the ECA and World Bank are in general agreement. First, the ECA's *Khartoum Declaration*[5] states that

> ... the political context for promoting healthy human development [in Africa] has been marred, for more than two decades, by instability, war, intolerance, restrictions on the freedom and human rights of individuals and groups as well as overconcentration of power with attendant restrictions on popular participation in decision-making.

Next, the Bank (1989 pp. 60–61) states that

> Underlying the litany of Africa's development problems is a crisis of governance. . . . Because the countervailing power has been lacking, state officials in many countries have served their own interests without fear of being called to account. In self-defense individuals have built up personal networks of influence rather than hold the all-powerful state accountable for its systemic failures. In this way politics becomes personalized; and patronage becomes essential to maintain power. The leadership assumes broad discretionary authority and loses its legitimacy. Information is controlled, and voluntary associations are co-opted or disbanded.

As both these quotations imply, a connection is seen between the prospects for development (and hence productivity of resource utilization) and the nature of political systems, with the ECA calling for greater political accountability and a more grass roots approach.

Political scientists have similarly noted a connection, with "patrimonial" states in many African countries, which are seen as inimical to economic efficiency and development. Patrimonial states refers to a system of personal rule based on communal or ethnic loyalties. In this view, the state becomes dominated by the pursuit of individual and communal welfare and does not act as the guardian of the national interest. Profits accrue to those who can manipulate the instruments of state, rather than through production, but this creates a self-reinforcing spiral of political and economic decay. Development and adjustment are frustrated. Take, for example, the following account of policymaking in an unnamed African country (Lamb (1987, p. 18)):

---

[5] United Nations (1989), page 7.

> A consistent and timely response to the deepening crisis was impeded by the fragmentation of information and decision-making. All major decisions . . . are visibly concentrated in the person of the Head of State, but many other decisions are taken in a dispersed, haphazard way throughout the administration . . . . What planning has taken place has largely been in a formal bureaucratic sense and rarely linked to what has actually to be done to make what is planned materialize . . . economic considerations are relegated to second priority, because first priority is granted to short-term political considerations, often in a disconcertingly erratic manner.

More than one country situation fits such a description.

We are not here suggesting that there is some simple connection between political systems and the quality of economic policies. But policies are the outcome of political processes, so that the nature of these processes can strongly influence the policy choices. Some regime types (which might have a range of different formal characteristics in constitutional terms) are so unrepresentative, unaccountable, ineffectual or corrupted that they are either not interested in using resources for development whose benefits are widely shared or are incapable of so doing. We do not imply that such regimes are universal, or even very common, in Africa, nor that reform is impossible. To quote Ndulu again (1986, p. 103):

> The current political-economic situation is not sustainable, but political constraints to change do exist. Nevertheless, the professed distribution of resources and power among various groups has been eroded and a more malleable situation has emerged as unofficial adjustments are being made by different groups in reaction to changing conditions.

There is much political diversity on the continent, and economic hardship does often set corrective forces in motion. In some countries, it is difficult to see a way forward without a revolution. In most, the position is less desperate, and in many it has been possible to make economic progress, so that even in the lean years of 1980–87 13 out of 41 sub-Saharan African countries for which data are available experienced positive per capita income growth.

Furthermore, the evidence does not support the view that the benefits of this are invariably concentrated in a small ruling group to the exclusion of the masses. Ultimately, bad governments that run down the economy are apt to be removed; the worst policies and practices tend eventually to generate counteracting forces. Nonetheless, it would be difficult to justify on developmental grounds continuing flows of finance to some of the governments of sub-Saharan Africa, and for those it is surely right to withdraw support pending political reforms.

My paper also looked at *OECD-country influences* on aid effectiveness. The hostile global economic environment, often aggravated by donor-country policies, is a major—but familiar—entry into our list of determinants. Of these, the adverse effect on Africa of trends and policies that worsen its terms of trade, debt-servicing burdens, and access to world savings should be particularly stressed. So also—and despite the enhanced structural adjustment facility—should the long-term difficulties that the IMF has experienced in tailoring its approach to balance of payments policy and the terms of its financial support to make them more appropriate to the circumstances of sub-Saharan Africa. We should note, however, that the donor community has responded to the region's special problems by devoting much increased proportions of total aid to it, and by special (although still inadequate) debt-relief initiatives.[6]

There is also a variety of donor-country policies and practices that reduce the quality of financial support offered and thus its potential developmental value. Many of the difficulties stem from the use of aid to promote foreign policy or commercial objectives. This leads to confusion and to practices that substantially reduce the real value of the assistance offered. Procurement-tying is the most obvious example. Most estimates put the direct cost of this, in terms of the higher price that has to be paid by buying from donor-country suppliers by comparison with the cheapest source, in the 15–30 percent range. But procurement-tying imposes indirect costs, too: adding to the bias toward capital and import intensity; placing additional demands on scarce administrative resources; creating an obstacle to aid coordination; and so on. Donor agency weaknesses further diminish the value of aid: inadequate staffing; pressures to spend; short time horizons; biases toward large, capital-intensive projects; and practices that undermine budgetary discipline in recipient governments. There are also various proliferation problems: of donors; of projects; of policy conditions. Donor coordination is also a weak spot, partly because both donors and recipients are ambiguous about it. The donors who so frequently urge policy reforms in developing countries need also to reform their own policies.

---

[6]While global aid flows increased only slowly in real terms (partly because of the collapse in aid from the Organization of Petroleum Exporting Countries (OPEC)), there was a major redistribution in favor of sub-Saharan Africa, with its share of total net aid receipts rising from 9.0 percent in 1960–61, to 18.7 percent in 1970–71, to 25.8 percent in 1980–81, and to 34.5 percent in 1987–88. Moreover, the terms were softened and many past aid loans written off.

Conclusion

In short, what is suggested here is that the many influences on the efficiency of resource use adumbrated above are of more immediate importance for the development of Africa than the volume of finance it receives. To put it another way, finance injected into an efficient economic environment will be highly potent, but there is little point—other than to meet humanitarian concerns—in channeling more to countries that do not meet minimum standards for productive utilization. The priority needs are to improve the policy environment among both African recipients and donor countries; and investments in education, training, health, financial sector and institutional reforms, and other key influences on absorptive capacity.

Politics arguably deserves even higher priority, however. On this it is for the peoples of Africa to determine—and secure—the political systems they want. They appear increasingly to want multiparty democracy, not merely for the greater freedom that it offers but also because of the safeguards it provides against self-serving governments insensitive to the aspirations of their peoples. Failing political reform, there is little developmental case for providing more finance in support of some existing governments. The task, in this case, is to apply scarce assistance selectively in those countries that have a demonstrated ability to put it to good use. Such selectivity is liable to be a more effective response by the donor agencies than attempts to impose policy—let alone constitutional—reforms by conditionality. But the donor community, including the IMF and the World Bank, have difficulties with country selectivity, and improvements in this area may themselves require a political breakthrough among the donor (and shareholder) countries.

Bibliography

Khan, Mohsin, and Malcolm D. Knight, "Import Compression and Export Performance in Developing Countries," *Review of Economics and Statistics* (May 1988).

Killick, Tony, "The Development Effectiveness of Aid to Africa," PRE Working Paper, No. 646 (Washington; World Bank, 1991).

———, Moazzam Malik, and Marcus Manuel, "What Can We Know About the Effect of IMF Programs?" ODI Working Paper, No. 47 (London: Overseas Development Institute, September 1991).

Lamb, Geoffrey, *Managing Economic Policy Change: Institutional Dimensions*, World Bank Discussion Paper No. 14 (Washington: World Bank, June 1987).

Ndulu, Benno J., "Governance and Economic Management" in *Strategies for African Development*, ed. by Robert J. Berg and Jennifer Seyman Whittaker (Berkeley: University of California Press, 1986), pp. 81–107.

World Bank, *Sub-Saharan Africa: From Crisis to Sustainable Growth* (Washington, 1989).

―――――, *World Development Report* (1990).

United Nations, Economic Commission for Africa (ECA), *African Alternative Framework to Structural Adjustment Programmes for Socio-Economic Recovery and Transformation*, UN Doc. No. E/ECA/CM.15/6/Rev. 3 (Addis Ababa, 1989).

Structural Adjustment Program: Lesotho's Experience in a Nutshell

A.M. Maruping

In 1988/89 the Government of Lesotho found it appropriate to engage in a structural adjustment program in partnership with the International Monetary Fund (IMF) and the World Bank Group. A three-year program covering the period 1988/89–1990/91 was adopted. The program commenced in April 1988. As the program nears an end (March 1991), this brief paper seek to answer such questions as the following: Why did the Government of Lesotho decide to undertake a structural adjustment program? What were the aims and objectives of the program? What steps did the Government take to achieve those objectives? What has been the outcome of the program? What is the prognosis regarding economic performance?

Situation Before the Structural Adjustment Program

Lesotho's real gross domestic product (GDP) growth rate was a mere 0.2 percent in 1986 and 7.9 percent in 1987. Capital expenditure as a ratio to total government expenditure was 29.1 percent in 1986/87. In 1987/88, the fiscal deficit as a percentage of GDP was 20.3 and as a percentage of gross national product (GNP) was 10.5; gross national savings as a percentage of GNP dropped from 25.5 percent to 20.0 percent; and the current account stood at M 72.6 million. Fixed capital formation declined from 44.8 percent of GDP in 1986 to 43.9 in 1987; and from 22.9 percent of GNP in 1986 to 22.5 in 1987. Domestic credit was rising at an alarming rate; it rose by about 88 percent from 1985/86 to 1987/88. Net foreign assets dropped by 12.13 percent between 1985/86 and 1986/87 and declined further by 6.5 percent between 1986/87 and 1987/88. External indebtedness as a ratio to GNP rose from 31.1 percent in 1986/87 to 34.8 percent in 1987/88. Inflation, using the consumer price index (CPI) stood at 19.7 percent (year-on-year) in January 1986; it dropped to 10 percent in January 1987, but rebounded to 11.6 percent in January 1988—it was, however, still at a double digit level. Clearly, the economic situation was deteriorating. Resolute intervention was needed to put matters back on track.

The movements of these economic indicators are in actual fact related. There is a definite chain reaction. For instance, as the fiscal deficit rises, both domestic credit (i.e., borrowing) and external borrowing rise, in order to finance the deficit. Imports increase. The current account deficit worsens. Net foreign assets are then depleted. This is the economic situation that led the Government to undertake a structural adjustment program.

Aims and Objectives of a Structural Adjustment Program

The structural adjustment program undertaken by the Government aimed at stabilizing the economy while at the same time (1) improving allocation of resources by correcting distortions in the system, (2) removing obstacles to growth, and (3) nurturing activities that lead to sound and sustained growth. These aims were to be attained by pursuing the following specific objectives: (1) reducing the Government's fiscal deficit to manageable levels; (2) narrowing the current account deficit (or preferably eliminating it altogether) in order to restore balance of payments viability; (3) striving for efficient allocation of resources; (4) curbing inflation; and (5) clearing the economy of structural impediments. These were considered guiding lights for specific measures to be adopted for achieving the intended end, the end being strong and sustainable growth under stable conditions.

Policy Measures Taken to Meet Objectives

Fiscal, monetary, incomes, and other policies were adopted as the means of meeting the set objectives. Fiscal policy aimed at reducing the fiscal deficit by raising revenue, containing recurrent expenditure, and encouraging well-planned capital expenditure. The raising of revenue was to involve an improved tax package and a strengthened revenue collection machinery. Increasing government expenditure was to be curbed by cutting from the budget dispensable items, instituting tighter controls, and monitoring the situation closely.

Tight monetary policy was pursued. Interest rates and domestic credit ceilings were preferred policy instruments. The Government's domestic borrowing in particular was to be drastically cut. The residual credit allocation could then be directed to the productive activities in the economy. This would follow as the fiscal deficit diminished. Public sector external borrowing on noncessional terms was limited. A ceiling was set. The rationale behind this kind of monetary policy is that when credit is curbed, the means of payment will be dampened and imports will be contained, therefore, mutatis mutandis, the current account balance will improve. In addition, in a situation such as that of Lesotho where inflation is largely imported, it (inflation) is somewhat arrested by this action.

Incomes policy involved orderly upward revision of wages and salaries. In the public sector, there was direct control. In the private sector, control was through the setting of a minimum wage. A number of policies were also adopted that aimed at eliminating structural impediments in the system and supporting directly productive activities of the economy in various sectors. They covered the agricultural, industrial, and public sectors, among others. Successful pursuit of all these policies was expected to stop and reverse disturbing trends in the economy.

Experience During Implementation of Policies

At the beginning of the program, there were delays in implementing adopted policies, in observing guidelines, in shooting for targets, and in keeping within the set limits. As a result, there were slippages. The slow start could have been due to the fact that the structural adjustment program, which presented a joint endeavor of the Government, the IMF, and the World Bank, was a new phenomenon in Lesotho and the usual human tendency to resist change—old habits die hard. Also, the groundwork for implementation of the program had not been adequate. Key players (i.e., key officials) in the public and private sectors had not been sufficiently educated about the program. Nor were members of the public adequately informed. Much was taken for granted. Consequently, there was an element of hostility on the part of some officials owing to the then prevailing anti-IMF sentiment internationally; there was also an innocent inability to grasp fully what the expectations were and how to begin implementing policies on the part of other officials. Administrative machinery in government and in other key institutions was slow to adjust and adapt. This was the effect of one of the raison d'êtres for structural adjustment programs, that is, the need to reorganize and reinvigorate administrative machinery.

Delays in adhering strictly to the adopted policies had consequences. The fiscal deficit worsened from M 160.5 million in 1987/88 to M 181.1 million in 1988/89. A chain reaction occurred. Domestic credit, going mainly to government, and therefore crowding out the private sector, rose by 42.8 percent. External indebtedness as a percentage of GNP rose from 34.8 percent in 1987/88 to 36.5 percent in 1988/89. Imports increased, mutatis mutandis, and the current account deficit deteriorated further from M 72.6 million in 1987/88 to M 109.3 million in 1988/89. Inflation rose to 14.9 percent (based on the (CPI)) in January and further to 15.9 percent in April 1989. Of course, the economy itself takes time to turn around because of response lags in the system.

The first year of the program was a period of learning and adjusting. Lessons regarding consequences of noncompliance were also learned. Midway through the program, cooperation increased. Fuller understanding of what the structural adjustment program was all about spread among officials. Compliance improved drastically.

Because of the hurry in formulating and adopting policies, the Government ended up agreeing to certain long-term courses of action that could not possibly be fully accomplished within a three-year period. Entrenched customs and traditions and the sensitivity surrounding the issue made it impossible to complete the process within the specified period.

It was also of interest to observe the change in attitude, among partners in the program, toward social issues. The program increasingly assumed a "human face" at every review. All parties were keener to protect vulnerable social groups. Health, education, and welfare were accorded special treatment during reviews. For example, food items used mainly by the poor were exempted from the general sales tax. One wonders whether this apparent change of heart midway was the result of international pressure to heed the plight of the vulnerable social groups during the program.

Situation Toward the End of the Structural Adjustment Program

Positive results of the structural adjustment program began to show in 1989/90. Success was greater with respect to stabilization policies. The fiscal deficit dropped from 17.3 percent of GDP in 1988/89 to 7.8 percent in 1989/90 (Table 1). Projections suggest it may be in the neighborhood of 3 percent in 1990/91. As a percentage of GNP, it declined from 9.5 percent in 1988/89 to 4.4 percent in 1989/90, with a projection of only about 1.7 percent for 1990/91. Fixed capital formation as a percent-

Table 1. Financial and Economic Indicators

	1983/84	1984/85	1985/86	1986/87	1987/88	1988/89	1989/90	1990/91
Fiscal deficit	−26.0	−19.0	−67.3	−87.8	−160.5	−181.1	−103.2	−48.7[1]
Fiscal deficit as percent of GDP	6.4	4.0	11.9	13.6	20.3	17.3	7.8	3.0[1]
Fiscal deficit as percent of GNP	3.1	2.0	6.1	6.9	10.5	9.5	4.4	1.7[1]
Domestic credit	127.7	122.3	172.6	223.4	324.4	463.3	480.1	426.2[2]
Net foreign assets	126.3	199.1	216.9	190.6	178.2	163.2	222.0	360.9[2]
Current account balance	−15.68	13.05	−16.47	14.40	−72.59	−109.37	−37.54	
External debt as percent of GNP	16.5	27.8	32.1	31.1	34.8	36.5	35.5	

Source: Central Bank of Lesotho.
[1] Projections.
[2] December 1990.

age of GDP rose from 46.7 in 1988 to 52.0 in 1989. As a percentage of GNP, figures are 25.2 for 1988 and 28.8 for 1989. Domestic credit rose by a mere 3.6 percent. This was necessary to accommodate real growth of the economy. The current account deficit narrowed by 65.68 percent, from M 109.37 million to –M 37.54 million. Inflation was down to 12.1 percent by April 1990 (CPI and year-on-year) and down to 9.1 percent in October 1990. Net foreign assets were up by 121.14 percent by December 1990, from the figure of 1988/89. External indebtedness as a ratio to GNP was down from 36.5 percent in 1988/89 to 35.5 percent in 1989/90. Evidently, the program was beginning to bear fruit.

In the area of removal of structural obstacles and support of directly productive activities, although deadlines were not necessarily met in a number of cases, some progress was being made. It was slow, however. Perhaps it is because of the nature of items that had to be attended to. Entrenched structures are not easy to change. In any case, as pointed out earlier, there were delays in setting processes in motion at the beginning of the program. It could be said, therefore, that while stabilization policies achieved commendable results, the actual restructuring of the economy moved rather sluggishly. Extra effort and determination should yield results.

Prognosis

The structural adjustment program came to an end in March 1991. There is still much work to be done, especially in the real sector. The fundamentals of the economy are yet to be truly restructured. Work is incomplete in this facet of adjustment. There is also need to round off and consolidate stabilization endeavors. It is therefore prudent to go for a successor program (1991/92–1993/94).

The Government is currently drawing up a new five-year development plan. It is an opportunity to ensure that the plan and the new economic adjustment program are in total harmony. It will be important to educate key players and members of the public right at the beginning. This will enhance appreciation and consequently cooperation. Vulnerable social groups should continue to be protected. Emphasis should be placed on the removal of structural impediments and promotion of directly productive activities in the new program. That is, concentration should be on the expansion of productive capacity and on full utilization of that expanded capacity.

Real GDP growth in 1988 was 10.8 percent and 6.3 percent in 1989. Growth in 1989 could have been stronger were it not for the excessive rains at the wrong time of the season, a cutworm epidemic, and an early frost that impaired the performance of the agricultural sector.

In the near future, progress that has already been made could slow down because of four factors:

(1) The high oil prices resulting from the Gulf conflict will adversely affect the current account. Elimination of the current account deficit could be postponed. The downward trend of inflation can also be halted.

(2) The drought during the planting season (September–December 1991) meant a poor harvest, necessitating the import of cereals. Again, that means that progress already made in the current account will be dampened somewhat. Curbing of inflation will be retarded.

(3) The impending general salaries review, which had to be undertaken to contain the brain drain, will have the effect of postponing elimination of the fiscal deficit. Imports are likely to rise as a result. Again, both the current account and the inflation rate are likely to be adversely affected.

(4) The general global economic slowdown is likely to affect Lesotho as well. This could be in the form of reduced demand for Lesotho's exports. Inflow of assistance from Lesotho's partners in development may also slow down.

Competition among developing countries for limited financial resources, given new entrants in the area, such as Central and Eastern European countries, has become more intense. The effect on the inflow of financial assistance should not be discounted.

On the positive side, commencement of construction on the Lesotho Highland Water Project, should contribute handsomely to the real growth in GDP. The only question is whether the impact will be strong enough to more than offset the negative influence of the factors catalogued earlier.

In the medium term a sizable number of migrant workers in gold mining face repatriation. This is due mainly to the price of gold, which has been sticky downward, given rising production costs. Granted that migrant workers' remittances contribute substantially to GNP and considering that it is by far the largest foreign exchange earning activity, consequences will be dire.

Prudent use of the proceeds from the Lesotho Highland Water Project should go some way in creating additional productive capacity that should absorb some of the workers. Retraining can also equip workers with skills still in demand.

Conclusion

The experience of Lesotho seems to indicate that the structural adjustment program does work. It shows that a happy combination of policies—fiscal, monetary, and incomes—tends to yield better results than when only one policy is burdened, usually the monetary policy. All pertinent economic policies should be brought into play in order to cope effectively with the rigors of the stabilization process.

While the structural adjustment program was to a reasonable degree successful with stabilization, progress in the removal of structural impediments and support for productive activities has been slower. The nature of some of the items falling in that category to effect meaningful change requires a longer period than the three years provided.

IV
Trade, Investment, and Growth
Prospects for Africa

A View from UNCTAD

K.S. Dadzie

Exports account for nearly one third of gross domestic product (GDP) in Africa. Obviously, such a regional figure masks substantial differences among countries in the region but is an important index of external trade dependence. On the other hand, Africa's share of world exports has dropped by a third, to less than 2 percent in the past thirty years. Meanwhile, dependence on one or two primary commodities for a large share of export earnings continues. Except for a few countries, there has been little real progress with diversification. The coexistence of high export dependence and low market shares indicates little influence on international trade and high exposure to changes transmitted through the global trading system. The region's vulnerability to external shocks is further exacerbated by its high dependence on a limited range of primary commodities as exports. The experience of the 1980s demonstrates the risks associated with such exposure.

Among the most significant features of this experience was the loss of foreign exchange earnings by many countries in the region resulting from the collapse of commodity prices. Neither the oil exporting nor the non-oil exporting countries were spared drastic falls in foreign currency receipts at various periods. The balance of payments difficulties associated with such developments and the reluctance of commercial lenders to permit roll overs of existing loans or to grant fresh ones created enormous reserve management problems. The average level of international reserves declined by half from 1980 to the equivalent of three months of imports in 1988. The distribution of international reserve holdings differed among countries, but even countries (such as Côte d'Ivoire and Kenya) that had been hailed in the late 1970s and early 1980s as models of prudent economic management were not spared the devastating effects of the collapse in commodity prices. Part of the income loss arose from reduced market shares, but, by and large, commodity price falls were the culprit for the difficulties faced by most African countries.

Loss of reserves, stagnating real resource flows, and mounting debt service forced many countries to resort to import compression. Reduction in imports affected not only equipment imports and important replacement parts, but in some cases even basic requirements, such as fertilizers, hospital supplies, and educational materials. Capacity utilization and output declined. Similarly, physical infrastructure in many distressed countries suffered neglect as trade-generated resources declined. In these circumstances, economic management in most countries was reduced to addressing problems of day-to-day existence with little scope to develop a long-term perspective on growth and development.

Stabilization, Adjustment, and Trade Expansion

Attempts to cope with external and internal shocks have taken various forms, ranging from price and earnings stabilization schemes to the use of market-based instruments. Lately, countries have also initiated a number of policy reforms under IMF- and World Bank-supported structural adjustment programs to correct some of the distortions in their economies and to promote trade expansion. Some of these efforts are discussed below

Given the supply and the price problems of primary products, it is no surprise that earnings variability has been a critical preoccupation of producers. Several multilateral initiatives have been pursued to mitigate the consequences of earnings fluctuations.

Stabilization of Prices and Earnings

Four main kinds of response to export earnings variability have been pursued. The first attempts to stabilize markets through intervention schemes, which, in their fullest versions, are embodied in international commodity agreements. The second utilizes available market instruments, particularly futures markets, to hedge against sharp price movements. The third and fourth mechanisms rely on outside institutions to provide compensatory financing when pronounced shortfalls of earnings actually occur.

The thrust of intergovernmental efforts has been toward international commodity agreements. At times, these have functioned reasonably well. Indeed, producers and consumers have in the past been able to agree on price ranges, financing of buffer stocks, exports quotas, and occasionally joint measures to improve market intelligence. But in recent years cooperation has waned. The severe difficulties of both the international cocoa and coffee agreements, covering two products of critical importance to Africa, highlight the problems inherent in such arrangements.

The establishment of the Common Fund for Commodities provides an avenue for promoting commodity measures (other than stocking), such as research and development, quality and productivity improvement, and market development, as well as local processing efforts and new uses for commodities. While stabilization measures are an important component of the Common Fund, they can be activated only when interested international commodity organizations elect to negotiate satisfactory terms to obtain financial support for their buffer-stocking operations. Nevertheless, the other measures mentioned above could make a vital contribution to broader programs of structural diversification of commodity-dependent economies in Africa. In this respect, the critical issues will be the extent to which the resources of the Common Fund (direct and through leverage) will be sufficient to finance suitable projects, the conditions that will govern the submission of projects, and the likely costs of operation.

The STABEX system for compensating unexpected falls in export earnings has been a constant feature of successive Lomé conventions. In principle, the entire eligible shortfall is to be covered through grants, but in practice the fixing of a total allotment with annual installments in each five-year convention period has meant that funds have not always been available. On three occasions during the 1980s, funding was inadequate despite additional efforts by the European Community (EC). The coverage of STABEX includes all African, Caribbean, and Pacific States (ACP); whereas the recent Swiss scheme of compensation in grant form has focused on the less-developed countries (most, though not all, of which are African countries). Under the Swiss program, shortfalls in the value of exports of a commodity to Switzerland can be accumulated over a few years to reach the prescribed minimum size for assistance. Subject to mutual agreement, the grant then made by Switzerland is treated as a supplement to a structural adjustment loan under World Bank-International Development Association auspices.

For several years, the IMF has had a compensatory financing mechanism designed to provide bridging facilities to help individual countries cope with a temporary shortfall in earnings. But this mechanism is not easy to employ. First, the need for relatively quick disbursement of foreign exchange is not usually met. Second, governments do not know in advance how large a drawing can be made. Third, if a country is experiencing a balance of payments disequilibrium independent of the shortfall, then the IMF makes the drawing of compensatory finance conditional upon reasonable assurance that adjustment measures will be undertaken. Fourth, any finance obtained bears a service charge and must be repaid according to strict schedules. The monetary and other costs of the facility, taken together, have made it less attractive to African countries.

Partly in response to this deterrence, a new compensatory and contingency financing facility (CCFF) was set up in August 1988 and was designed to help members of the IMF maintain Fund-supported adjustment programs in face of unforeseen external shocks. The basic features of compensatory financing were otherwise maintained although access limits were reduced. No African country has negotiated the inclusion of a contingency element in its IMF short-term assistance, and therefore no country has been eligible to draw under the contingency heading. Access is in any case complicated by the statistical conditions that have to be met. The recent events in the Persian Gulf area have led to temporary improvements in the CCFF, which are most welcome. These temporary improvements remain constrained, however, by quotas and give rise to market-related charges and relatively short repayment periods.

Structural Adjustment Programs and Trade Expansion

Economies in Africa face formidable constraints in their efforts to achieve adjustment with growth and concomitant export expansion. In countries facing acute macroeconomic disequilibria over extended periods, these efforts have helped to remove inefficiencies and to encourage export expansion up to a point; however, the scope for increasing exports quickly by a combination of cuts in consumption expenditure and devaluation—the principal policy measures usually recommended by major financial institutions—has tended to be narrow in most African countries. The scope for export expansion has generally been circumscribed by rigidities in domestic consumption and production patterns and by external demand factors. For many products, the domestic market remains the sole or main outlet. Where production could be switched to foreign markets, export supply capabilities have often proved inadequate for various reasons. One has been a neglected productive apparatus, owing to the lack of foreign exchange to buy imports of spare parts and new machinery to maintain the existing capital stock or to operate it at reasonable utilization levels. Also, reduced demand has resulted in idle plant and subsequent declines in production.

Furthermore, resource mobility across sectors—required to enlarge the production of tradables at the expense of other goods—is particularly low in African countries where sectors are highly disparate on account of the uneven and incomplete introduction of modern techniques and where the degree of product and market diversification is limited. Poor infrastructure and high transport costs to major overseas markets also continue to hamper export expansion and export market diversification.

The experience of African countries has demonstrated the acute difficulty of reconciling payments balance with other major policy objectives, namely, price stability, growth, and social peace, simply through devaluation and expenditure reduction. In fact, there are no short-term solutions, whatever the policy mix applied. It is the longer term that provides greater scope for increasing export supply capabilities through growth-oriented structural adjustment.

The level of new investment clearly has to play a commanding role in the process of the restructuring of output patterns required to strengthen export supply and external balance. Moreover, acquisition of technology at an accelerated pace, broad-based development of human resources, and rehabilitation and improvement of essential infrastructure are indispensable prerequisites for a growth-oriented adjustment process. Hence, sufficient external finance must be available, on terms and conditions conducive to the enlargement of production capabilities. Development aid and meaningful debt and debt-service reduction will be crucial as commercial borrowing capacity to finance increased imports beyond export revenue is constrained by debt problems for most of the African countries—and will continue to be so for some years. If, on the other hand, long-term adjustment is postponed for want of foreign exchange, economic stagnation will be inevitable and many African economies will remain trapped at a low level of income.

Furthermore, in an environment of extreme poverty, the effectiveness of economic policies in promoting structural change and sustained growth rests, in large part, on their social acceptability. Specific targets for improvements in the human condition, however, have not been featured in any of the stabilization and adjustment programs, although more recently there have been indications of greater attention being paid by adjustment efforts to mitigating social conflict. In the past, cuts in subsidies for basic necessities, in real wages, and in real health and education expenditures have had high social cost; poorer groups who have little, if any, access to safety net provisions have particularly suffered.

Liberalization generally promotes a more efficient allocation of resources, but little consensus exists on the optimal phasing and sequencing of market liberalization measures. Considerable uncertainty remains as to what outcome can be expected, in particular, for those many African economies at early stages of industrialization that have insufficient resources of human capital and an inadequate or debilitated infrastructure. Successful liberalization depends crucially on closely coordinated liberalization measures and industrial policies and, more particularly, government programs for the promotion of individual production sectors. The timing and phasing of reductions in protection would need to take account of the degree of competitiveness reached by individual industries and the seriousness of constraints on the further development of their competitive strength. Hence, the lowering of protection should provide an additional stimulus to improving efficiency, but its pace would have to be adjusted so as to allow sufficient time for government assistance and efforts of entrepreneurs to develop international competitiveness. As many African economies are still highly uncompetitive, rapid and indiscriminate liberalization could disrupt, rather than promote, economic development.

Finally, even relatively minor external shocks can easily threaten modest gains. The impact of the Persian Gulf crisis could have adverse effects for most of the African countries that are dependent on oil imports, income from migrant workers, and tourism and could seriously compound their existing difficulties in implementing structural adjustment programs and expanding export supply capabilities. Many countries in Africa are likely to suffer major losses in export revenue if the recessionary tendencies already evident depress world demand for their products. Moreover, more stringent austerity measures, including a fresh wave of reductions in imports of intermediate and capital goods, may become necessary in a larger number of non-oil exporting economies. Renewed retrenchment would further constrain investment and thwart efforts to build up competitive supply potential. For many countries in Africa the setback could be dramatic.

Diversification and Market Access

Structural adjustment programs have emphasized the improvement of supply conditions in order to maximize returns from commodity production. This is predicated on the assumption that the central problem is the inability of African output to maintain its market share, both in quantity and quality, vis-à-vis other producing regions. Even if that premise is accepted uncritically, it is essential that the international trading environment should not undermine the efforts of Africa.

Exports of commodities from Africa have traditionally been directed to Western Europe much more than to other markets. In 1988, the EC alone absorbed more than 60 percent of exports for many commodities. Intraregional trade was less than 6 percent of the total. Although allowance for unrecorded trade may well increase that proportion considerably, it is less than the corresponding figure (15 percent) for Latin America's intraregional transactions and way below the figure for Asia (43 percent). The concentration on Western Europe has generally been considered an advantage for Africa in the sense that a very large share of its exports enjoys duty-free access, even when sales from other developing countries face tariffs. This is because almost all relevant products, which would otherwise be most-favored-nation dutiable are covered by the Lomé convention and bilateral EC agreements with non-ACP countries, such as Algeria, Egypt, Libya, Morocco, and Tunisia. Nevertheless, the market access issue requires more careful assessment.

Preference margins that Africa currently receives are small because its exports are items facing low most-favored-nation rates. In terms of their practical value, the Lomé preferences can be examined by dividing Africa's exports to the EC into three broad groups. The largest of these, accounting for over 70 percent of the value of such exports, enters the EC duty free but would do so even without the Lomé convention. The second group refers to items on which both most-favored-nation and Generalized System of Preferences rates are positive and which do not compete directly with European production. Here, African states do receive a genuine preference over third-party exporters to the EC; coffee is an example of such a product. The third group is the smallest in terms of African export value and consists of goods produced within Europe for which European suppliers obtain substantial protection. Key examples are items falling under the Common Agricultural Policy (CAP) and the Multifiber Arrangement (MFA). Here, Africa's preferences are valuable in that they shield the region's exports from competition by other third-party suppliers and allow the region to benefit from the artificially high prices in the European market brought about by the restriction of supply. Nevertheless, it is in just these areas that nontariff barriers severely diminish the value of tariff preferences.

The dynamics of tariff preferences are particularly important at the moment. Prospective changes emanating from the current Uruguay Round would reduce or even eliminate preferential margins and could, therefore, be quite costly to African exporters. Elimination of EC duties on all unprocessed tropical commodities plus significant reductions on processed items could well reduce the export earnings of sub-Saharan Africa. African countries would undoubtedly respond by changing their production patterns and improving their competitiveness. In the end, it is not entirely clear that they would lose in the long run. Indeed, some observers hold that developing countries will gain in the long run, especially from liberalization of agricultural products.

The second major aspect of the market access issue refers to the definition and application of the rules of origin that any product must satisfy before it can qualify for preferential treatment. These rules are particularly relevant to items that embody inputs from non-EC and non-ACP countries. The EC recognizes African origin if the inputs from third parties have been sufficiently processed so as to warrant a change of the four-digit tariff heading. In practice, what happens is that simple assembly is excluded; for manufactures a maximum share for nonoriginating materials of 40–50 percent is set; for textiles and clothing, the starting material for transformation is defined as yarn, and for fishery products they must be taken from the sea by ships registered in the EC or Africa and be at least 50 percent owned by nationals of those states. These criteria are exceptionally restrictive for countries in early stages of industrialization.

Although the EC has offered derogations from these origin rules, the procedures for examining cases are laborious. Even if a derogation is granted, the maximum period is three years (renewable for a further two years for the less-developed countries). After that, the African exporter must conform to the normal rules of origin. The complexity of interpreting origin rules and then applying for derogations from them is unquestionably costly for the African entrepreneur. While recent evidence of a few applications for derogation is interpreted by the EC as a positive sign, a more likely explanation is that the administrative procedures involved reduce the value of these concessions.

The third problem with market access is the prevalence of nontariff barriers. These apply to processed items and increase sharply with the degree of processing for certain products, such as vegetable oils and tropical fruits. Commodities from Africa that compete with European production, such as those covered by the CAP, along with goods falling within the MFA, face a battery of variable import levies, countervailing duties, quotas and, voluntary export restraints. For some commodities this array of control instruments is supplemented by regulations that permit access only at certain times of the year. In still other instances, such as with beef, the terms of the Lomé convention provide only partial remission from import duties and even then require that the exporting country impose a tax on its own sales abroad. As commodities move up the processing chain and are qualified as manufactured goods, the EC imposes a number of nontariff barriers against imports. Although some of these measures have yet to impinge directly on African producers, they have been invoked against other ACP states. That fact certainly influences foreign investor perceptions of the prospective opportunities that the Lomé trade system may offer; by introducing uncertainty, it does not encourage optimism about new export-oriented investments.

One obstacle to trade comes from the barriers affecting products in their primary state; another is the escalation of barriers against processing of these items. On the whole, developing country exports of manufactured goods face 50 percent more nontariff barriers than do such commodities traded among industrial countries themselves. The obstacles often extend to such simple operations as packaging, which are among the means whereby low-income countries try to capture a little more of the value added.

Many African countries are not yet seriously affected by these barriers simply because they do not produce and export the processed items concerned in sufficiently large quantities. But the position may alter as they move closer to the trading frontier in a significant way. This point is of particular interest with regard to the MFA. Its application and, in particular, the great stress laid on controlling market channels have unquestionably restrained the rate of growth of exports from developing countries. Their share of the apparel and clothing market has fallen in recent years, at a time when the market as a whole has grown quite quickly. For African countries, much will depend on the extent to which future arrangements in this area encourage greater investment in production. Even so, the existence of these barriers must be regarded as a long-term constraint on expansion of export earnings.

Regional Cooperation

Many African countries are too limited in market size, resources, infrastructure, or geographical conditions to be economically strong and viable on their own. While the Lagos Plan of Action sets the blueprint for the necessary cooperation at the regional level, progress toward the attainment of its objectives has been limited. Efforts to integrate markets at the subregional level have been hampered by a combination of exogenous and endogenous (mainly structural) constraints. African economies are generally characterized by little differentiation owing to their low level of industrialization, and little complementarity owing to their similar commodity-based production structures. This characteristic limits the extent to which economic interaction can take place and the prospects for sustaining trade expansion over the long term.

The economic crisis and the macroeconomic imbalances that have afflicted the African economies and the consequent adjustment measures applied during the 1980s have also affected their capacity to cooperate. These influences diverted attention away from long-term development and economic integration goals to short-term macroeconomic policy considerations. Moreover, instead of adopting common positions and joint measures to resolve pressing economic problems, member states of economic communities have had to resort to purely national measures that have often undermined their obligations to their subregional communities. As a result, the intratrade of all subregional economic communities declined significantly between 1981 and 1985, although by 1988 a slight improvement had been recorded; and the volume of transactions channelled through the subregional clearing and payments arrangements was drastically reduced.

Yet there is little doubt that economic cooperation and integration, in the long-term, is crucial to the economic development and survival of African countries. Indeed, very few of them possess the resource and market size necessary for viable industrialization and accelerated development. Fewer still can participate on their own in the rapid technological revolution that is sweeping the world today.

One development that will have major implications for the economic integration process in Africa, and which has its origins in the Lagos Plan of Action, is the decision of the Organization of African Unity (OAU) heads of states and government summit in July 1990 to establish an African Economic Community by the year 2025. This decision was based on the summit's conclusion that intra-African cooperation is crucial to the economic survival of the region in the coming years. In the same resolution, the OAU summit agreed to merge the proposed Community with the OAU into a single organization with one secretariat.

The Association of African Central Banks with its subregional branches aims to promote exchange of views on policies relating to trade finance, macroeconomic policies, and harmonization of policies in relation to these areas. So far, given the diversity of currencies, trade links, different levels of development and variances in policy stances, cooperation among African central banks has been good but cautious. Meanwhile, attempts to promote an African Monetary Fund have stalled. Most central banks regard the idea as somewhat premature in view of the very disparate levels of performance and policy stances of member states.

In the area of multilateral clearing and payments arrangements, the performance of the three established clearing arrangements has also been poor. One of the arrangements has been suspended, and the volume of transactions cleared through the two operational clearing arrangements has been minimal. Recently, a fourth clearinghouse was established by the Economic Community of Central African States. Almost half of the African countries, however, do not participate in these arrangements and are not members of similar operational arrangements. The operations of the subregional clearing and payments arrangements have suffered from the small volume of cleared transactions, which is directly associated with weaknesses in the intratrade of subregional economic communities; restrictions on the type of trade to be cleared, which has generated asymmetry in the trade exchanges of member states; payments difficulties manifested by persistent debtor-creditor patterns leading to unsustainable accumulation of arrears; and the avoidance of the clearing system on account of foreign exchange problems.

In brief, specially renewed efforts will be required to implement the main ideas embodied in the Lagos Plan of Action. Regional cooperation efforts would also have to take account of the vast potential of South Africa and the evolution of the political process there. If the best expectations are realized, and a democratic South Africa emerges in which all its citizens have the same rights, duties, and opportunities, the region will be confronted with an important economic and industrial power at its southern tip with which it will wish to have normal economic relations.

Foreign Direct Investment

Since the onset of the debt crisis, African countries have made considerable effort to improve the policy environment for foreign direct investment. Like other developing countries, they have sought to expand rapidly the role of foreign direct investment as a means of redressing the imbalance between debt-creating and non-debt-creating flows, but also to compensate for the virtual cessation of commercial bank lending to the region. New flows of foreign direct investment would also substitute for low and declining domestic savings and rapidly deteriorating investment stocks, and contribute to the reactivation of the declining export sector.

Encouraged by international financial institutions and bilateral donors, the result of these efforts has been a net improvement in the investment climate in the region. Many African countries have seriously pursued the liberalization of their investment regimes and introduced new incentives and other programs such as debt-equity swaps and privatization, to attract foreign direct investment. Although these changes have coincided with an upsurge in worldwide flows of foreign direct investment, the volume of net foreign direct investment flows to African countries in real terms was still, by the end of the 1980s, only about half the level reached before the eruption of the debt crisis. Indeed, at the best of times the volume of these flows to African countries has never been more than modest. This has now dwindled to a mere trickle, or about $0.7 billion in 1989. Debt-distressed African countries have been particularly hard hit. Although most of them have introduced the necessary policy reforms, the debt crisis has continued to stifle foreign direct investment by feeding the general perception of high risk, diminished profitability, and poor prospects for growth. An expansion of these flows would undoubtedly alleviate some of the financial problems faced by debt-distressed countries. But as long as the debt overhang persists, it will continue to dampen foreign direct investment, as well as other private flows to these countries.

The comparative unattractiveness of African countries to foreign investors is also a reflection, however, of weaknesses in their basic economic structures and institutions. Though the region is endowed with substantial natural resources and abundant cheap labor, most domestic markets are small; technological and managerial bases are weak; and the labor force is largely unskilled. These deficiencies are often compounded by geographical and climatic problems and by inadequate administrative and juridical processes.

At the global level, depressed commodity prices during much of the 1980s and overcapacity in a number of industrial sectors, including petrochemicals, also contributed to the fall in net foreign direct investments flows to Africa. Innovations in labor-saving technologies, new materials, and techniques aimed at the reduction of energy and raw materials consumption have also had adverse consequences on foreign direct investment in commodity-exporting African countries. The risk factors of the 1980s further encouraged investors to rely increasingly upon risk-averting techniques, such as joint ventures and licensing agreements, which allow firms to earn attractive returns even in troubled countries while minimizing equity participation and exposure to the commercial and political risks associated with traditional foreign direct investment. Recently, cross-border investment opportunities within countries of the Organization for Economic Cooperation and Development (OECD) have been expanding, supported by improved economic performance, financial deregulation, and intensified business competition in view of the unified EC market after 1992.

Such problems, including the pervasive negative perception of foreign investors concerning Africa, combine to create an unpromising situation. Nevertheless, the picture is not altogether dismal for, as the recent liberalization efforts demonstrate, there is an increasing will on the part of African leaders to improve the prospects for foreign direct investment, in a region where the opportunities for sound investment are not inconsiderable. Not only are there good opportunities for investment in the traditional resource-intensive sectors but also in the rehabilitation of existing industries, debt-equity swaps, the privatization of state-owned enterprises, and the flexibility of techniques, such as joint ventures, production and profit-sharing arrangements, franchising, leasing, and commodity-linked securities. Equity markets are also regarded as promising avenues for foreign investment in developing countries and African countries have begun to establish stock exchanges, although the current possibilities in Africa are rather limited.

While there is need for African countries to continue to improve their policy environment for foreign direct investment (and other non-debt-creating flows), for instance, by reassessing the remaining barriers to it, especially in those sectors with substantial export potential, they can also seek ways to minimize the possible negative effects of bidding against each other. Improved cooperation among African countries through stronger and more stable regional common markets could provide additional incentives for both African and foreign entrepreneurs. Regional and multicountry investment funds, like the African Enterprise Fund (AEF) and the Commonwealth Equity Fund (CEF) could also provide a more stable and attractive framework for investors.

If efforts by African countries are to be successful, they will need to be complemented by adequate and timely action by multilateral financial institutions and countries exporting foreign direct investment. OECD countries could consider putting in place special guarantee arrangements to encourage their investors to locate in Africa. In this regard, France's recently established guarantee fund to protect French investments in Africa is a welcome initiative. Nevertheless, OECD countries should examine the possibility of strengthening such initiatives by the elaboration of a comprehensive framework involving trade, investment, and debt-reduction incentives, backed by adequate financing. Such initiatives should aim, inter alia, at strengthening the role of regional institutions, especially the African Development Bank and the African Enterprise Fund.

Investment promotion efforts also need to be intensified. African governments could make better use of the services of the International Finance Corporation (IFC), the Multilateral Investment Guarantee Agency (MIGA), the Africa Project Development Facility (APDF) of the United Nations Development Program (UNDP), and the IFC-initiated African Management Services Company (AMSCO). Indeed, IFC's capital base should be quickly expanded in order to enable it to increase its operations in developing countries as a whole, and particularly in Africa, and also to enlarge its technical assistance role. The encouraging development that 18 African countries have already joined MIGA (with 11 others in the process of doing so) should enable MIGA to play an increasingly dynamic role on behalf of a larger number of African countries. Finally, a stronger sponsorship role by the World Bank Group on behalf of a larger number of African countries would send to investors an unmistakable signal of confidence in the future of these countries.

Conclusion

In addressing the subject of trade, investment, and growth prospects in Africa, one must start with the high external trade dependence of countries in the region. Although this phenomenon poses difficulties, several countries in other regions, notably Southeast Asia, have turned such dependence to great advantage. They have enjoyed substantial export-led growth in their economies and a significant measure of development by adopting policies that permit flexible responses to shocks in their economies.

In the case of African countries, a major constraint derives from the limited range of unprocessed primary commodities that forms the basis of their high export trade dependence. This has been exacerbated by structural problems and, until recently, by a reluctance to adopt corrective policy measures early, in order to cushion economies against external shocks.

Since the second half of the 1980s, however, many African countries have introduced extensive and courageous measures to correct policy mistakes of the past. Some successes have been recorded, but on the whole the structural adjustment programs under which these measures have been introduced have been too constrictive and have not taken sufficiently into account the structural limitations of the countries applying the programs.

Some of the limitations of these programs now appear to be accepted, and it is to be hoped that a new generation of structural adjustment programs will be broader in scope and more growth and development oriented.

Continued action to strengthen commodity markets—through improved consumer producer cooperation, policies to enhance the competitive position of raw materials vis-à-vis synthetics, and supply rationalization schemes—and to expand and stabilize commodity export earnings—through new or enhanced compensatory financing facilities—is of course necessary to mitigate the effects of the commodity export dependence of African countries. However, the problems associated with dependence on a limited number of commodities—particularly vulnerability to changing market conditions and unstable export earnings—can only be solved in the long term through diversification. African countries need to develop new export products, stimulate the processing of commodities, and increase their participation in, and returns from, the marketing and distribution of their exports.

The diversification efforts of African countries could, however, be severely constrained by market restrictions, especially as they relate to processed goods or even agricultural products of trading interest to the industrial countries. Therefore, it is important that trade restrictions, especially on tropical products of export interest to African countries and in the area of nontariff barriers, be removed. Agricultural trade liberalization deserves every support because the long-run benefits of such liberalization in the context of an appropriate domestic policy environment could be substantial, despite the fact that some African countries might experience short-term welfare losses. Net food-importing countries, in particular, would need to give priority to promoting domestic food production over imports and would need expanded development assistance, including balance of payments support to cope with higher imported food prices.

In addition to trade liberalization by the industrial countries and the improvement of access to their markets, foreign direct investment is essential to Africa's growth and development. Local investment will not be enough at this stage to promote growth and development. Despite the region's efforts to create a more attractive environment, foreign direct investment has declined. The catalytic role of IMF and World Bank programs for external resource flows has yet to yield substantial results, nor have the various institutional arrangements put in place to promote foreign direct investment. Meanwhile, the globalization of markets and institutions and the risk, often denied, of Africa's interests being adversely affected by new regional trading blocks, including major trading partners, threatens to extend Africa's overall marginalization in trade and resource flows.

To counter these tendencies, African states need to pursue more vigorously their objective of self-reliance and to intensify regional cooperation in trade and development. Cooperation in trade, industry, research and development, technology, and infrastructure development will enable countries to realize the region's potential more fully, and draw the attention of the rest of the world to the region as a serious partner in global trade, growth, and development. The evolution of South African as a nonracial democracy could offer particularly attractive prospects for cooperation between countries of the region.

In the long run, Africa's growth and development will have to come through trade expansion, judicious investment policies at the sectoral level, and prudent management of macroeconomic variables at the national level. Africa cannot rely for its future growth solely on external aid. Growth must also be funded from trade-generated resources, and this must be a central consideration in Africa's economic policies. In the process, regional cooperation, as well as foreign direct investment and market access, must play a more significant part than hitherto.

A View from Africa

Bekele Tamirat

The topic on which I have been invited to comment combines three development issues of great complexity, namely, trade, investment, and growth.

Theoretical Tenets

Trade, thanks to the time-honored Ricardian theory of comparative advantage, has had pride of place in the economic literature in being described as the "engine of growth." Simply stated, the theory maintains that under free trade assumptions international trade conducted according to comparative advantage increases the welfare of all trading partners.[1] Of course, reality is generally more complex than theory. For one thing international trade, especially in recent years, is anything but free. As you know, the contemporary international trade scene is plagued by a plethora of tariff and nontariff barriers of one sort or another. As a result, the ongoing Uruguay Round of trade negotiations shows all the signs of foundering on the issue of protectionism, especially in the area of agricultural commodities.

Turning to concepts regarding investment, we observe that investment is a major determinant of growth along with other factors, such as natural resources and technology.[2] Investment or capital formation, as it is sometimes called, is essentially a function of savings, domestic and foreign, that in turn depends upon income, current and expected. Although the magnitude of investment as indicated by the investment/GDP ratio is important in determining the rate of growth, equal importance should be attached to the productivity of capital (as may be measured by the capital/output ratio),

---

[1] See, for example, Peter Newman, in *The East African Economic Review*, Vol. 1, New Series 1964, pages 22–23.

[2] Melville J. Ulmer, *Economics: Theory and Practice*, 2d ed. (Houghton Mifflin Co., 1985), page 102.

to the sectoral distribution of investible resources, and to the synchronization of investment decisions. Further, in analyzing investment issues in the African context, the sources and terms of investment financing should also be taken into consideration, especially as nonconcessional foreign loans all too often give rise to debt and balance of payments problems.

The last of the trio of development issues in my comment is growth—the ultimate goal to which the first two contribute in a very significant way. Most economists agree on the various factors that constitute the sources of growth, such as natural resources, the quality of population, capital, technology, cultural values, and the like, but as to which of them is decisive or all important is controversial. For example, capital investment was considered to be the most decisive factor of growth, especially in the 1950s and in the 1960s. Current thinking, on the other hand, accords no less importance to the issue of human resource development. Similarly, in the wake of the relative success of export-led growth strategies, the existence of a growing external market for the products of a developing country has also increasingly become the focus of attention for many development theoreticians and practitioners alike.

As nearly always in economics, there is inevitably another school of thought that holds the opposite viewpoint. Export pessimism nurtured by the resurgence of protectionism, the secular nature of the terms of trade deterioration for developing countries, and the persistence of impediments to the transfer of technology has lent credence to the advocacy of a development strategy that is essentially inward looking and relies on internally located sources of growth, such as import substitution. In reality, there is no such thing as a purely export-led or a purely import-substitution growth strategy. The question is really one of degree rather than of exclusiveness. The issue can also be seen as a question of what priority to accord to alternative avenues of growth in any given historical period of a country's socioeconomic development.

With this rather brief sketch of some of the theoretical considerations that enter into the discussion of trade, investment, and growth, I would like to examine in very general terms Africa's performance in these areas in the recent past before attempting to put forward some ideas regarding the prospects for the foreseeable future.

Africa's Experience

The record of Africa's growth performance in the 1980s is well known and is generally quite bleak. Caused by natural, internal, and external factors alike, massive setbacks struck the economies of Africa, particularly those of sub-Saharan Africa. The average annual rate of growth of gross domestic product (GDP) of sub-Saharan Africa during the period 1980–87 was a minuscule 0.5 percent. Agricultural GDP grew by only 1.3 percent and industrial GDP actually declined by an average rate of 1.2 percent against an annual population growth rate of over 3 percent. As a consequence, output per capita dropped by 2.8 percent a year. As averages usually mask individual differences, there were some exceptions to these broad trends: A handful of countries, such as Cameroon, Botswana, and Mauritius, did manage to attain growth of output in per capita terms during the 1980s. But the fact remains that 13 African countries (comprising not less than a third of the region's population) are reckoned to be poorer now than at the time of independence.[3]

The foreign trade picture of sub-Saharan Africa was equally dismal. During 1980–87, exports declined annually at a rate of 1.3 percent and imports by 5.8 percent. Similarly, the terms of trade in 1987 were estimated to have deteriorated by about 16 percent compared with 1980. Large current account deficits plunged the continent into a deepening external debt crisis. Sub-Saharan Africa's total external debt stood at $134 billion by 1988 and was equal to the region's gross national product (GNP). The debt-service ratio rose pari passu to a high of 47 percent. Debt arrears are now a common feature of the external economic profile of sub-Saharan Africa.

The record on the investment front was also unfavorable. During 1980–87 gross domestic investment fell at the rate of 8.2 percent a year, bringing the investment ratio down to 16 percent from 20 percent in 1980. The ratio of gross domestic savings to GDP also dropped from 22 percent in 1980 to 13 percent in 1987. As important as the decline in the relative magnitude of investment was its falling productivity.

In identifying the major causes behind the generally dismal economic performance of Africa during the past decade, one must not get bogged down in the question of whether domestic factors were more important than external factors, or vice versa. I believe both, within a reasonable margin of error, contributed to the worsening situation. Drought, unfavorable terms of trade, protectionism, inadequate concessional resource inflow, high oil prices and global recession at the beginning of the decade,

---

[3] World Bank, *Sub-Saharan Africa: From Crisis to Sustainable Growth* (Washington, 1989), page 18.

exchange rate instability, intermittently high world interest rates, etc. were all external causative factors over which the continent had virtually no control. On the other hand, internal factors, such as uncontrolled population growth, inefficient public enterprises, uneconomic public investment projects, poor macroeconomic management reflected in fiscal indiscipline, price distortions, overvalued currencies, excessive monetary expansion, and the like, had a direct negative bearing on overall economic performance.

The deep crisis into which Africa was plunged has prompted a response in many African countries that has produced some encouraging, if somewhat faltering, signs of improvement. Since around 1985, there have been some firm indications of recovery in output, particularly agricultural output, and exports.[4] The economic reforms undertaken included macroeconomic and structural measures, such as exchange rate adjustment, fiscal austerity programs, control over the growth of money supply, correction of price distortions, a general movement toward liberalization, and the active encouragement of the private sector and restructuring of public sector enterprises. While the reforms have generally been in the right direction and are therefore to be commended, the social costs of adjustment that came in their wake have at times threatened to outweigh their benefits, occasionally forcing reversals. The donor community has responded with increased assistance, albeit still far from adequate, and some measure of debt relief. We should remember, however, that the reforms that have been taken are only beginning to show some positive signs; one does not yet know whether they are sustainable. Therefore, Africa's social and economic woes of the past decade are far from over.

Africa's Prospects

Let me begin with Africa's trade prospects. I am afraid there is no ground here for optimism. Africa's terms of trade have continued to be unfavorable despite considerable economic expansion in the industrial countries for most of the 1980s. Price forecasts for Africa's major commodities up to 2000 are not encouraging; they imply no justification for any hope of an improvement in the terms of trade.[5] The development of synthetic substitutes and new production techniques for new materials is

---

[4] Ibid., page 35.
[5] Ibid., page 32.

believed to be an important factor behind the depressed world demand for some natural industrial inputs.

At the same time, the resurgence of protectionism and the rather inauspicious manner in which the problem is being tackled under the current Uruguay Round of trade negotiations do not augur well for the region's trade with the rest of the world. It is ironic that we in Africa are constantly being told to heed the teachings of Adam Smith and David Ricardo in managing our domestic economies, while those same tenets are being flagrantly flouted on the international trade scene by none other than the leading champions of free competition and enterprise. I submit that there is a case of double standards here.

On the investment front, too, one can hardly be less pessimistic. Population growth and massive debt-service obligations have eroded the saving and investing capacity of the region, and no major revival in the investment ratio need be expected unless incremental resources from the donor community on very concessional terms could be obtained. The problem here is that since the far-reaching changes that took place in the Soviet Union, Eastern Europe, and elsewhere, Africa has had to compete with these regions, which in many ways may be more attractive to the donor and investing world community than Africa, for external assistance and foreign investment. Indeed, it is not without reason that these days the fear of Africa's marginalization is frequently being echoed.

If trade and investment prospects are not likely to be good, neither are those for overall growth, generally speaking. I must, however, hasten to point out here that we in Africa are pinning great hopes on the structural reforms that we have undertaken. But here, too, the social costs of adjustment and the magnitude of investable funds required to reverse years of decline and stagnation are proving to be beyond the resources of the continent.

The odds do not seem to be very good, but this should not lead to despondency. On the contrary, we should strive to implement economic reform programs with commitment and renewed vigor. In so doing, among other things, emphasis should be given to the following measures in international trade, investment, and growth.

International Trade

- Intensify efforts to take advantage of whatever opportunities are available from the existing world trade system or reforms that may be forthcoming.

- Expand trade among African countries using mechanisms such as countertrading and regional clearinghouses and enhance the trade harmonization processes at subregional levels.
- Continue to protect viable infant industries, not only to support Africa's industrialization program but also to maintain employment.

Investment

- Give priority to investments aimed at self-sufficiency, particularly in the area of food crop production and processing.
- Establish industrial production facilities based primarily on domestic raw materials and catering for domestic markets, where such markets are of a reasonable size, but also gradually expand the facilities to produce goods for the world market based on the production experience gained in satisfying domestic demand. (Such a strategy may enable African countries to absorb any shocks arising from the failure of the international trade system and to protect jobs.)
- Assign priority to manpower development so that African countries will not remain marginalized in the world economic system. (The only guarantee for African countries to continue to have a say in future developments of world affairs, be it economic or political, is to develop skilled manpower that can face the challenges of uplifting African societies from the darkness of underdevelopment. Education and training and health are key areas in this respect.)
- Invest in carefully selected export-oriented production facilities to cater to the world market where there is an obvious comparative advantage. (Attracting external capital for this purpose from the private sector will be important.)
- Give priority to infrastructural development, such as roads, ports, etc., to create and facilitate internal markets.
- Give due consideration to the use of domestic resources and, in particular, to the creation of jobs when selecting technology.

Growth

In addition to the trade and investment measures suggested above, which I think will contribute significantly to overall growth, ongoing and new stabilization and structural economic reform programs in Africa will need to emphasize the following:

- Restructuring and rationalizing existing public sector enterprises, with a view to making them more efficient and competitive.
- Increasing the efficiency of investment in public sector projects.
- Creating an effective incentive system, and generally an enabling environment, in order to promote private enterprise and initiative.
- Gradually correcting macroeconomic distortions, such as inappropriate pricing practices and excessive budget deficits.

Some of the steps outlined may appear to be somewhat restrictive and inward looking in nature when viewed from a free trade point of view, but it should be appreciated that these are transitional measures until African economies achieve a level of development that enables them to integrate into the international economic and trade system on a more equitable basis.

Finally, let me emphasize that, however gloomy the trade, investment, and growth prospects for Africa may seem now, the degree to which the problems are going to be alleviated or intensified will, in large measure, depend on whether or not we can muster the will to take appropriate measures and pay the sacrifices that these may entail. I believe that the shape of the final outcome is partly within our control. Hence, although an uphill task, we must be prepared to change the failure of the past decade into success in the 1990s and beyond.

A View from Africa

Kerfalle Yansane

Africa's Experience of Development

As humankind enters the last decade before the third millennium, most African countries are still facing the problem of choosing an appropriate strategy for development. After more than thirty years of independence, Africa's economic performance is still the weakest of all the developing regions of the world, and the constraints of development are being increasingly felt. In light of this situation, and bearing in mind the precarious, not to say, dramatic, circumstances of the people of Africa, there is every reason to express concern about the choice of economic policies implemented in Africa, and above all, about the way in which they have been implemented.

Analysis of Development Strategies

The economic strategies adopted during the first decades of independence in Africa considered industrialization to be the engine of economic growth and the key to the transformation of traditional economies, essentially because of the uncertainty over the outlook for commodity exports and the acknowledged desire to reduce dependency on imported manufactured goods. African policymakers also felt that governments should play a major role in implementing these strategies; consequently, and generally with the full support of creditors, multiyear development plans were devised, involving investments in vast basic industries, concomitantly with the implementation of an arsenal of price control regulations, exchange restrictions, and credit and foreign exchange allocations.

For some observers, the reasons for the weak economic performance of African countries are linked to factors over which they have no control:

bad weather, low world commodity prices, and insufficient aid flows. Others, however, blame the policies implemented, especially the inadequate macroeconomic framework and the weakness of the economic incentive structure. Studies of this question have analyzed in depth the reasons for the failure of development strategies in Africa. They especially emphasize the inadequacy of development spending compared with the needs of such productive sectors as agriculture, industry, mining, etc., underscoring the fact that not enough attention has been given to agriculture, in particular to measures to encourage small-scale producers to raise their productivity and to appropriately modernize their operations.

With regard to international trade, which is a powerful stimulus to domestic demand and the dissemination of technical progress, the strategy implemented in most African countries was based on exporting one or a few primary commodities while importing a broad variety of inputs and processed products. This led to a dramatic decline in Africa's share of world exports, especially commodity exports, and a considerable rise in its volume of imports. Moreover, given the preponderance of primary commodities in African exports, the terms of trade have exhibited a long-term tendency to deteriorate, which, with few exceptions, has almost always become a reality.

Lessons of Investment Policies

With investments, the main problem lies not in the drying up of sources of investment that has been observed for a number of years now, but rather in their low yield, which is itself a result of the drop in African productivity.

What happened in Africa is easy to understand; like all developing regions, the African countries enjoyed a substantial flow of investments while investments were profitable. Very rapidly, however, the particular circumstances of Africa started to reduce their profitability. Even so, the flow of investments to the African continent continued, as long as the favorable world economic situation managed to conceal the falling real performances there. With the onset and the persistence of the world economic crisis, investments were increasingly directed toward the countries and regions that showed satisfactory economic performances. The African countries thus became locked into a recessionary spiral, in which lower general economic performance generated a smaller investment flow that, in turn, accentuated the falling economic growth rate.

Trade and Development Strategy

Where the Problem Lies

Empirical observations in African countries over the period 1971–87 show a relatively weak but positive correlation between exports and general economic performance. It would be a little hasty, however, to draw the conclusion that the link of causality between exports and economic performance is a one-way phenomenon. The availability and allocation of foreign means of payment constitute one of the key elements of this link, to the extent that all the sectors of the African economies, including the export sector, need to import products necessary for their activity. It so happens that the African countries' ability to import was sharply curtailed after the drop in their export earnings and their subsequent difficulty in gaining access to external sources of capital.

The African countries were therefore dragged into a recessionary spiral in which the decline in their export earnings had a negative effect on the level of investment and consequently on the general performance of the economy, which, in turn, contributed to weakening their export potential. Given the economic crisis the African countries have undergone since the end of the 1970s, opinions vary as to the economic options for reviving growth, and the proponents of an export-oriented strategy contend, in an intricate theoretical debate, with those favoring a domestic-market-oriented strategy.

Initiatives for Solution

Beyond the purely academic approaches that establish the theoretical foundations of the theories proposed, we will be addressing the debate that has arisen among economic policy decision makers.

The Lagos Plan

The Assembly of Heads of State and Government of the Organization of African Unity, meeting in its second Extraordinary Session, held in Lagos in April 1980, adopted a document entitled the "Lagos Plan of Action," with a view to implementing the Monrovia Strategy for the economic development of Africa. The preamble of this document states, "Faced with this situation (the failure of earlier policies), and determined to undertake measures for the basic restructuring of the economic base of our continent, we resolved to adopt a far-reaching regional approach based primarily on collective self-reliance." It is thus clear that the Lagos Plan's approach is one based on a domestic market-oriented strategy, which, however, goes far beyond the limited framework of the national economies of the states concerned. The basis of this approach is an explicit rebuttal of the development models used in Africa during the first two decades after the surge of independence, which tended to be, in many ways, a continuation of the prevailing economic system during the colonial era. In this connection, the Lagos Plan clearly indicates that ". . . rather than result in an improvement in the economic situation of the continent, successive strategies have made it stagnate and become more susceptible . . . to the economic and social crises suffered by the industrialized countries."

The Lagos Plan of Action thus proposes a progressive reduction in the economic dependence of the continent on the industrial nations and the expansion of regional economic cooperation. But the question we may then ask is the following: What form should this reduction of dependence take? As the most striking aspect of this situation is the dependence of African economies on one or a few primary commodities, the main buyers of which happen to be the developed countries, does this mean that these exports have to be halted?

The World Bank Plan

Just a few months after the appearance of the Lagos Plan, the World Bank published a report entitled "Accelerated Development in Sub-Saharan Africa." The aim of this report was also to define a strategy for the 1980s in Africa. In the preamble, the President of the World Bank states, "The report accepts the long-term objectives of African development as expressed by the Heads of State of the Organization of African Unity in the Lagos Plan of Action." The report falls within the range of neoclassical analysis. Without neglecting the impact of the postcolonial situation and the weight of external factors, it covers factors that are inherent in the problems of the continent and, as a result, the solutions it proposes are appropriate.

Although the Lagos Plan has not been broadly implemented, the World Bank report, because of the Bank's significant financial resources, has, on the contrary, had a considerable impact on African economies during the period under review. The World Bank report may, in fact, be considered as the basic document for the structural adjustment policies implemented in Africa and one can, without risk of error, assert that the

1980s have proved to be the years of structural adjustment for African countries.

At the end of the 1980s, it is possible to offer, with hindsight, a tentative assessment of structural adjustment in Africa. While it is generally agreed that structural adjustment has achieved little, there is considerable disagreement as to what the reasons were. For some, the reasons lie in errors in the design or external constraints; others emphasize the way programs were misapplied. So should structural adjustment and its corollaries, liberalization and economic openness, be rejected? Certainly not!

Lessons of Foreign Experience

Because the conditions under which the development of the industrial nations of Western Europe and North America took place were somewhat special, it is very unlikely that any developing country will be able to make use of similar conditions for its industrialization. It would, therefore, be interesting to examine the experience of developing countries or countries that have attained industrialization more recently. In this respect, the experience of a number of countries that, thanks to their remarkable performance and, above all, to the rapidity of the process by which they have moved up through the ranks of the underdeveloped to those of the industrial nations, is pertinent in more ways than one.

About a dozen economies in Europe, America, and Asia are usually known by the generic name of newly industrializing economies. They are those of Brazil, Greece, Hong Kong, Mexico, Portugal, Singapore, South Korea, Spain, Taiwan Province of China, and Yugoslavia. The newly industrializing economies of Asia are the ones in this group that have shown the most remarkable economic performances. Since 1960, they have had sustained gross domestic product (GDP) growth, made the demographic transition, and have become industrialized at an outstanding rate. At the same time, the growth of their exports has been coupled with a sharp redistribution of the structure of exports in favor of manufactures. Today, these four Asian economies, the largest of which supports a population of about 42 million on a territory no greater than 99,000 square kilometers accounts for over 50 percent of manufactured exports from developing countries.

What is the explanation for the exceptional success of the economic policies implemented by these four? The reasons given are linked to both external and domestic factors, and it is their simultaneous appearance and combination that explain why the four have performed so well.

Like all other economies at the lift-off stage, the Asian four had to face the problem of investment. In the lift-off initial phase, they had to call on domestic saving, encouraged by government incentives, especially those involving high nominal interest rates. However, it was foreign aid, the availability of an abundant supply of manpower, low wages, and, last, foreign investment that enabled them to start up and then to consolidate their industrialization process. Significantly, American aid provided a total financial input of between 5 percent and 10 percent of GDP.

The success of industrial policy in Korea, Singapore, and Taiwan Province of China can to a large extent be attributed to government policy in directing investment and in defining the stages and priorities in the process of industrialization. The initial phase in the development strategy implemented by the Asian four aimed at satisfying domestic demand by diversification and the creation of an integrated heavy industry. This strategy, labeled as one of import substitution, was followed by what was called an export promotion policy, which was started as soon as the two following conditions were met: the rationalization of industrial enterprises with highly labor-intensive innovations and the modernization of agriculture that sharply increased productivity.

The performance of these economies underscores the fact that the promotion of exports produced more satisfactory results than those obtained during the import substitution phase and at a lower cost. There are three main reasons for this: (1) With the export promotion strategy, the costs are borne by the general government budget; whereas with import substitution, it is the entrepreneur and the consumer who pay. (2) Faced with international competition, export enterprises have to innovate and offer products at international prices and of international quality. (3)With a mainly inward-looking strategy, the economy is liable to severe inflationary pressure, the usual sign of which is an overvalued exchange rate.

It can be seen from this analysis that the Asian four—outstanding examples of economies that are highly integrated into the international market—are in the vanguard of those that have achieved industrialization and development in the second half of the twentieth century. Is this sufficient, however, to allow us to conclude that an outward-looking policy would have the greatest development potential?

A World Bank study using data from 41 developing countries over the period 1963–85 yields the following conclusions: After classifying the countries in four categories according to their trade orientation, it found that the links between trade strategy and economic performance are not absolutely clear. This uncertainty is related to the question of the direction of the causality link: Does an open policy lead to better economic performance or does excellent economic performance favor greater openness to the outside? The figures show that the economic performance of outward-looking strategies has, on the whole, proved better than that of inward-looking strategies, in almost every respect.

The Outlook

To overcome the economic difficulties the African countries are facing and to pave the way for lasting sustained growth in Africa, the solutions being considered should restore the conditions for running the economic infrastructure more efficiently; progressively expand the scope of subregional relations so as to optimize the distribution of factors; and progressively merge into the international market channels. To do this, policies will have to focus mainly on pursuing reforms in the African economies; promoting intra-African trade and subregional integration; and continuing efforts to preserve acquired positions and to conquer new positions in the international market.

Pursuit of Reforms in the African Economies

The results of economic reforms in Africa over the past decade have been very moderate. For the coming years, these reforms should, above all, try to improve the effectiveness of development policies. With this in mind, the most important element to be urged is political will. The need and the will to implement reforms should be felt by and emanate from Africans themselves. Consequently, they should play the main role in designing and implementing them.

Once defined and felt by all economic agents, the need for reform should lead to concrete, practical, and easily valuable measures. Such measures should be directed, inter alia, at putting in place an administration inspired by the need to undertake reforms and to back up economic agents; rehabilitating the macroeconomic framework; removing all domestic trade barriers; directing the economic incentive infrastructure at reducing the remaining distortions in the African economies; and placing special emphasis on making the best use of human resources and improving the physical infrastructure, so as to provide private sector producers with the necessary conditions for success.

In implementing these reforms, the African countries should, as far as they can, avoid being lured into the tempting expedient of reducing the education and health budgets. The fact is, most growth theories put the development of human resources among the priorities in any viable and lasting development process.

Promotion of Intra-African Trade and Subregional Integration

In the area of intra-African economic cooperation, neither the will nor the initiatives are lacking, for there are more than 200 regional cooperation organizations, of which more than three fourths are intergovernmental. A glance at the current situation, however, reveals how far below their potential they are performing. The fact is that the ratio of intraregional trade to the whole has not grown for at least twenty years and accounts for only 5 percent of the trading of African countries. A study by the International Trade Center has estimated that potential intra-African trade is on the order of ten times its present size.

The inescapable reality is that most African countries are sparsely populated and possess limited economic resources. As a result, their development options, taken individually, are particularly fragile. Balanced development and, especially, any strategy based on significant structural changes, will require both access to larger markets for agricultural and industrial products and international policy coordination for a whole range of areas of activity.

The Lagos Plan of Action is the most ambitious and complex initiative for economic integration ever undertaken in Africa. Its approach consists of dividing sub-Saharan Africa into three subregional groupings (Western Africa, Central Africa, and Eastern and Southern Africa), which would each pass through three stages: free trade, customs union, and economic community. Three sets of obstacles will have to be removed for integration to be attained in this manner: the reduction of transport costs; the liberalization of trade; and the resolution of problems related to money and finance.

Another approach is to forget about integration through trade and adopt a new approach emphasizing the promotion of regional means of production. This approach would focus on regional investment in heavy industries and transport and communications. Whatever ways are chosen for the march toward economic integration in Africa in the coming years, they will have to be allowed for in any reform programs designed and implemented jointly with the international financing agencies.

Preservation of Acquired Positions and Conquest of New Positions in the International Market

The strategy to be implemented to preserve acquired positions and conquer new positions in the international market depends to a large extent on the success of reforms and of economic integration. To preserve such acquired positions, support will have to be given to commodity price stabilization agreements, such as the commodity fund put in place by the United Nations Committee on Trade and Development (UNCTAD), in order to consolidate and initiate sufficient financial assistance to facilitate commodity price stabilization through the implementation of such international agreements. Other financing mechanisms, such as the IMF's compensatory and contingency financing facility and STABEX will also have to be promoted. These mechanisms should only be considered, however, as temporary and complementary to the other measures taken to adapt to international market conditions.

The export revenue stabilization process is all the more important for the African countries in that it is virtually a prerequisite for the overall success of the recovery strategies in Africa, to the extent that commodity exports will, for some time into the future, constitute the most important source of foreign exchange for the region.

Last, as for the conquest of new shares of the export market, the main prior condition to be met is a quality product at a competitive price. This objective will not be met without greater efficiency in the economies of the African countries and maximum coordination of action by the public and private sectors.

Once the internal conditions have been met, the strategy to be implemented should concentrate on three main points: (1) targeting the promising market openings in which the countries concerned possess unquestionable comparative advantages; (2) focusing efforts on occupying these openings by developing the necessary skills and, subsequently, conquering ever growing markets; and (3) once these openings are occupied, seeking to dominate the whole economic branch through a policy of expanding both up and down it.

Panel Discussion

Adjustment, Resources, and Growth: How to Manage in the 1990s

Robert J. Berg

The great political challenge for North-South relations in the years ahead will be to foster mature and balanced political relations in the midst of continuing unequal economic relations. Nowhere will this be more difficult than with Africa, since the disparities are so great. We must build from the present, and the present has political and economic inequality of striking proportions. The political agenda is now thin. The economic agenda dominates relations through structural adjustment and, to a lesser extent, through development dialogues.

The assigned task of this paper is to suggest how Africa and the donors should manage development in the 1990s. There are a wealth of assumptions in this impossible charge, but suggestions are always possible to offer and might be of some small value if at least the lessons of the 1980s are clear.

The 1980s

The last ten years of development and development finance demonstrate some striking lessons that can be drawn from these basic observations:

- The key aim of the adjustment decade, to restore economies to creditworthiness, has not been achieved. Debt has grown over the decade to the point that it now equals Africa's gross national product (GNP) at about $147 billion, and payments to private creditors have been virtually suspended by most African countries (World Bank (1991)).

- Rescheduling exercises have improved in content, but still can fairly be characterized as a stop-gap procedure that has postponed, not solved, the problems of the external sector.

- Economies have declined over the decade, leading to a deterioration in both the quantity and quality of key public services. Critical declines in the education and health sectors have severe implications for the decades to come.

- The most severe decade-long phenomenon has been the deterioration in the fundamentals of sub-Saharan Africa's development, characterized by substantial erosion of the physical environment, deteriorated capital investments, continued high population growth rates, and a consequent further imbalance between the supply and demand of foodstuffs.

- There have been clear bright spots, particularly renewed emphasis to foster pluralistic forces in societies and the reform of many poor practices of macro-policy, but the impact of these on the human condition is yet to be clearly seen.

These trends have led to the characterization of the 1980s as the "Lost Decade of Development" and, of course, to the questions of who lost it and how—an investigation which, thankfully, is not the topic of this paper, but perhaps of future economic historians.

Parallel Agendas

A clue in this direction can be found in the development for most of the decade of parallel agendas—one for adjustment and one for development.

Adjustment of Economies and Policies

The adjustment agenda aimed at creating a soft landing and at setting up the pre-conditions for growth. The development agenda normally would be aimed at the growth of economic and social well-being—an expansionist agenda. For much of the decade, the donors combined these agendas so that donors normally engaged in long-term development work (e.g., the World Bank and United States Agency for International Development (USAID)) and diverted their efforts to reinforce IMF-type actions. Lately, this unified agenda has begun to move apart.

For much of the decade, one could not look at donor relations with Africa without being led to questions of how aid to Africa was or should be conditioned. There is no such thing as unconditioned aid, but prior to the 1980s aid was generally conditioned on project- and program-specific matters. In the 1980s, the adjustment agenda was incorporated by many aid givers in two respects: a move toward balance of payments assistance and linking assistance to IMF-type conditionality.

The practice of imposing conditions based on structural adjustment by donors of development assistance seems now to have run its course for two reasons: (1) to a large extent macro-policies have been changed, but (2) they have not led to the growth expected from their imposition. This is most clearly seen in the case of investment rates. Rather than kindling a blaze of domestic and international investment in Africa we have seen continued low domestic investment and international disinvestment. This is true even for such well-touted cases as Ghana where the domestic savings and investment rates remain among the lowest in the world. And it means that many components of the structural adjustment cure, for example, privatization of public enterprises, lack the wherewithal of private investment to succeed. Perhaps this is a key reason that the number of public enterprises in Africa has remained steady during much of the 1980s (Swanson and Wolde-Semait (1989)).

Donors are now saying that the conditions of structural adjustment are necessary but not sufficient. Currently, donors are moving to making aid conditional on reforms in the systems of governance. They believe that not since the birth of independent states in Africa has there been such a chance to foster the forces of political pluralism and even, as U.S. Assistant Secretary of State Cohen put it, "Western-style democracy"[1] (Bretton Woods Committee (1990)).

One has to ask whether the donors are clearer now about this new wave of conditionality than they were when they instituted conditions relating to structural adjustment. My own view is that they are less clear. Still to be clarified are such basic questions as (1) Is the aim to improve governance or to shift political systems toward democracy, or both? (2) What model(s) of governance and democracy are to be instituted? (3) What Reforms are to be introduced? (4) Who are the best agents to introduce reforms? (5) What is the appropriate time frame for reforms to take place? (6) How is success to be measured?

Democracy is a particularly hard concept to define, far more difficult to define and measure than, say, market pricing. It has no theory to export, has taken many forms, and has used many devices to reach the elusive goal called human freedom; even those forms of democracy in existence today are in a state of flux (Barzun (1986)). In addition, it is by no means clear that the modern political science theorists (i.e., aid officials) have thought through what the relationship is of their new conditionality to the development goals they (and presumably their host countries) wish to pursue. Is it clear that promoting democracy and improved governance will expedite structural adjustment and development agendas? Is it not possible that elites already antagonized by portions of the structural adjust-

---

[1] Subsequently, U.S. policymakers have conceptualized their efforts as aimed at fostering pluralism.

ment agenda will have additional reasons to fight donor policies once they can be seen to be at the losing end of political conditionality as well?[2]

To those who wonder where this kind of conditionality will lead in the 1990s, it can be predicted that conditionality looks like it will branch out into other lines. Some are now holding that political conditionality is necessary, but not sufficient. They think human rights conditionality is also needed (e.g., Waller (1990–91)).

It would seem that the good intentions of donors to foster political freedom via aid conditionality has confused three questions: (1) What are appropriate considerations for a donor in choosing which countries to support? (2) What conditions are appropriate to link to specific aid programs or projects? And, (3) might not a specific "condition" be better pursued as an aid project or program?

In my view, political and human rights conditions are appropriate for donors to have in mind when they decide which countries to aid and what levels to extend to a country. They are inappropriate as conditions of specific aid projects and programs and might better be both more achievable and palatable through specific technical assistance. It is more straightforward to assist a country's judiciary directly than to condition an aid program on an improved judiciary.

Fundamental Development

This new conditionality indicates, at least to me, a second departure from Africa's fundamental development crisis, the first being structural adjustment itself.

In the 1980s, the international community may have lost sight of key issues that may well have more of a bearing on the future well-being of Africans than the current agenda. The largest such issue surely is whether Africa can feed itself. The imbalances of population, natural resources, and agricultural systems are likely to grow in the 1990s. This will imperil millions. To meet the needs of its unusually fast-growing population, Africa must triple its food production during the next 30 years. During this time, it must also find employment opportunities for 300–400 million working age persons and find first-year educational placements for approximately 30 million young persons each year, about triple the abso-

---

[2]For an excellent discussion of these questions see Lancaster (1990).

lute number facing the combined nations of the Organization for Economic Cooperation and Development (OECD) (Wheeler (1987)).

Africa must pursue these immense tasks in the midst of considerable civic instability. Civil wars still disrupt numerous economies, setting back the development calendar by uncounted years. The instability of communities and families is shown by the highest rate of external and internal migration of any continent. Sub-Saharan Africa with 10 percent of the world's population contains 35 million international migrants, nearly half the world's total, and this may increase as the climate in OECD countries for Third World migrants deteriorates.[3] With the lowest proportion of urban residents of any continent, Africa has the highest proportion of landless or near landless families, 63 percent of total households (Leonard (1989)). All of these factors alter adversely the fundamentals of African development.

Africans also face severe issues in the external sector, in addition to its debt crisis, which argue for attention in the 1990s. In assessing Africa's trade prospects, a considerable amount of attention has been given to the future of its exports. There are major issues of composition and some real issues of access. Unfortunately, less concern is being given to the import side. One must be struck with the results of the World Bank's 1989 study documenting the huge premium Africa pays for its imports. Analyzing 1986–87 iron and steel exports by certain countries to their former colonies, the study found premiums over what these countries charged developed countries of 31.5 percent for Belgium, 53 percent for the United Kingdom, 66.5 percent for France, and 72.6 percent for Portugal (Yeats (1989)). Valid explanations no doubt can be offered for some of these spreads, but certainly the issue is suggestive, indicating that management of the import side requires far more attention. (Indeed, one can hardly be in Botswana without paying homage to the results of sensible management of imports.)

Realism on the investment side also is required. The prospects for foreign investment in Africa are exceptionally poor, because the competition will be even stiffer in the 1990s than it was in the 1980s. The U.S. governmental debt of $2.9 trillion and its corporate debt of $2.1 trillion will alone cause huge distortions. At the same time, others are seeking tens of billions of dollars of new investment: the U.S.S.R., the new democracies of Eastern Europe, the Latin American nations undertaking major structural reforms, and the dynamic economies of Asia. Several large Latin

---

[3] See Russell, Jacobsen, and Stanley (1990).

American nations are hoping between them to attract new capital of $20–25 billion in the next three years through varying privatization plans. Environmental projects will require formidable amounts of capital over the next decade (Hormats (1990)).

Surely the major emphasis will need to be on domestic investment and the return of flight capital. The adjustments and actions necessary for these potential investment flows may well be substantially different than those taken in pursuit of investment from the far less likely source, the international private sector.

Implications for Donors in the 1990s

Substance

Should the parallel agendas of structural adjustment and development continue to be merged in the 1990s? Two answers are being offered. The World Bank is moving away from the structural adjustment agenda but is still linked to it in many ways. At the same time, there is an effort among African leaders to link the two types of agendas but to shift the content of the development agenda to the African Alternative Framework.[4]

In my own view, both agendas are important, but they should be delinked much further. Perhaps this is best seen in the context of the stakes of not addressing the fundamental development crisis. Survival issues must be addressed whenever politically possible: even if civic conflicts are reduced or eliminated. Programs to increase food production, decrease population growth, and arrest environmental deterioration must be pursued. These must be achieved if Africa is ever to have a hope of self-sufficient, sustainable development. They necessitate long-term investments that cannot be made hostage to short-term policy ups and downs. While it is perfectly reasonable to link funding of endeavors in these sectors to sectoral performance, ways must be found to delink these sectors from the adjustment conditionality of the 1980s and the political conditionality of the 1990s.

This is not to say that the internal and intra-African political and transformational agendas are unimportant: they are crucial. But donors

---

[4]As occurred at the meeting of African LDC ministers of economy and planning, Tripoli, May 14–15, 1990.

have other ways of assisting these issues through direct technical assistance and peer support.

In any case, the "political" issue that may be hotter in the 1990s than many of the political issues now on the agenda is land tenure and the related issue of water rights. Courageous actions, many of which may benefit from international collaboration, will be needed in a number of countries.

Process

Whether or not the substance of the donor system is changed in the 1990s, the system itself is badly in need of repair. An agenda of donor reform should have at least three items: improved technical assistance, aid coordination, and the quality of personnel.

Technical assistance to Africa, estimated to be about $4 billion a year in direct costs, may well provide needed help, but its distortions are also large. A typical example is found in Tanzania. The annual cost of the 1,000 expatriate experts there is $300 million a year, three times that for Tanzania's entire civil service. Shifts should be made toward cheaper and less intrusive assistance: hiring short-term rather than long-term consultants and taking the resultant savings to carry out sound ideas recommended by the technical assistants rather than continuing to pay for ever-more-technical assistance and ever-more ideas that cannot be tried out (Jolly (1989)).

Coordination issues are so well-known as to not need amplification. The question is whether the 1990s will bring a better record than the past. Some African states have been skittish about encouraging aid coordination lest they organize the "opposition." Others have taken steps to corral the system. There is much to be said for co-opting the donors. The issue is how to do it best. Study of countries that are doing well in this matter, for example, Cape Verde, could be instructive. Joseph Wheeler, chairman of the Development Assistance Committee of the OECD, points out that countries ought to try to link aid to long-term problems and that a way to reinforce this is to have aid coordination managed by those involved in a country's internal long-term planning.

Finally is the question of the quality of staff working on African assistance. This is more a problem in the private sector, particularly in banks, than in the public sector. As Africa faces yet another decade of crisis, donors and those in the private sector working with Africa should pay particular care to assign the best possible staff. Ways to stimulate this should be a matter of dialogue within the donor community.

Debt Issues

Management of the debt crisis has already resulted in many special steps benefitting Africa. But, undoubtedly, further steps are needed. (1) The stock of debt needs to be further reduced, including the debt of the multilaterals, as many—for example, A.W. Clausen—have urged. (2) Net flows to Africa from the Bank and Fund should be managed in a way to provide strong positive flows during the 1990s. It might even be useful to establish net positive annual targets for the 1990s. (3) While several bilaterals have reduced official debts considerably, there is still unused authority in a number of bilateral institutions that should be exercised soon. (4) A more fundamental step would be to amend the Toronto Accords to permit their use in combination rather than singly. (5) Finally, some feel that a cadre of very high-level experts in financial negotiations, independent individuals not attached to existing major institutions, should be created to provide states wanting such assistance with authoritative, institutionally unbiased advice.[5] Perhaps this last idea could be addressed by the new international effort to build capacities in Africa.

Donor Roles

In the years ahead, donors should act more as specialists in proven areas of worth rather than in herding together from trend to trend. In my view, the World Bank should direct more of its efforts toward long-term sectoral issues. Conditionality should be aimed at assuring sector-specific performance. Performance in population planning and environment should be a far greater basis for deciding on programs than structural adjustment criteria. I would also urge the Bank to take a lead in assisting countries to better manage their imports, advising on ways to procure more economically. The Bank should be active at the Paris Club, noting the development impacts of various proposals, and being an active voice for development, but leaving to the IMF its necessary imposition of adjustment policies.

The Bank should also creatively work on issues of land tenure, water rights, and the other basic resource allocation problems that are likely to play such a major future in internal and intra-African relations in the decades ahead. Finally, the Bank and many other donors ought to be looking at employment issues far more closely and creatively in the years

---

[5] Drawn from the Bretton Woods Committee discussions, April 25, 1990.

ahead. The need is less for strategies—shelvesful abound—than for taking bold actions.

If I were to suggest new work for the IMF in the 1990s, it would be to pay greater attention to fostering an environment conducive to greatly enhanced domestic savings and investment. I would also hope the IMF could play an active role with African countries and Northern bankers in devising ways to attract flight capital for development purposes in Africa. But the most fundamental step the Fund could take would be to make its long-term role in Africa clear. It is all too easy to feel that the Fund may be keeping its arrangements in Africa to the short-term in the hopes that Africa's problems will clear up soon and then the Fund would be able to delink from Africa. The IMF must make clear its long-term view of relationships with African finance.

The bilaterals should delink fully from structural adjustment programs. They should stop being all things to all people and work more conscientiously to specialize where proven performance is demonstrated. Among the tasks bilaterals could take on that would have major impact on the future of African development would be to take far more active roles in helping to settle civil conflict in Africa. A sad example from my home country is the failure of the United States to forcefully act to settle the civil conflict in Liberia. The bailout will be far more expensive than any conceivable political solution that would have involved the United States. Bilateral donors also should examine their own trade regimes to institute reforms aimed at helping promote African exports.

There may well be specific steps that donors can take to foster pluralism in Africa by working on the specific aspects of pluralism: encouraging decentralization, fostering the private sector, helping give women a more equal chance in societies, and strengthening nongovernmental development institutions.

Northern nongovernmental organizations care deeply about Africa's future. Over time more of them will heed the call of African nongovernmental organizations to be less active as direct agents of development and more active as peer promoters of the internal mobilization of skills and institutions fostered by their African counterparts.

Conclusion

Pursuing donor-African relationships in the 1990s will be difficult. Crafting politically more equal relations in the midst of dramatically different levels of economic happenstance calls for mature creativity on both sides. Relations will focus on economic issues and uppermost will be whether the structural adjustment and the development agendas should remain as merged in the 1990s as they were in the 1980s.

In my view, the agendas need to be further delinked. There is a need for IMF-like actions, but the main development challenge is not reform of the external sector, pricing, and the public sector, valid as these issues are, but of survival. The development agenda, focused strongly on the nexus of population, environment, and food production, needs to take center stage among the donors. Surely political development is also worth concern, but more as a target of peer concern than as a condition for assistance. And surely, too, there is plenty of room for reform on both sides.

Some years ago I came up with the idea of a "compact" for African development. The idea was to have the donors offer major new resources in exchange for which Africa would offer major economic reform. The idea found favor with the United Nations Economic Commission for Africa (UNECA) and the UN Special Session on Sub-Saharan Africa. Major new resources did not materialize for Africa, but the requirement of major new reform did.

Now I do not speak of a compact involving major new resources for Africa, as substantial new aid flows are even less likely in the 1990s than they were in the 1980s. Instead, I would hope a new compact could be based at a political level on mutual commitments for improved performance. The new compact would have industrial countries offer significant reform of their assistance systems in ways indicated, including the need for targeted positive flows by the multilaterals throughout the 1990s. For the African states, it would call for commitments on the fundamentals for survival without which the development prospects for the next century are dim.

How can a package of mutual reform be put together? Clearly, it will need political impetus for which African unity and the mobilization of Africa's friends in the West will be necessary. The lesson of the 1986 Special Session should be clear: hard political homework is necessary on both sides before final deals are proposed. Intricate politics will be necessary, as will deft handling of public relations.

It would be liberating to be able to see a reduction of aid relationships in Africa, as one can in much of Latin America and with a number of countries in Asia. But that day is far off. The 1990s will be a very rough decade, and Africa will need all the constructive help it can find. If the financial and development history of the 1990s is to be better than that of the 1980s, there is much work to do. No one doubts the dedication shown on all sides during the 1980s. But the human stakes have gone up and so will the cost of delayed change by the donors and by Africa itself.

Bibliography

Barzun, Jacques, "Is Democratic Theory for Export?" (New York: Carnegie Council on Ethics and International Affairs, 1986).

Bretton Woods Committee, "Africa's Finance and Development Crisis," a conference held April 25, 1990 (Washington, forthcoming).

Hormats, Robert D., "The Contest of the '90s — for Capital," *Economic Insights* (November/December, 1990).

Jolly, Richard, "A Future for UN Aid and Technical Assistance?" paper presented to the North South Roundtable, Uppsala, 1989 (unpublished).

Lancaster, Carol, "Governance in Africa: Should Foreign Aid be Linked to Political Reform?" in *African Governance in the 1990s*, Working Papers from the Second Annual Seminar of the African Governance Program (Atlanta: Carter Center, Emory University, 1990).

Leonard, H. Jeffrey, "Environment and the Poor: Development Strategies for a Common Agenda," in *Environment and the Poor* (New Brunswick, New Jersey: Transaction Books, 1989).

Russell, Sharon Stanton, Karen Jacobsen, and William Deane Stanley, *International Migration and Development in Sub-Saharan Africa*, World Bank Discussion Paper, No. 101, Vol. 1 (Washington: World Bank, 1990).

Swanson, Daniel S. and Teferra Wolde-Semait, *Africa's Public Enterprise Sector and Evidence of Reforms*, World Bank Technical Paper, No. 95 (Washington: World Bank, 1989).

Waller, Peter P., Berlin: German Development Institute. Personal communications, 1990–91.

Wheeler, Joseph C., "Sub-Saharan Africa and the International Community," presented to the UNECA conference on "Africa: The Challenge of Economic Recovery and Accelerated Development," held in Abuja, Nigeria in June 1987.

World Bank, *World Debt Tables, 1990–91* (Washington, 1991).

Yeats, Alexander J., *Do African Countries Pay More for Imports? Yes*, World Bank Policy, Planning and Research Working Paper, No. 265 (Washington: World Bank, 1989).

G.K. Helleiner

The discussions at this symposium have been rich. Let me try to summarize my reactions to them under five broad headings: (1) the changing meaning of "adjustment," (2) humility about what we know concerning optimal program design, (3) the need for home-grown programs, technical capacity, and technical assistance, (4) the need for external finance, and (5) debt relief. All except the need for external finance have received substantially more emphasis, and agreement, in this symposium than they did in the last one five years ago in Nairobi.

The Changing Meaning of "Adjustment"

There has been evolution in what analysts typically mean by the word "adjustment." The "mind set" that accompanies terminology *does* matter. It is unhelpful to suggest, as some have done here, that it does not. Among the real issues lurking behind the terminology are the following.

(1) *What is the relevant time horizon?* Is the long run really just a series of short runs? The Governor from Ghana (Ghana, after all, is a relative success story, however fragile it may still be) said no; he said clearly that Ghanaian programs would have been different had they been able to use the longer time horizon that he clearly preferred. Upon reflection, that seems an obvious proposition. Any elementary business course teaches that much about the selection of an appropriate time horizon in planning for organizations. Why should it be any different for national economies?

(2) *What is the analytical basis for the term?* Stephen O'Brien was admirably precise about three alternative possible analytical interpretations: (1) increased capacity utilization, (2) a shift along the production frontier toward more tradables, (3) capacity expansion, particularly in tradables. The Group of Twenty-Four's conception of adjustment was, from the beginning, a matter purely of tradables supply and capacity utilization. It was the World Bank that added everything else that might be related to capacity expansion—thereby converting it into an apparent synonym for development itself. Early in this symposium, our moderator, Mr. Patel, expressed the view that adjustment should now be seen as equivalent to "development." That, of course, raises the old, and still controversial, question of the meaning of development.

(3) *Might the term refer to governmental capacity?* Mr. Boorman argued that all countries are "adjusting" all the time and the word adjustment should be understood as relating simply to the quality of economic management, particularly macroeconomic management. Non-adjusters are bad managers.

The word adjustment has become, in my view, a weasel word. Its meaning is no longer clear, if indeed it ever was. If we are to use it, let us at least try to agree as to what we mean: good economic management, or development, or balance of payments adjustment, or something else.

Humility About What We Know Concerning Optimal Program Design

Everyone is now groping toward better program design. The IMF's Managing Director set the right tone at the beginning of the symposium: questions remain, he said, and there is room for improvement. In the search for better design, it should be obvious that there will be high returns from a greater volume and variety of inputs. No one has a monopoly of good ideas. The main requirement, in the view of many here, is that there be more non-Washington perspectives in the competition of ideas. The international financial institutions should be more open to outsiders and be willing to listen to all. At the end of the symposium five years ago, the then-director of the Africa Division of the IMF promised the governors greater openness, pragmatism, and flexibility. The governors will be in a better position than I to judge whether this promise has been kept.

Greater humility and uncertainty about the appropriate pace, sequence, and timing of policy reforms (among other matters) have implications for conditioning of loans and performance targeting. It would seem to me that there is room for *more* intrusive debate about the details of domestic programs but, at the same time, that there should be *less* external insistence upon the fine-tuning details about which there remains legitimate argument.

The Need for Home-Grown Programs, Technical Capacity, and Associated Technical Assistance

There is now agreement that local "ownership" of programs is absolutely fundamental to their success. The Managing Director called attention to the need for home-grown programs in Africa. Home-grown programs require the building of greater independent African technical capacity. The building of such capacity requires a long time horizon and steady effort (such as that of the African Economic Research consortium). There are no quick fixes in this realm. Although the Managing Director appeared enthusiastic about the prospect of expanded technical assistance, some governors expressed concern about recent cuts in such programs. I trust that the governors will be able to hold the IMF to the implicit promises offered at this symposium.

It is worth reminding ourselves, however, that technical assistance costs and productivity need to be monitored carefully. Technical assistance programs have attracted more criticism than virtually any other sphere of official development assistance, and sub-Saharan Africa gets a relatively high proportion of this form of assistance. It is also important that such assistance efforts not interfere unduly with "learning by doing." Political leaders are under pressure to think for the short run, and thus to seek the best available advice, and hope the long-run problem of capacity-building eventually just works itself out. Where one sees increasing numbers of expatriates in senior positions, or even merely failure of their numbers to fall, as one sometimes does in Africa, one must wonder about the efficacy of local capacity-building.

In order to provide encouragement, it will be important that the IMF and World Bank not continually insist upon trying to "improve" every detail in home-grown programs. Local policymakers must be allowed to learn. To take a recent specific example, when high quality exchange rate analysis is offered by African policymakers (even when agreement on its detail is not complete) it should not be taken by the Fund staff as a challenge to "parental" authority but, rather, as a welcome sign of growing independent analytical capacity, deserving the benefit of any doubt.

The Need for External Finance

External resources are of course not the only constraint upon adjustment or development; and that is why correlations such as those to which Professor Killick called attention frequently do not turn out well. Where good programs are in place, however, adequate funding unquestionably greatly affects both investment levels and the productivity of investment. Donor constraints on the uses of funds and limited coordination among them can also be extremely costly. There has been a call at this symposium for "perseverance" on the part of African governments undertaking adjustment programs. There must also be donor perseverance: steady and predictable support, in appropriate form, of deserving programs.

The fragility of most sub-Saharan African countries' economic prospects, on which all agree, implies that the risks of failures on this front are very great. Nor has this symposium devoted much attention to the impact of adverse developments in external trade barriers or world commodity prices upon the prospects of success. There is a strong case for building in waivers or contingency clauses to allow for unforeseen external circumstances.

It seems that external resources will be scarce. How should they be rationed? Should more go to the demonstrably deserving once they have clearly shown their determination? Should more ESAF (enhanced structural adjustment facility) money have been directed in the past year to a relatively few African countries with strong programs rather than remaining unutilized? If so, tighter country selection seems called for. But we had better be sure about the selection process—removing all hints of bias based upon politics, ideology, or great powers' strategic interest. *Can* we be confident about the selection process? Are not many governors already saying the process of selection is inappropriate, or too tight, or both? Particularly in the light of the discussion in this symposium and elsewhere of the prospect of "political conditionality," there is an obvious danger of increased and inappropriate politicization of the selection process.

Debt Relief

I have deliberately put the question of debt relief last so that no one could suggest that it was receiving disproportionate attention. During the symposium, Mr. Samuel-Lajeunesse of the Paris Club said debt relief was not "a miracle cure." Mr. Boorman of the IMF also emphasized that it was not "*the* solution." But I heard no one suggest that it was either; these were attacks upon a straw man. Purely pragmatically, given where the majority of Africa's countries are now, debt relief—especially by the Paris Club—would be enormously helpful. It has so far been much too little and much too late. A great deal of economic damage and human suffering could have been avoided had the need for debt relief been recognized earlier. While the Paris Club members have been fiddling, Africa has been burning. On both economic and humanitarian grounds, the case for rapid and effective action on debt has been far stronger in Africa than in Egypt or Poland, where strategic considerations have generated a relatively lightning-like response. There seems to have emerged a genuine consensus at this meeting that debt relief for Africa, while certainly not sufficient for the attainment of agreed objectives, is now necessary. There have also been constructive suggestions for improving Paris Club procedures. I believe that a major outcome of this meeting has been the general plea from all its participants that the world at last get on with serious African debt relief.

Matthew Martin

African central bankers and IMF officials have shared at this symposium a wish to improve the preparation, negotiation, and monitoring of adjustment and external finance. There are two key ways to achieve this: by reducing transaction costs and by improving information. The first means rationalizing the staff time—and funds—both groups spend in interminable rounds of multiple negotiations. The second means improving the timeliness focus, and accuracy of economic data and analysis behind adjustment programs. The two obviously interact: rationalizing negotiation would free time and money for analysis and monitoring; and better information would save time in negotiations.

Reducing Transaction Costs

To put together a typical package of adjustment and finance, most African governments have to negotiate with the following groups: (1) the IMF and the World Bank, for adjustment loans; (2) the Paris Club, for (usually only Organization for Economic Cooperation and Development (OECD)) bilateral debt; (3) the London Club, for rescheduling (usually only long-term) debt to banks—and more recently, for reducing the debt; (4) consultative groups, for (largely OECD) aid disbursement; (5) each non-OECD creditor and donor government separately, for debt relief and aid plans; (6) many other commercial creditors, for short-term debt, uninsured suppliers credits, and import and bridging facilities not in the London Club; and (7) OECD government export credit agencies, for new loans. Each requires extensive preparation, negotiation, and monitoring.[1]

Preparation

For adjustment agreements, the government must provide accurate and up-to-date data and analysis on recent and future economic policy; a letter of intent for the IMF; a letter of development policy for the Bank; and (for low-income countries) a policy framework paper (PFP). The Paris Club demands a memorandum on economic policy, a request for relief terms based on recent data, and a speech on these issues. The London Club asks the same as the Paris Club, but data and possible terms are different, and

---

[1] Most of this section is based on Martin (1991).

the economic policy memo has usually to be rewritten, owing to poor coordination (of which more shortly). Consultative groups require a report on economic policy, assessing aid needs, usually two or three other reports (on public investment or social sector programs, individual policy issues)[2] and several speeches. Other creditors need data, requests and speeches, and sometimes formal documents. Each separate meeting can take three or four days to prepare.

The workloads of the IMF and the World Bank are equally heavy. They involve IMF staff in Article IV talks, on reports of recent economic developments in the country, briefing papers, draft letters of intent, and (usually annual) requests for loans under a stand-by arrangement, the structural adjustment facility (SAF), or the enhanced structural adjustment facility (ESAF).[3] World Bank country staff write initiating memoranda, draft letters of development policy, and president's reports (one or two a year) for adjustment loans; public investment programs, country strategy papers, and country economic memoranda. Both institutions have to agree on a joint policy framework paper for low-income African countries.[4]

They also have to attend meetings of the Paris Club, London Club, and consultative groups (and often those of other commercial creditors). For each of these, the IMF and World Bank prepare a separate assessment of the government's debt relief or aid needs and a speech. Their data specialists often have to help the Paris and London Clubs reconcile debt data with those of the government. The Bank also writes a report on the economic program for consultative groups and usually several accompanying documents to match those of the government.

Negotiation

Adjustment negotiations can take three years on an initial program, but more usually last from 9 to 15 months. IMF missions spend 10 to 15 weeks a year in the country, and government staff are in Washington for up to 10 weeks. World Bank structural adjustment loans require more

---

[2] For example, at a recent meeting, one country had to prepare reports (with the World Bank) on the economic program, food security, debt prospects, and foreign exchange management.

[3] For a few countries, it has also involved assessing export shortfalls and requesting loans under the compensatory and contingency financing facilities.

[4] One government with large London Club debt spent almost three months in constant negotiations (as did three staff members of the IMF and World Bank) in 1986.

missions and longer stays. If the initial program is implemented as planned, monitoring of implementation and negotiation of the next program run in tandem: each quarter sees one or more IMF review missions, several Bank visits, and several government trips, with the frequency mounting as a new program approaches. Countries with implementation problems may have from 6 to 12 months between programs, with three or four missions each way. Paris Club formal multilateral talks are mercifully short—only one or two days, though prior lobbying by African governments and the IMF and the World Bank may occupy several days. African governments then discuss as many as 19 bilateral follow-up agreements with creditor governments. The Paris Club sets deadlines for concluding these talks, but not one of these was met in 1981–90. Most agreements take from 6 to 24 months, due largely to data reconciliation and administrative problems on both sides (including difficulty in scheduling talks between other debtor negotiations).

London Club rescheduling talks took as much as 30 days over a period of 12 to 18 months, depending on the degree of disagreement between the banks and the government.[5] However, banks and African governments are experiencing a long and frustrating delay in the International Development Association (IDA) buy-back facility, due to data and legal problems, and to creditor bank reluctance to reduce debt: negotiations have taken 45 days or more, and 24 months to conclude.

Consultative group meetings are also short (two or three days) but World Bank and government staff face lengthy prior bilateral lobbying of donors (sometimes even pre-meetings to test likely pledges) and subsequent talks to confirm that pledges will be committed and commitments will be disbursed. Other talks can take several years of intermittent meetings, depending on the number of creditors, the insistence of other creditor governments on preferential terms, and the divergent interests of commercial creditors.

Monitoring

In theory, monitoring should occupy several staff full-time in tracking Paris Club bilateral agreements, debt-service payments, aid commitments

---

[5]The one notable exception was at the consultative group meeting for Mauritania in March 1985, where Arab donors attended and made pledges on both aid and debt relief for 1984–85—though OECD donors did not follow their example.

and disbursements, balance of payments changes, trade finance and export credit availability, and import costs. In practice, it often has lowest priority, owing to the simultaneous demands of preparation and negotiation. The exception is adjustment program implementation (as described above). As one senior African policymaker said to me in 1987: "In order to meet IMF targets, and prepare and negotiate new programs and finance, our team needs to be in five places at once and have 36 hours in a day. Where do we get the time to monitor finance?"

Poor Synchronization and Coordination

Each group of creditors makes decisions separately from other groups and discusses rescheduling and new money separately;[6] in addition, many creditors will only talk bilaterally. This raises major hurdles for synchronization and coordination.

IMF and Paris Club talks usually mesh fairly well, with the Club meeting just before or after the IMF formally approves a loan. London Club talks are often badly out of sequence: banks delay signing when the IMF suspends disbursements, until a new program is agreed; sign agreements just before programs break down (and have to abandon them); or do not sign before programs break down (and therefore receive no payment). The same applies to agreements with other commercial creditors—though occasionally they occur just before an IMF-supported program, and are made part of its arrears reduction target. Many consultative groups meet just before IMF loans are formally approved, to maximize donor pledges of aid, due to faith in the country's commitment to adjustment. But others are held later, and therefore are delayed or undermined by program implementation problems. Many are held when programs have been (or are about to be) suspended, and most donors respond by minimizing new aid pledges.

Paris Club, London Club, and consultative group meetings have no predetermined order, but their actual order can be a key influence on whether the adjustment program is adequately financed. If the Paris Club or consultative group meets after formal IMF Executive Board approval of the program, the program starts with an unfilled "financing gap," not calculated to inspire Board or creditor confidence. If the Paris Club comes before the consultative group, Club refusal of softer terms can put an extra

---

[6]As happened for Zambia in 1984; see Jaycox and others (1986).

financing burden on aid. But the reverse order is worse: aid pledges at consultative groups then have to be made assuming a certain level of debt relief and if the Paris Club is less generous than expected, programs may be underfunded before they begin.[7]

Poor synchronization and protracted talks can have severe negative effects on packages. Given the frequent sudden changes in the balance of payments experienced by many African countries, results of the different talks cannot fit together into an integrated "financing gap" calculation unless they end almost simultaneously. So the IMF and Bank have to recalculate gaps for each meeting. This can undermine creditor confidence in the calculation, reduce debt relief or aid, and leave a gap to be closed by import or reserves cuts or arrears on debt service.

Transaction costs in adjustment and financing negotiations are far too high, due largely to lack of synchronization and coordination. They place an inordinate burden on the staff time of all sides, and encourage duplication of data compilation, analysis of the economy, and document writing. They also encourage a short-term outlook where African governments and the IMF and the Bank cannot plan beyond the current annual program, and creditors look for short-term repayment. Thence the "short-leash" approach of reschedulings with one- to two-year consolidation periods, aid pledges for only one or two years, and annual SAF or ESAF programs, which further increases the workload for all sides.

A recent IMF paper described the resulting overwork and frustration of many African government officials: "In many African countries, policymaking has deteriorated to a state of constant crisis management...," with beleaguered government officials scrambling from day to day to meet debt-service obligations (Greene and Khan (1990, p. 13)). Many IMF and Bank staff interviewed also criticized current procedure. As one said in Washington last November: "We are here to help African governments design adjustment policies which will enable long-term development, not to rush from meeting to meeting with little time for in-depth analysis." In other words, the cumulative burden of constant talks leaves everyone less time to focus on the key issues: identifying and monitoring economic policies that are feasible for African governments and external finance gaps which creditors can fill.

---

[7] The meeting could also include pledging an amount of export credits—as export credit agencies did for Nigeria in 1986.

Reducing the Costs

In the 1980s, governments, the IMF, and the World Bank often helped each other to reduce the workload. The institutions sometimes drafted letters of intent or development policy for governments to adapt, or advised them on preparing for meetings. Governments provided the institutions with data and information on bilateral contacts with donors and creditors.

As a first step, such cooperation could be formalized in the joint preparation of a single document and data for each negotiating meeting of the Paris or London Clubs and consultative groups. Though adding some time to reconcile different positions, this would save time in separate document-drafting and data compilation. It would make data and analysis authoritative and put them largely above further negotiation, freeing manpower to design and monitor adjustment.

A single negotiating meeting on finance would be preferable. Precedents are available from Mauritania in 1985, where Arab donors pledged aid and debt relief at the consultative group; and from several round table meetings where donors pledged aid and an overall amount of debt relief (which was later confirmed in bilateral talks). It could include all commercial and government creditors that now negotiate bilaterally and all multilateral creditors. It could have separate caucuses for different groups—or agencies of creditor governments—if needed to retain confidentiality.[8]

The World Bank's recent effort to discuss debt informally at consultative group meetings and to include non-Paris Club creditor governments could be a precursor for a single meeting in Paris, with administrative support from the IMF, the World Bank, ex-Paris Club Secretariat, key banks, and other data experts. If the average meeting lasted from 7 to 10 days and agreed on outline terms with creditor governments, it would save 10 to 20 days of annual time.

Finally, joint monitoring of finance would give it much more priority: a joint team could track balance of payments developments, export credit and aid, new loan flows and terms, aid disbursement, and debt-service arrears. This would build on the current work of donor-government, joint monitoring committees on aid disbursement.

---

[8]Most of this section draws on Martin and others (1991), which presents the findings of the External Finance for Africa Project, a joint study between five African governments and the International Development Centre, Oxford.

Improving Information

Quality of Existing Information

Economic data and policy analysis on African economies improved dramatically in the 1980s, owing to strenuous efforts by governments and the IMF and the World Bank. However, most countries still face major faults and omissions in both areas.[9]

Data

A recent Bank paper described the unreliability, absence, and lack of timeliness in much of the data on Africa, owing to the new demands of multiple users and budgetary, resource, training and staff constraints (Chander 1990). Oxford's External Finance for Africa (EFA) project has gone into detail on balance of payments and external finance data and found that nobody can be expected to know how much external finance an African country needs.

Trade data are often inaccurate when compared with trade partner statistics,[10] or initial statistics have to be revised repeatedly by factors of 25 percent for two or three years. Many countries compile disaggregated data only on one or two nontraditional exports. In many cases we do not know the percentages of world market prices that countries actually receive for their export products. African countries routinely pay 30 percent or 40 percent more for their imports than other developing countries, but in many countries no actual import price series are available, and we do not know enough about import composition or sources to identify causes of overcharging. The same is true of service payments, where detailed figures are often estimated or delayed. Loan and grant disbursement schedules are often unknown. Debt service is underestimated, due partly to creditor reluctance to divulge data until rescheduling talks. Efforts and omissions are therefore large and frequently revised, and some balance of payments items are derived as residuals.

Onto this are built problems with projections. It becomes impossible to project potential nontraditional exports in detail, leading to projections of aggregate percentage rises. Aggregate import data allow only broad elasticity-based analysis of import needs and import use efficiency. Import

---

[9]See also Yeats (1989a).
[10]See also Yeats (1989b).

prices are assumed to fall with liberalization and rationalization; trade-related services are assumed to correlate with trade levels; and external finance is projected based on subjective assumptions about negotiations. In all of our project countries, actual data have not lived up to these assumptions: projections have been systematically optimistic. The actual shortfalls have necessitated import and reserves shortfalls or debt service arrears, undermining the feasibility of (and donor confidence in) the adjustment program.

Economic Analysis

Tony Killick's forthcoming book, *Adjustment Policies in Low-Income Countries*, reinforces the case that on adjustment policies for the exchange rate and the agricultural, industrial, or financial sectors, there is still considerable uncertainty on details of implementation methodology, scale and timing for individual countries. As Elliot Berg (1991) has recently put it: "Many of the intellectual underpinnings of 1980s-style adjustment lending are contested—such fundamentals as the feasibility of export-led growth, the efficacy and beneficence of deregulated markets, and the desirability of market-determined interest rates or exchange rates."

The EFA project has examined policies to promote exports, rationalize imports, and mobilize external finance. It has found that successful export policies stress overcoming structural (payment, processing, marketing and transport) problems, export promotion and market development, foreign exchange retention, and import-duty drawback, as well as devaluation and producer price incentives. Results are often distorted by switches from parallel to official market exports, or by weather, and have usually been disappointing because they paid too little attention to price incentives or to the motivations of farmers (particularly smallholder) and manufacturers (particularly small-scale).

Import rationalization has been equally elusive. Market allocation of foreign exchange and imports has had to be gradual. This was partly for political reasons, but also reflected the illiquidity of private sector importers; their inability (or unwillingness due to competing sources of foreign exchange) to cope with the complex specification, tying, procurement and letter-of-credit procedures necessary to use market-allocated funds and their lack of access to imports due to domestic distribution problems. Amounts and forms of external finance often remain incompatible with adjustment priorities and needs. Import support aid to governments is delayed by problems with procurement, documentation, tying, counterpart funds, donor or recipient implementation capacity, and poor coordination leading to duplication, which delay disbursement. The Bank is still having difficulty convincing donors to provide aid directed to the private sector through liberalized import systems. The Program of Action to Mitigate the Social Costs of Adjustment (PAMSCAD) in Ghana, and similar social programs elsewhere in Africa, face slow project design and implementation. There is no mechanism to provide trade credit on local currency terms most importers can afford or foreign currency terms central banks can afford.

Improving the Information

These findings argue for more work on data compilation, analysis, and projection. This can be helped by expanding practical, closely focused technical advice and training, institution-building for specific units, and incentives for data compilers and analysts. The newly established African Capacity Building Foundation (ACBF) could play a lead role here. Equally, we need to rationalize the demands of multiple users and the work programs of data compilers.[11] The aim should be to establish one authoritative data base (for example on balance of payments, debt, and finance), using all available expertise of the IMF, Bank, OECD, Commonwealth Secretariat, debtor governments, and other independent advisors. The stress should be on key data needed for adjustment and development apart from those on standard targets, closer identification of interactions between investment, import composition, and growth.

One key mechanism can vastly reduce external finance and balance of payments shortfalls: the deliberately pessimistic balance of payments scenario and the contingency mechanism in Zambia's program of 1989–90, which allowed excess copper earnings to offset finance shortfalls, should certainly be repeated. In addition, rescheduled debt and new loans could be denominated in SDRs to reduce interest and exchange rate fluctuations. However, other nations will require cheap, total, and timely contingency and compensatory finance; and the compensatory and contingency financing facility fulfills only the last of these characteristics.

Many other participants at this symposium have suggested more humility in recommending policies, and more caution in implementing them: similar safeguard mechanisms to offset unexpected results or ex-

---

[11] Chander (1990) also suggests that data improvements, and how to organize and fund them, should be a main item on the agenda of consultative groups.

ogenous events could easily be devised for other standard adjustment program targets.

Programs need still more stress on overcoming structural export supply problems and on gradualism in import liberalization. They also need to focus on the precise motivations of exporters and importers, the effects of the parallel market, how to optimize import composition without distortionary policy, how to diversify import sources and end-users, how to reduce import prices, and how to increase service earnings and reduce service payments.

The 1988–91 successes in untying aid in the World Bank's Special Program of Assistance, for example, establishing prototype standard procurement, documentary, and counterpart methods in Mozambique, show how much can be achieved relatively quickly. But more work is needed to raise donor implementation capacity and channel donor funds to priority projects and liberalized import systems. This implies greater consultation between recipients and donors in deciding priority projects and routes to import liberalization: lower transaction costs in existing negotiations could provide the time. Importers also require extensive training in using liberalized import systems. We need to find ways to get aid rapidly to the poor, to the social sectors and to environmental protection and institutional reform. Finally, we need to replace commercial or ECA trade finance loans, which most low-income countries cannot afford, with concessional trade credit.

The Wider and Longer-Term Picture

For most individual African countries, these problems are daunting and the solutions are urgent. They cumulate for the continent and the world. In terms of transaction costs, many IMF, World Bank, and donor/creditor staff cover several countries and face constant meetings. They also have to attend overall "tour d'horizon" sessions of the Paris Club, which discuss recent developments in individual countries' packages—for these they have to prepare assessments of ten or more African countries, based on constant monitoring; and methodology sessions that decide possible changes in terms and operating procedures—for these they have to decide their positions and whether they wish to lobby for changes. Bank staff have to assess recent developments for each country to prepare meetings for the Special Program of Assistance. Staff of both institutions have to assess developments in country and regional lending in order to make internal decisions on their lending program (or on arrears clearance).

In terms of information, putting together faulty data from individual countries makes it impossible to analyze sufficient needs for debt relief and new money or the need of other low-income, poverty-filled, or debt-burdened developing nations. As data improvements through the SPA have clarified the needs of low-income Africa, so the pressure has grown to find additional finance to minimize rationing among countries. In other words, there have been two problems with "adding up" individual countries' needs: (1) country estimate + country estimate = continental guess; and (2) better estimate + better estimate = continental shortfall.

Coordination, synchronization, and better information in individual countries' talks will provide the time to study the continental and global picture. They will also provide more security for all sides to plan for the long-term, encouraging debt relief and new finance, and adjustment programs for periods of five to ten years. Such planning would replace day-to-day crisis management and enable more analysis of how to raise the quantity and quality of domestic savings and investment; to enhance regional cooperation; to reduce dependence on import, aid and commodity exports; to improve human capital, basic needs, income distribution and prospects for the poor; to protect the environment; and to maximize political freedom. By improving negotiating procedure now, we can free resources to focus on these key issues for African development in the 1990s and beyond.

Bibliography

Berg, Elliot, "Comments on the Design and Implementation of Conditionality in Adjustment Programmes," in *Restructuring Economies in Distress: Policy Reform and the World Bank*, ed. by Thomas Vinod, and others (Oxford; New York: Oxford University Press, 1991).

Chander, Ramesh, *Information Systems and Basic Statistics in Sub-Saharan Africa: A Review and Strategy for Improvement*, World Bank Discussion Papers, No. 73 (Washington: World Bank, 1990).

Greene, Joshua, and Mohsin Khan, *The African Debt Crisis*, AERC Special Paper No. 3 (Nairobi: African Economic Research Consortium, February 1990).

Jaycox, Edward, and others, "The Nature of the Debt Problem in Eastern and Southern Africa," in *African Debt and Financing*, ed. by Carol Lancaster and John Williamson, IIE Special Report No. 5 (Washington: Institute for International Economics, 1986).

Killick, Tony, *The Adaptive Economy: Adjustment Policies in Low-Income Countries* (Washington: World Bank, forthcoming).

Martin, Matthew, *African Debt Negotiations: No Winners* (London: Macmillan Press and New York: St. Martin's Press, 1991).

———, and others, *External Finance for Africa Project: Overall Report* (Oxford: International Development Center, June 1991).

Yeats, Alexander, *On the Accuracy of Economic Observations: Do Sub-Saharan Trade Statistics Mean Anything?* PRE Working Paper WPS 307 (World Bank, November 1989).

———, *Do African Countries Pay More for Imports? Yes*, World Bank PRE Working Paper WPS 265 (World Bank, September 1989).

G. E. Gondwe

The challenges for economic adjustment and growth facing Africa in the 1990s are daunting in their scale and pressing in their social and political implications. Indeed, it is easy to be discouraged by the enormity of the task, particularly in view of the unsatisfactory economic performance of many African countries in the 1980s and the inadequate economic structure against which programs and policies in the 1990s must be fashioned. On the one hand, it is possible to be overly sanguine and complacent about the ability to cope with these challenges; on the other, one can be unduly critical of the structures and mechanisms inherited from the 1980s to deal with the issues involved. A position somewhere in the middle seems to be warranted, one that promises a more balanced approach. With regard to the role of the international financial institutions—including the Fund—in this adjustment process, adaptations have indeed already occurred in response to the experience of the 1980s, but flexibility and imagination are needed to meet the demands of the decade ahead.

Claims have been made that the Fund is (1) focusing too much on the short term and too little on the long run; (2) emphasizing economic concerns without due regard to social issues; (3) dealing too much with internal policy matters, with inadequate attention to the promotion of external funding, and; (4) imposing their own policy packages without regarding the input of the local authorities. It seems to me that such sharp distinctions are not especially helpful and do not properly reflect the evolving role of the institution. Nevertheless, in view of the currency of these views, I shall address each of them briefly and then go on to discuss more broadly some key adjustment and growth challenges for the 1990s.

Some Adjustment and Growth Issues

Short-Term and Long-Term Adjustment

As widely acknowledged, African economic difficulties are reflected in serious macroeconomic imbalances and severe structural weaknesses and distortions. As for the former, major imbalances in the government's fiscal position are frequently a central concern, usually exacerbated by sizable losses by parastatals, subsidized in full or in part by the state. These imbalances are typically reflected in monetary expansion at a rate well in excess of growth in the country's productive resources, promoting not only an inflationary environment but frequently resulting in scarce savings being directed to less efficient forms of economic activity. These, and related, imbalances must be redressed if medium- and long-term growth is to proceed on a firm foundation. Although this point seems self-evident, it can surely be obscured by the repeated stress from critics that the shorter-term objectives are being overemphasized by the Fund. In fact, medium- and long-term adjustment is unlikely to be realized unless based on a sound macroeconomic framework. Monitoring by the Fund of the short-term aspects of macroeconomic programs is not therefore an end in itself but a necessary step in ensuring a background more conducive to longer-term economic growth. To decry this shorter-term aspect of programs is to miss part of their rationale.

This said, it is equally true that short-term adjustment objectives must be constructed in a manner consistent with longer-term economic and social aims. It is perhaps a matter for debate as to whether or not the Fund was as early to recognize and incorporate these longer-term elements into its programs as it might have been, but it is certainly now an important feature of African programs supported by the Fund. Indeed, the structural adjustment facility (SAF) and the enhanced structural adjustment facility (ESAF) strongly emphasize longer-term components; furthermore, while it is true that these facilities support programs with terms limited to periods of up to three years, the design of the programs stresses the need for viability in the subsequent years. Consistent with this increased focus on mutually reinforcing short- and longer-term objectives, Fund negotiating missions endeavor, for example, to formulate fiscal targets with the authorities that give due attention not only to the level but also to the composition of the fiscal aggregates. Thus, on the revenue side, emphasis is placed, where needed, on tax reforms that not only help realize stabilization objectives, but also promote structural efficiencies in the tax collection and administrative process. Equally, on the expenditure side, attention is focused not only on the level and timing of expenditures, but also on the respective composition of recurrent and developmental outlays.

Other examples can be given of this joint concern with stabilization and structural objectives. Take an example from my own country, Malawi. The import liberalization program—now recently completed—was a major structural component of the program supported by the Fund under a three-year ESAF arrangement. An important objective of this program for liberalizing the system of prior exchange approval for imports was to ensure much wider access to supplies, including capital equipment and factor inputs, needed for capital formation and increased productive capacity. Apart from this essentially structural objective, the import liberalization program also played an important role—in conjunction with appropriate financial policies—in facilitating the slowdown in inflation by increasing the availability of supplies and improving competition, and has had important implications when establishing appropriate external reserves targets, including those for the short term. The import liberalization element of the program, therefore, clearly had both structural and stabilization aspects. These examples can be multiplied but support the position, in my view, that short- and medium-term objectives should be formulated in a complementary fashion. Too much emphasis on one or the other can lead to policy distortions and ineffective implementation. The Fund is fully aware of this need for complementarity, which is an essential element in program design, and is somewhat sensitive to the unwarranted criticism that these issues are being discounted or underemphasized.

These considerations have necessarily required a wider degree of coordination between the major international financial agencies. Cooperation between the Fund and the World Bank has been of central importance, particularly in the context of the policy framework paper, which brings together, in conjunction with the national authorities, the macroeconomic and structural issues and policies involved. Apart from program construction, coordination is also being increasingly emphasized in monitoring arrangements. To promote improved cooperation between the Fund and World Bank in constructing and monitoring programs, arrangements are being developed for joint participation in missions and in briefing and debriefing discussions, and coordination in the timing and staffing of missions. More recently, the Fund has been emphasizing improved cooperation with United Nations' (UN) agencies and is participating in a range of UN working committees, thereby enabling programs to be formulated on the basis of a wider range of data and opinion.

Appropriate attention to the time horizon of adjustment is also important from the perspective of the country's ability to meet timely debt-service payments; this is a particularly important issue in view of the difficulties experienced by many countries in this area over recent years. A program for restoring a country's external viability therefore needs to be phased so as to ensure that debt-service payments are made in a timely fashion, thereby enhancing the country's creditworthiness. The Fund has been giving particular attention to this aspect of program design, not surprisingly in view of its own experience. Self-interest, at the very least, and the need to ensure the revolving nature of Fund resources would surely argue against such a narrow perception of adjustment objectives. More broadly, of course, the Fund sees improved external viability as a central focus of any adjustment and structural reform effort. It is for this reason that export expansion and diversification—and possibly a degree of import substitution in certain cases—are viewed by the Fund as major elements in any policy package. Such an objective will obviously require maintenance of external competitiveness and appropriate and enabling financial policies, but will at the same time also necessitate structural reforms that support a shift in productive resources toward export- and import-competing activities.

Need for Emphasis on Both Economic and Social Concerns

The Fund has at times been criticized for not placing sufficient stress on social concerns and issues—including poverty alleviation, redressing of income inequalities, and environmental concerns—in its programs formulated with member countries. There is no doubt that greater effort to address major social issues is now being made in the context of Fund programs, with strong encouragement from the Fund's senior management. On this point, it needs to be emphasized that the economic and social problems facing Africa are not the making of Fund-supported programs but are typically deep-seated and long-standing. Furthermore, it must also be acknowledged that while economic policies and reforms involve social costs and sacrifices, the costs of forgoing adjustment are much higher still. It must be clearly understood that the Fund believes that the social implications of economic programs must be adequately recognized and major social priorities duly incorporated into the policy framework, even if macroeconomic objectives need to be modified to some degree. Failure to do this certainly complicates the whole process of policy formulation and acceptance, and mitigates strongly against the chances of effective implementation of the program. At the very least, programs need to protect the most vulnerable population groups from difficulties stemming from adjustment.

Against this background, the Fund has been focusing on means by which these legitimate social concerns can be met. An important emphasis has been on the social composition of government expenditures, ensuring that due emphasis is given to spending in areas of higher social priority. Conversely, restraint in budget expenditures when needed to meet appropriate fiscal objectives needs to be fully focused on areas of lower social priority. In such policy formulation, the Fund staff works closely with national officials to ensure that this general aim is realized. As a further example, revenue-generating measures need to be reviewed with respect to their nature and form, be they regressive or otherwise, to ensure an appropriate recognition of social concerns. Because program policies typically have an important impact on various prices in the national economy—both for goods and services—increasing attention is being given to the impact of price changes on the various population groups, specifically the poor who are obviously most vulnerable to price movements. Of course, the Fund's emphasis in this area is still evolving, but there can be little doubt that it will assume increasing importance in the period ahead. Effective incorporation of these features—including appropriate steps toward poverty alleviation—in programs supported by the Fund will require inputs from a range of organizations and agencies, as well as the countries themselves. The Fund is paying particular attention to improved collaboration with the World Bank, the UN, and other organizations to ensure that a practical collaborative approach is taken in dealing with these social concerns.

Having stated the Fund's broad intentions, it is nonetheless important to note policies in the social area that the Fund considers inappropriate for this task. In particular, price controls, budget subsidies, and exchange and trade restrictions are frequently envisaged as a means by which, inter alia, social issues can be addressed. Such policies have clearly been found wanting in the past and have led to inefficient and costly bureaucratic difficulties; the Fund considers such policies ill-suited for the realization of social objectives, despite their frequent appeal for political or bureaucratic reasons. The Fund believes that both efficiency and equity objectives can be better served by more appropriately conceived adjustment policies, including policies that incorporate greater scope for private sector initiative.

Internal Policy Issues, Relative to Promotion of External Financing

It is certainly true that most of the Fund's financing over the past decade has been conditional, contrasting with experience in the 1970s when certain facilities—notably the oil facility—provided significant funds virtually without conditionality. The question therefore arises as to the appropriate relationship between external financing and conditionality, particularly as a guide for the 1990s. The issue focuses most particularly on the extent to which current difficulties facing African countries, including the problem of payment arrears, has resulted in creditors calling for heightened conditionality to ensure appropriate policy reforms. To press the point, observers have argued that conditions often warrant an increased intrusion into domestic policy management, with greater scope for exacting increased conditionality from countries weakened by their economic difficulties. Such a view is good for polemics but not very useful for policy formulation and implementation. Experience in Africa, as elsewhere, has shown that there must be a workable nexus between creditors and borrowing countries. The Fund believes that such a coordinated approach is the only possible means of achieving successful adjustment and growth. Many instances are at hand to indicate that too ready an access to external finance, without an appropriate macroeconomic policy framework, can result in short-lived economic benefits, with attendant waste, mismanagement, and lost opportunities. Indeed, ensuing external debts can often negate or seriously qualify any immediate economic gains. Conversely, an economic program, no matter how well conceived and desirable its objectives, must remain on the drawing board if the requisite external assistance is not forthcoming. Formulation of internal objectives consistent with available external resources is therefore a prerequisite for an effective economic program.

The Fund plays a major role in this endeavor and doubtless will continue to do so in the 1990s. As for the developing countries, the need for meaningful adjustment is now evident, particularly after a decade of disappointing performance in many cases, and with delays in policy formulation and implementation proving very costly, both in economic and social terms. To assist low-income countries, notably in Africa, the Fund established the SAF, despite opposition from certain constituent member countries. This development was followed by the establishment of the ESAF, which has provided resources on highly concessional terms, including longer repayment periods. Middle-income countries are supported through stand-by and extended Fund facility (EFF) arrangements. Of the 30 programs supported by the use of Fund resources, 20 now involve SAF or ESAF arrangements. The essence of these arrangements—formulated closely in cooperation with the World Bank—is the promotion of growth and adjustment, while acting as a catalyst for financing from other creditors. Indeed, the catalytic role of the Fund's involvement in country programs has been essential in mobilizing external support, and more could be done in this regard if a larger number of African countries were to embark on strong adjustment programs. The Fund's approach therefore focuses on a complementary—rather than antagonistic—relationship between internal policy issues and the promotion of external financing. A further concern requires due regard to ensuring appropriate absorptive capacity of the member country to external assistance and financing. While the challenges remain as acute as ever, the benefits and results already emerging from the approach should not be underemphasized.

Input from Local Authorities

This issue has already surfaced in the preceding comments, and can be dealt with fairly briefly. Despite statements to the contrary, local participation in the construction of programs supported by the Fund is not just rhetoric, but the very nature of the negotiating process. Fund-supported programs take into account the particular features of each country, the priorities of the authorities, and their administrative constraints. In designing a program, a balance must be struck between the need for appropriate adjustment and legitimate social and political concerns, without which such a program has little chance of success. This task can only be accomplished by a comprehensive and open dialogue with the authorities on program objectives and policies.

General Issues

Having commented on some specific issues relating to adjustment and growth in the 1990s that impinge on Fund programs, I would like to make a few broader observations about the role of the Fund in Africa in the period ahead.

While it is true that the difficulties and challenges for economic progress in Africa are indeed formidable, it must be remembered that the international environment is improving in certain respects, including many instances of intensified adjustment and structural efforts in both developing and developed countries. In these circumstances, the prospects for improved economic growth and lowered inflation in the world economy are encouraging. Of course, there are always major uncertainties and downside risks, not least the implications—both in the short and long run—of the situation in the Middle East, that qualify the outlook for economic development and stability. Furthermore, vulnerability to economic downturns in developing countries remains a problem, and progress on world trade liberalization continues to be disappointing. Nonetheless, many aspects of the situation—including a strengthened will in many developed and developing countries to grapple with their economic difficulties—seems more favorable than a decade earlier.

Against this background, the Fund sees itself as playing an important role in Africa in encouraging countries to adopt appropriate macroeconomic frameworks and policies on the basis of which sustained economic growth can take place. A major priority is to ensure that strengthened macroeconomic performance will lead to improved creditworthiness, both with respect to official and private sectors. Once these macroeconomic frameworks and policies—with needed external support—are in place, scope is provided for meaningful structural reforms. Within this context, the Fund will support credible macroeconomic programs designed to increase domestic savings and investment, raise productivity, and achieve increased export diversification. As regards external financing, while the Fund will continue to help reforming countries to mobilize adequate external resources, it is clear that African countries will need to place greater emphasis than in the past on the generation of domestic savings to meet their financing requirements. A number of African countries have already benefitted from progress in these areas, and it would be unduly pessimistic not to see promise of comparable improvements elsewhere in Africa. All together, Africa needs to fear marginalization only if it chooses to stop or reverse the economic adjustments on which it has embarked.

The Fund has continually adapted its programs to help deal with the particular circumstances of African countries. Criticism that the Fund has imposed ready-made "solutions" on its African member countries does not reflect the facts, as the detailed construction of individual programs clearly shows.

As regards debt issues, vital for many African countries, the Fund continues to support a strategy that is based on international cooperation. It believes that all initiatives to alleviate the debt burden of developing countries without undermining further flows of external financing to these countries deserve support. Recent initiatives have provided significant debt relief to African countries, through, for example, improved debt rescheduling (Toronto). Further efforts, supported by the Fund, are under way to finalize agreements between the creditor banks and some middle-income countries. It needs to be remembered, however, that medium-term solutions to the debt problem remain dependent on other elements, including efficient mobilization of domestic savings, restoration of confidence, ability to attract external private investment, and export diversification.

Finally, it needs to be stated that the Fund has a clear mandate to assist sound adjustment and developmental efforts in Africa, as with other member countries. It obviously needs adequate resources to support these programs of reform, and the recent increase in quotas will be an important help in this direction. The quality of analysis and commitment to program design from its own staff are recognized as critical, and cooperation with other financial institutions—particularly the World Bank—is also central. But the Fund does not shrink from its responsibilities, nor accept claims that it should diminish or even relinquish its role.

List of Participants

Chairman
Abdul R. Turay
  Governor
  Bank of Sierra Leone
  President
  Association of African Central Banks

Moderator
I. G. Patel
  Former Governor
  Reserve Bank of India

Algeria
Abderahmane Hadj-Nacer
  Governor
  Central Bank of Algeria

Angola
Antonio Grasa
  Manager
  National Bank of Angola
Marinela Ribas
  Manager
  National Bank of Angola

Central Bank of West African States (BCEAO)
Charles K. Banny
  Governor
Mbaye Diop Sarr
  Director
  Central Department of Research and Forecasting
Latégan Lawson
  Acting Director
  Central Department of International Relations
Amadou Sadiekh Diop
  Assistant Governor

Central Bank of Central African States (BEAC)
Jean-Edouard Sathoud
  Deputy Governor

Botswana
H.C.L. Quill Hermans
  Governor
  Bank of Botswana

Burundi
Isaac Budabuda
  Governor
  Bank of the Republic of Burundi

Djibouti
Luc A. Aden
  Governor
  National Bank of Djibouti

Ethiopia
Bekele Tamirat
  Governor
  National Bank of Ethiopia

The Gambia
Abdou A.B. N'Jie
  Governor
  Central Bank of The Gambia

Ghana
G.K. Agama
  Governor
  Bank of Ghana

Guinea
Kerfalla Yansane
  Governor
  Central Bank of Guinea

Guinea-Bissau
Pedro A. Godinho Gomes
  Governor
  National Bank of Guinea-Bissau

Kenya
M.J.P. Kanga
  Director of Research
  Central Bank of Kenya

LIST OF PARTICIPANTS

J. K. Kinyua
Central Bank of Kenya

Lesotho
A.M. Maruping
Governor
Central Bank of Lesotho

Liberia
Thomas D. Voer Hanson
Governor
National Bank of Liberia

Madagascar
Blandin E. Razafimanjato
Governor
Central Bank of the Republic of Madagascar

Malawi
Hans Joachim Lesshafft
Governor
Reserve Bank of Malawi

P. W. Mamba
Assistant Director of Research and Statistics
Reserve Bank of Malawi

M. Ganiza
Research Officer
Reserve Bank of Malawi

Mauritania
Ahmed Ould Zein
Governor
Central Bank of Mauritania

Mozambique
Eneas Da Conceicao Comiche
Governor
Bank of Mozambique

Namibia
Wouter Benard
Governor
Bank of Namibia

Nigeria
Mallam Ismaila Usman
Deputy Governor
Central Bank of Nigeria

E.A. Ajayi
Director, Office of the Governor
Central Bank of Nigeria

Alhaji G. Ahmed
Special Assistant to the Deputy Governor
Central Bank of Nigeria

Rwanda
Gerard Niyitegeka
First Vice-Governor
National Bank of Rwanda

Joseph Ntamatungiro
Director of Research and Statistics
National Bank of Rwanda

Sao Tome and Principe
Manuel de Nazaré Mendes
Governor
National Bank of Sao Tome and Principe

Arlindo Afonso de Carvalho
National Bank of Sao Tome and Principe

Sudan
El Shiekh Sid Ahmed el Shiekh
Governor
Bank of Sudan

Swaziland
H. B. B. Oliver
Governor
Central Bank of Swaziland

Tanzania
Gilman Rutihinda
Governor
Bank of Tanzania

Tunisia
Mohamed El-Beji Hamda
Governor
Central Bank of Tunisia

Uganda
C.N. Kikonyogo
Governor
Bank of Uganda

Zaïre
Citoyen Pay-Pay wa Syakassighe
Governor
Bank of Zaïre

Ongona Elongo
  Division Chief
  Research Department
  Bank of Zaïre

Zambia

Jacques A. Bussieres
  Governor
  Bank of Zambia

Zimbabwe

Kombo J. Moyana
  Governor
  Reserve Bank of Zimbabwe

International Monetary Fund

Michel Camdessus
  Managing Director

Mohamed Finaish
  Executive Director

L.B. Monyake
  Executive Director

Corentino V. Santos
  Executive Director

Omar Kabbaj
  Alternate Executive Director

Ahmed M. Abushadi
  Senior Information Officer
  External Relations Department

Peter Andrews
  Personal Assistant to the Managing Director

K. Burke Dillon
  Assistant Director
  African Department

World Bank

J. Ayo Langley
  Executive Director

Authors, Discussants, and Panelists

Franciso Abbate
  Chief
  Development Finance Program
  UN Conference on Trade and Development

Robert J. Berg
  International Development Conference

John T. Boorman
  Director
  Exchange and Trade Relations Department
  International Monetary Fund

Kenneth K. S. Dadzie
  Secretary General
  UN Conference on Trade and Development

G. E. Gondwe
  Deputy Director
  African Department
  International Monetary Fund

Gerry Helleiner
  Professor of Economics
  University of Toronto

Tony Killick
  Senior Research Fellow
  Overseas Development Institute
  Regents College

Matthew H. Martin
  Research Fellow
  International Development Center
  University of Oxford

Percy Mistry
  Vice Chairman and Finance Director
  International Development Center
  University of Oxford

Andrew K. Mullei
  Director-General
  Association of African Central Banks

Benno J. Ndulu
  Research Coordinator
  African Economic Research Consortium

F. Stephen O'Brien
  Chief Economist
  Africa Regional Office
  World Bank

Denis Samuel-Lajeunesse
  Chief
  Office of International Affairs
  Ministry of Economy, Finance, and Budget

A. O. Sangowawa
  Director
  Country Programs Department
  African Development Bank

O. Teriba
  Chief
  Socio-Economic Research and
    Planning
  UN Economic Commission for
    Africa

Mamoudou Touré
  Counsellor and Director
  African Department
  International Monetary Fund

Special Guests

Louis Emmerij
  President
  OECD Development Center

Kenneth S. King
  Regional Director, Africa
  United Nations Development
    Program